Peachpit Learning Series

Microsoft Windows Vista

Larry Magid

Dwight Silverman

Peachpit Press

Microsoft Windows Vista: Peachpit Learning Series

Larry Magid

Dwight Silverman

Peachpit Press
1249 Eighth Street
Berkeley, CA 94710
510/524-2178
800/283-9444
510/524-2221 (fax)
Find us on the Web at: www.peachpit.com
To report errors, please send a note to errata@peachpit.com
Published by Peachpit Press, a division of Pearson Education

Project Editor: Cliff Colby
Editor: Jill Marts Lodwig
Production Editor: Jonathan Peck
Copyeditor: Kathy Simpson
Compositor: Dovetail Publishing Services
Indexer: Patti Schiendelman
Cover Design: Charlene Charles-Will
Cover photograph: Jason Reed / Getty Images

ISBN 13: 978-0-321-44192-8
ISBN 10: 0-321-44192-3

9 8 7 6 5 4 3 2 1

Printed and bound in the United States of America

My half of this book is dedicated to my older sister, Carol Magid, who has supported me for longer than I can remember.

—Larry Magid

My half of this book is dedicated to Scott Clark, my boss and friend, whose faith in my abilities and infinite patience helped make me the geek I am today.

—Dwight Silverman

Acknowledgements

A project as big as a book must be a labor of love. The writer must love doing it, and those around the writer must love him in order to put up with the process. Those around me—my wife, Lisa, and children, Jack and Jessica—have shown me a lot of love and patience as I skipped meals and other family events to get this done. Thank you, and I love you!

I also owe tons of gratitude to my co-author, Larry Magid, who brought me aboard this ship to help him write about Windows Vista. I've wanted to write a computer book for some time, and I couldn't be happier that the very first one I wrote was with Larry. Let's do it again some time!

Special thanks also to Jill Marts Lodwig, this book's editor, who was a solid hand during some rough times. This book's as good as it is largely because of her.

—*Dwight Silverman*

As always I must thank my wife, Patti, for her patience during those many evenings when I was glued to the computer toiling over this book. Thanks also to Dwight who rescued me by agreeing to become my co-author. His contributions can only be described as enormous. Thanks also to our editor Jill Marts Lodwig for her patience and diligence, and to Peachpit's Cliff Colby for signing the book.

—*Larry Magid*

Contents

Contents

Contents

1

GOALS

Learn how Vista is different from XP

Learn about new interface features in Vista

Learn about security and performance enhancements to Vista

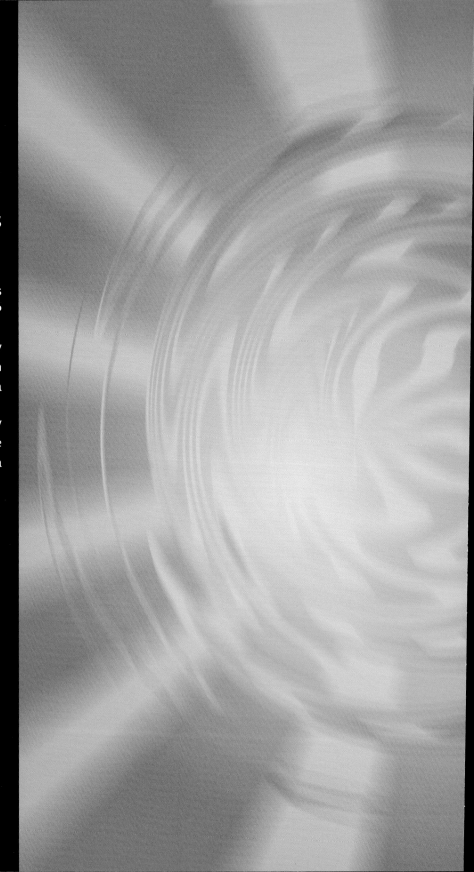

Meet Vista

When it comes to Microsoft Windows Vista, "Why should I care?" is a legitimate question. After all, you've been using Windows XP for years and, despite some issues, it's probably serving your needs. Besides, you most likely saw plenty of early reviews about Vista that were less than enthusiastic.

Still, the introduction of a new version of Windows is a big deal. The last time Microsoft released a major version was in 2001 with Windows XP. With a share of the personal computer operating system market that is above 90 percent, Microsoft's decisions affect hundreds of millions of people and probably even have an impact on the world's economy. Software and hardware companies have to retool to make sure their products are compatible. Corporations, organizations, and even governments have to weigh the merits of adapting to the new operating system versus sticking with what they already have, and consumers have to decide when and whether it's time to upgrade.

Ultimately, the decision is made for us because Vista isn't really about choice—it actually replaces Windows XP as the operating system that PC makers will include with their new machines. Of course, one could always avoid Windows entirely by getting an Apple Macintosh, a PC running Linux, or shunning computers altogether, but for better or worse, the overwhelming majority of us will wind up using a Windows PC.

Better than XP?

As authors of this book and technology columnists, we have been working with Vista for months and have both concluded that it's a significant improvement over Windows XP. We appreciate the new look and feel—Vista is definitely more attractive than XP. We like the fact that we can peer into running programs without having to switch to them. We find the new gadgets fun and handy, and we love the new search feature that makes it a breeze to find our files, email and even photos. While it's hard to get too excited about enhanced security or even parental controls, it's reassuring to know Vista users have some additional protections.

Some critics have dismissed Vista as just an upgrade, but it's far more than that. True, it doesn't revolutionize the way you use Windows, but a revolutionary change might have been more disruptive than useful. Yes, we have found some bugs in Vista, and we're sure more will emerge. In addition, despite increased security, we're pretty sure Vista users will continue to be plagued by hackers, viruses, malicious software, and other security problems.

There's more to like

Still, as we pound on Vista, we continue to find more things we like, including things that Microsoft hasn't even trumpeted in its massive marketing campaign. As you'll soon learn, there are definitely some great new features in Vista. For example, you can now run programs by typing their names in the Start menu's search box, which can sometimes be a lot quicker than hunting for an icon. Vista also introduces a dramatic and inexpensive way to boost performance, combining a feature that anticipates what you're going to do next with moving data off the hard drive and into an inserted flash drive or memory card.

Reviewers have also pointed out that Microsoft borrowed a lot of features from Apple's Macintosh OS X, but we think that's a good thing because it means that Windows users can now enjoy some of the features that Mac users have had for awhile. It's true that Vista's "gadgets" are a lot like Apple's "widgets" and that Mac users had high-speed indexed search way before Windows users did. The same is true of the ability to peek into windows without having to switch to them. Whether or not Microsoft is as innovative as Apple is something pundits can debate, but one thing is for sure—users benefit from healthy competition, and we're happy to see Microsoft finally add some long overdue features to its operating system.

But think before you buy

Despite all the things we like about Vista, we don't necessarily think that everyone should rush out and upgrade their PCs. Before you take the plunge, you should think about whether the benefits are worth the hassle. If your XP machine is working well and you don't have an immediate need for Vista's new features, you might be better off waiting till it's time to buy a new machine. Besides, by the time you add the cost of the Vista upgrade plus any possible hardware upgrades, it might be better to get a new machine anyway.

If you've just bought a new PC, then this discussion is probably a moot point, since it probably came with Vista installed. If this is the case, you may not have to think about whether to buy Vista, but you may still want to read the rest of this lesson so that you know what Vista has to offer.

Regardless of your situation, this book contains useful information for any Vista user or prospective Vista user—it can help you decide whether it's time to upgrade, how to upgrade and how to take advantage of all that Vista has to offer.

Vista in a Nutshell

Vista represents years of development by Microsoft engineers and includes millions of lines of new code. A major reworking of Windows, it includes multiple new features, a new look and feel, and some "under the hood" upgrades for stability and security.

Like any other operating system, Vista provides the basic code your computer needs to communicate with you and with the outside world. During the 1980s when most people used MS-DOS (*DOS* stands for *disk operating system*), the operating system had virtually no features visible to the user other than a place where you could type commands to load software or work with files. But today's operating systems provide far more than just the basics. Windows Vista is no exception; it's loaded with features, including some pretty powerful application programs.

Vista still handles the way your computer functions, controlling the display, the audio, the positioning of windows on your screen, the keyboard, and the mouse. It lets you copy, move, and delete files; it provides resources used by software and hardware, including printers, scanners, and MP3 players. But Vista also does a great deal more—certainly enough to let you start enjoying your computer right away, even before you start to load additional software.

New Features

With each successive version of Windows, Microsoft loads in more and more features. In fact, *features* may be the wrong word; a better phrase might be *applications,* because Vista now ships with bundled software that people used to have to purchase. Vista includes a very nice new calendar program, for example, along with a new email program and a personal contact manager. Windows XP

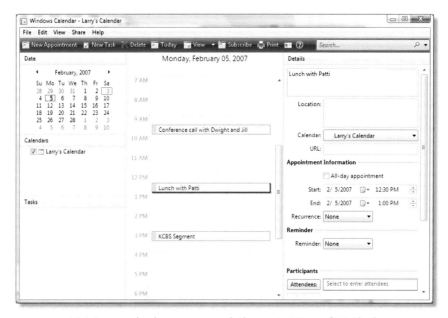

Vista's new calendar program rivals the one in Microsoft Outlook.

had email (Outlook Express) and a Windows address book but lacked a calendar. Together, these three free programs in Vista do pretty much what the full-scale Microsoft Outlook does, and you don't have to pay extra for them.

Vista also has an improved version of Windows Movie Maker for editing videos and burning them to DVD, as well as a new program called Windows Photo Gallery, which rivals Apple's acclaimed iPhoto as a photo-organizing-and-editing program.

The Home Premium and Ultimate editions of Vista include Windows Media Center, which you can use to play video clips, DVDs, music, and audio; view photos; and (if your PC has a tuner) watch TV or record TV shows to your PC's hard drive. Some PCs even have remote controls, allowing you to use Media Center from your easy chair rather than your desk. Although Media Center isn't a new feature, until Vista it was available on specially equipped PCs bundled with the Media Center Edition of Windows XP.

Other new programs include a backup utility and a program called Sync Center, which helps you synchronize your PC with mobile devices like smartphones, as well as with network drives. Microsoft also has added speech-recognition capability to Vista, which makes it possible to dictate text instead of type. This sure came in handy for Larry after he broke his elbow and was unable to type for a few weeks while working on this book!

Security

Years before it released Vista, Microsoft had been putting greater emphasis on security. In 2002, Chairman Bill Gates issued a memo to Microsoft employees where he declared that when "we face a choice between adding features and resolving security issues, we need to choose security. Our products should emphasize security right out of the box, and we must constantly refine and improve that security as threats evolve."

Two years later, Microsoft released Windows XP Service Pack 2—a free upgrade to XP that represented a major effort by Microsoft to shore up some pretty serious Windows security problems. Yet Windows XP continued—and continues—to be plagued with problems.

It's not uncommon for Microsoft to issue a free upgrade or patch to deal with critical security issues, such as the possibility of hackers taking remote control of your PC. If hackers can control your PC, they can do whatever they want with it, including stealing information; turning your machine into a zombie that sends out spam or infects other people's machines with viruses; and installing *spyware,* which is malicious software that can install itself on your computer, resulting in potential security breaches and slower performance.

Behind-the-scenes security enhancements

Microsoft claims it has done extensive security testing and emphasizes that Vista is its most secure operating system ever. It's difficult for us to validate behind-the-scenes security features for several reasons: We can't independently examine every line of code to determine exactly what flaws have been fixed, and we wrote this book during and shortly after Vista's release, which is too soon to know the operating system's security status.

However, even if Vista is the most secure Windows version to date, one thing we know for sure is that attacks against it will continue. Windows is a high priority for hackers simply *because* it's so popular. An attack against Windows can affect a huge number of people around the world. If the attack involves a financial crime, then all the better for the hacker, as it can be extremely profitable.

As a result, Windows users, as always, need to remain vigilant. The good news is that in Vista, users will find significant new security protections.

In Vista Microsoft has introduced Windows Service Hardening, which limits the damage attackers can do if they do gain access. For example, it now limits the number of automatic "services" that can potentially allow an intruder to damage someone's machine. Microsoft also introduced technology that makes it easier for companies to develop smart cards, biometrics technology, and other methods to keep unauthorized users from accessing protected computers.

Security features you can see

Although some of Vista's security changes are behind the scenes, others are right there in your face, like the Windows Security Center.

Vista now has what Microsoft calls User Account Control (UAC), which occasionally requires you to give Windows permission to carry out certain tasks, such as installing or uninstalling a program or deleting certain files or folders.

Some people find this feature annoying, because it puts a burden on users by requiring them to interact with Windows a bit more than they did in the past.

Vista's Security Center provides tools to keep your machine safe.

But UAC increases security by making it less likely that an automated piece of malicious software or a hacker will get remote control of your PC to do something destructive or dangerous.

By default, new accounts that are set up on a machine running Vista do not have administrative privileges, which means the owners of those accounts must get permission before performing certain potentially dangerous tasks. The person who sets up the machine does have administrative privileges, of course, but UAC sometimes asks even the administrator to verify that some commands are deliberate and not a result of someone taking remote control of the PC.

NOTE —— In Lesson 6, we tell you how you can disable UAC–complete with a warning that doing so also makes it easier for malicious software to damage your computer or jeopardize your security.

Another security feature, Windows Firewall, has been beefed up from the XP days, when it protected you only against inbound threats. Now it also protects against outbound threats, in case a piece of malicious software tries to "phone home" by sending data from your PC to a rogue server somewhere.

Vista also includes Windows Defender (formerly called Microsoft Anti-Spyware), which protects your PC against spyware. You'll find more details about Windows Defender and security settings in Lesson 6.

The business editions of Vista include Windows BitLocker Drive Encryption to protect data against prying eyes.

Additional security features are built into Windows Internet Explorer 7 (which comes with Vista but is available as a download for XP users) to help protect against phishing schemes and fraudulent Web sites that try to trick you into revealing personal information or contain code that could damage your PC or jeopardize your security.

Performance

Microsoft has added several performance features that can increase your productivity, assuming that you have a machine with a sufficient amount of memory (we discuss these requirements in Lesson 2).

SuperFetch

SuperFetch is a new feature that, over time, determines what programs you are likely to run at any given day or time and loads portions of those programs into memory so that they execute faster and more reliably. SuperFetch uses what Microsoft calls an "intelligent prioritization scheme," which can determine when you run certain programs and prioritize those programs. It's like having a butler who can anticipate your every need and bring you your robe and slippers just when you need them. Well, it's not quite that good, but it does help reduce the time that it takes to load some applications. SuperFetch will also prioritize the applications you need to run over background tasks, such as virus checking or defragmenting your hard drive.

ReadyBoost

You know those little USB thumb drives? Until recently, they were used just for transporting data from one machine to another, but now they can be used to speed your PC's performance. Windows can use the memory on that device as a cache (storage area) for data.

The principle is simple: Although the nonvolatile memory in a thumb drive is a bit slower than the RAM (random access memory) in your computer, using this type of memory is still much faster than retrieving data from your hard drive. So Vista improves performance by storing, or *caching,* data on that device. When Vista needs the data, it grabs that data from the thumb drive, secure digital (SD) card, or other nonvolatile memory and brings it into RAM so that it can be processed.

A thumb drive like this one from Sandisk can speed your PC.

Don't worry if you need to remove the drive. The data on the drive is only a copy; it's also safely stored on your hard drive. Also, Microsoft says that the data is encrypted in case the wrong person gets his or her thumbs on your thumb drive. You'll find details on how to set up ReadyBoost in Lesson 15.

ReadyDrive

ReadyDrive takes advantage of a new generation of hybrid drives that include nonvolatile memory as well as the hard disk itself. The idea is that data can be stored in that built-in flash memory so that the mechanical drive doesn't have to work so hard. This arrangement has three advantages:

- It saves time because data is fetched from memory instead of the hard drive.

- It saves wear and tear on the mechanical parts of the hard drive because Windows doesn't need to access them as much.

- It saves energy, which is terrific for laptop computers. By having Windows access the solid-state memory—which has no moving parts and therefore can be accessed with much less energy—ReadyDrive reduces the amount of work the hard drive's motor has to do to move the heads and spin the disk.

Although SuperFetch, ReadyBoost, and ReadyDrive are separate features, they still interact. Vista looks for the fastest way to store the data it will access, for example. It checks the computer's system RAM first; then it checks a Ready-Drive, a ReadyBoost flash drive, and finally the hard drive. Information about the programs used by SuperFetch may be stored in the ReadyDrive or the Ready-Boost device, depending on which is available.

The bottom line, however, is that your computer should run noticeably faster than it did with Windows XP if ReadyBoost is enabled or a ReadyDrive is available.

User Interface Enhancements

Microsoft also made some changes to Windows' look and feel.

Welcome Center

When you first start Vista, you'll probably notice Welcome Center, which is designed with new Vista users in mind. Welcome Center contains information about your computer's hardware, a tool for transferring files and settings, another tool for additional users if you plan to share the PC, a tool for connecting to the Internet, and information about what's new in Windows Vista.

This window also contains some commercial messages from Microsoft. A check box at the bottom of the window lets you decide whether to run Welcome Center at startup. If you elect not to run it at startup, you can always display it by clicking System and Maintenance in the Control Panel or just typing welcome in the search box at the bottom of the Start menu.

The first item in Welcome Center is View Computer Details. Click it, and you'll see which version of Vista you're using and a summary of your hardware, including the type and speed of your CPU and the type of graphics adapter you have.

Windows Welcome Center provides links to common tasks for new Vista users.

You can get more details, including a performance rating called the Windows Experience Index, by clicking Show More Details in the top-right corner. This rating is based on the performance of your processor (CPU), memory (RAM), graphics adapter, gaming graphics, and data-transfer rate of your primary hard drive.

The rating isn't actually a summary or an average of all your components, but the score of the component that ranks the lowest. You can get a complete report by clicking Windows Experience Index to the right of the numeric score. We explore the Welcome Center further in Lesson 3.

The Aero interface

We suppose this is a matter of taste, but to our eyes, the Windows desktop has gotten a lot prettier with Vista. Microsoft spent quite a bit of effort designing the eye-pleasing backgrounds and wallpapers.

Assuming that your hardware can handle it (see Lesson 2), the most stunning aspect of the desktop is the new Aero (sometimes called "Aero Glass") interface, which Microsoft describes as glasslike.

The first thing you'll notice about Aero is that the borders of windows are trans-lucent: You can see what's under them. At first, you might think that the Aero interface is (literally) window dressing—a gimmick to make the computer just a little prettier. But it has a functional aspect.

If you press Alt+Tab, for example, instead of seeing icons to represent each run-ning program, you see a thumbnail of the program's actual window, with the content exposed.

You can see actual images of running programs when you press Alt+Tab.

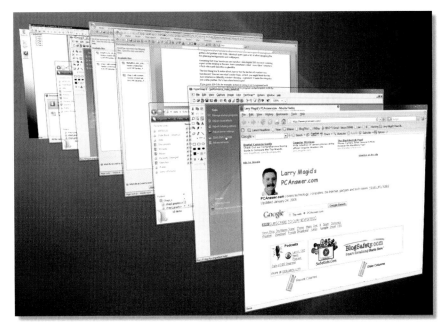

Hold down the Windows key and press Tab to view all the programs that are running.

This feature is called Flip 3D. If you press the Windows key+Tab (or click the Switch Between Windows icon in the taskbar), you'll see stacked windows that you can flip between or select with the mouse.

The thumbnail icons in the taskbar are live if you hover over them with the mouse. You can even see live video in those thumbnails if a video is playing in the background. Whether Aero is eye candy or a productivity tool lies in the eye of the beholder, but for those of us who use multiple windows, it can be handy to see inside a window without having to open it.

Bear in mind that the least expensive edition of Vista, Home Basic, doesn't support Aero; neither do some older or low-cost PCs. See "Is Your Existing PC Vista-Compatible?" in Lesson 2 to find out whether your PC is able to run Vista Home Premium and other editions that support Aero.

The Start menu

The Start menu has been redesigned in Vista to make finding and launching programs easier. When you first open it, it looks pretty much like the Start menu in XP, with a small number of programs immediately available.

But, unlike earlier versions of Windows, Vista doesn't make you hunt around or use cascading menus to find your programs. You can get a list of all your programs immediately when you choose Start > All Programs.

There is even an "old" new way to launch programs: Just like in the days of MS-DOS, you can run a program by typing its name in the search bar. You can use the search bar to find just about anything on your computer; we delve into a lot more detail on it in Lesson 5.

The new Start menu.

 As in previous Windows versions, the Start menu in Vista is your gateway to Windows Control Panel, which you access to do things like adjust your hardware settings, uninstall software, and turn on some of the "ease of access" features. We discuss the Control Panel in more detail in Online Resource A, which you can access by visiting www.peachpit.com/vistalearningseries.

NOTE —— You can access additional lessons on Vista's Control Panel and the Media Center by visiting www.peachpit.com/vistalearningseries and registering your copy of this book.

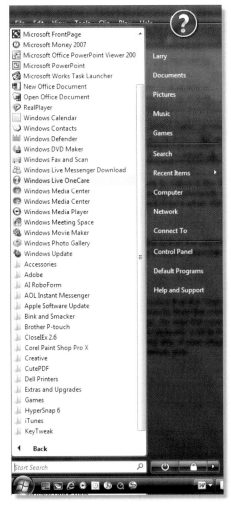

When you choose All Programs, you get a complete scrollable list of all your programs.

Five Versions of Vista: Which Is Right for You?

Vista now comes in five flavors: Vista Home Basic, Vista Home Premium, Vista Business, Vista Enterprise, and Vista Ultimate. Depending on which version comes on your machine (or which version you buy), you may be able to upgrade later.

Consumer versions

Home Basic edition

Windows Vista Home Basic edition ($199 for the complete installation; $99 for the upgrade) provides the basic tools you need, including the new search system; parental controls; many of the security upgrades; and most basic accessories, such as email and a calendar.

This edition, however, lacks some of the cool and useful features that you get in the Home Premium edition, which is why we don't recommend it for most people. If you do opt for this edition or buy a machine that has it preinstalled, you can upgrade later to one of the other editions (assuming that your hardware is capable of running them).

Home Premium edition

With the Home Premium edition, you get everything the Home Basic edition provides, plus the new Aero interface and the ability to burn movies to DVDs and use Windows Media Center to organize and play your media files. If your PC is equipped with a tuner, you can also watch and record TV programs. Home Premium supports Tablet PCs (laptop computers with a pen interface and a touch-sensitive screen)—a feature that's important only if you happen to have a Tablet PC.

If you want to use SideShow—a service supported by some hardware that gives you access to information on external screens—you'll need the Home Premium edition.

The Home Premium edition costs $239 ($159 for the upgrade).

Business versions

Microsoft has developed two editions especially for businesses. While consumers aren't likely to purchase these editions for home use, it is possible that you might encounter them at work.

NOTE —— Prices of the various editions of Windows Vista can vary, depending on where you get the product. If you get Vista with a new PC, the operating system will be included in the purchase price. Check with the vendor to see what version of Windows is included with the product you are thinking about buying. Microsoft has a chart of the different Vista editions you can view at www.microsoft.com/windows/products/windowsvista/editions/default.mspx.

Business edition

The Windows Vista Business edition includes additional business-related features, such as software to send outgoing faxes (an old-fashioned telephone modem and phone line are required), as well as some additional security features and diagnostic tools that Microsoft claims can help predict and prevent hardware failures, such as a hard-disk crash.

Like the Home Premium edition, the Business edition has the Aero interface and SideShow, but it doesn't have Windows Media Center.

The upgrade from XP for the Business edition is $199, or $299 for the complete installation.

Enterprise edition

The Windows Vista Enterprise edition has bells and whistles that are of interest mostly to large companies. These features include enhanced security and networking; the ability to install the operating system on multiple PCs within the company; and BitLocker, a technology that helps protect sensitive data if it gets lost or stolen. The Enterprise edition also lets you run Unix applications on your PC and has support for multiple languages.

Prices for the Enterprise edition are based on volume licensing agreements.

The best of both worlds: The Ultimate edition

Windows Vista Ultimate, which we used when researching this book, has all the features of the Vista Home Premium edition as well as the business features of Windows Vista Business.

At $399 for a complete installation or $259 for an upgrade, however, this edition is an expensive proposition. For most consumers, we recommend the Home Premium edition.

Now that you know what Vista is, it's time to get started. In Lesson 2, we cover how you can determine whether your machine is Vista ready and, if so, how to install the new operating system. We also explain how you can upgrade existing hardware to be Vista compatible.

What You've Learned

- How Vista is different from Windows XP

- New features that give Vista better performance, ease of use, and security

- Changes to the Windows interface, including Welcome Center, the Aero interface, and the new Start menu

- The various editions of Vista and which is right for whom

2

GOALS

Determine whether
your PC can handle
Windows Vista

Consider whether
buying a new PC is the
best approach

Learn about upgrade
options for Vista

Upgrade to Vista

If you want Windows Vista, there are two ways to get it. Depending on how you feel about shopping for computer equipment, one way is lot more fun and interesting than the other.

The simplest way to start using Vista is to buy a new computer with the operating system already installed. This way, you can be sure that everything will work on your new PC. You might have some issues with software you install or with your old peripherals, such as printers and scanners, but chances are that Microsoft will have worked out most of those issues by the time you're ready to roll. With regard to the PC itself, all you need to do is simply fire it up, sit down at it, and . . . well, read the rest of this book first. It will make your journey much easier.

The other way is to get Vista is to install it on your existing PC. This method requires some planning and research on your part, because you'll need to find out whether your computer's various components are compatible with Vista, whether the necessary hardware drivers are available, and whether your PC has the muscle to handle some of the updated operating system's features.

Whether you upgrade or buy new, in fact, you need to pay attention to the specifications, because they will help you determine what edition of Vista you should consider—or have to settle for.

Is Your Existing PC Vista-Compatible?

The minimum configuration to run the Home Basic edition of Vista is a PC with the following:

- 512 MB of memory

- 800 MHz CPU

- A graphics card that is compatible with DirectX 9 (as most graphics adapters sold in the past several years are)

The vast majority of PCs that have been purchased in the past few years are capable of running this stripped-down version of Vista. Just because a PC is able to run Vista, however, doesn't necessarily mean that upgrading is worth the cost, effort, and potential compatibility problems with existing software and peripherals. So read on!

To use the Aero interface, you need the Home Premium edition, one of the business editions, or the Ultimate edition. You also need a PC with the following minimum configuration:

- 1 GB of memory.

- 1 GHz CPU.

- A DirectX 9–compatible graphics card with a Windows Vista Display Driver Model (WDDM) driver.

- 128 MB of graphics memory and Pixel Shader 2.0. (Pixel shading is the ability of your graphics processor to render the surface properties of an image, including lighting, shadows, and other visual qualities.)

- 40 GB hard drive with 15 GB free space.

- DVD-ROM drive and audio output. (Vista is available on store shelves only on DVD; if you need it on CD, you must order it from Microsoft.)

The Easy Way to Check

If your machine is running Windows XP, an easy way to determine whether it's Vista-ready is to download the Windows Vista Upgrade Advisor from Microsoft's Vista Web site (www.microsoft.com/windowsvista/upgradeadvisor/).

The program will scan your PC to determine which, if any, edition of Vista can run on your machine. Be sure to plug in all your external peripherals—such as printers, scanners, and external hard drives—as they, too, need to be evaluated by the upgrade tool.

When the Upgrade Advisor finishes the scan, it lists the edition(s) it recommends. You don't necessarily have to buy the recommended edition, though—so long as you buy a version your system can handle. The left side of the screen will list other editions; click the ones you're considering and scroll down to see what changes you might have to make to run that edition.

The Windows XP Upgrade Advisor lets you know whether your system is compatible with each edition of the operating system.

Don't panic if the Upgrade Advisor tells you that some device drivers on your system aren't compatible; chances are that new drivers are available. You should also perform a Windows Update (see Lesson 2) to ensure you're using the latest drivers and visit the Web sites of your peripheral makers for any updated drivers you should be using.

> ## Upgrading to More Vista Features
>
> Want to move to a higher plane in Vista? To do an Anytime Upgrade, choose Control Panel > Windows Anytime Upgrade. A wizard will walk you through the process of finding an online store, buying a new product key, inserting your original DVD, and typing the product key. All the features for all the editions of Vista are on every DVD sold, and the product key unlocks the new features. You won't have to download anything or replace your original Vista installation disc. Anytime Upgrade is available for all editions of Vista except Ultimate, because there's nowhere to upgrade from there.

Buying a New PC

Most new PCs sold since Vista's consumer launch include Vista and are labeled as such. You may still see some budget or older systems available that run Windows XP, but most likely, you will be able to upgrade those systems to run Vista. Some vendors may continue to sell XP machines for customers who prefer to stay with the older operating system.

If you buy a new PC in a store or online, it likely will come with one of the Vista editions discussed in Lesson 1. If you're buying online and can configure your dream system, you may have a choice of editions. Think about the hardware you're buying and what you'll be doing with the computer; then choose wisely. Be careful not to overbuy. You may not need to pay for Vista Ultimate when Home Premium will do.

If you end up not having made the best choice, you're not stuck with what you have. Vista has a feature called Windows Anytime Upgrade, in which you can pay more and then install the software needed to get a more feature-rich version.

Vista installs different features on a notebook computer, making it easier to use on the road or during a presentation. It also has settings that can extend battery life. We'll go into more detail on Vista's Mobility Center, which groups many of these features in one handy control panel, in Lesson 13.

Upgrading an Older PC

If you're happy with your current PC, and if it can handle Vista's hardware requirements, you can buy a copy of the operating system and install it in any of several ways: an upgrade install, full install, or clean install.

Each type of installation requires a different process. The following sections walk you through these processes in detail.

> **NOTE** —— As always, it's extremely important to back up your data files before you upgrade, just in case something goes wrong. This precaution should include the upgrade install; don't presume that your files will come out the other side intact. In addition, watch out for this Vista gotcha: If you use Windows XP Professional and Media Center's built-in backup software, be aware that Vista's new backup program can't read the .bkf files that store your data. Microsoft has released a restore utility for Vista that can extract files from XP backups. Search Microsoft's Web site for `Windows NT Backup-Restore Utility`.

Upgrade install

An upgrade install keeps all your settings and existing programs that don't have conflicts with Vista. It's the simplest Vista installation but also the one that's most susceptible to inheriting problems (such as spyware) from your existing Windows setup.

Although conventional wisdom states that a clean install is preferred over an upgrade, that may not be the case with Vista. Microsoft says an upgrade installation is handled differently than in past versions, with steps taken to prevent applications from breaking and settings being lost. The result is that, if you've backed up your data and have a healthy system, an upgrade install may be an acceptable choice.

Perform an upgrade install

1. Put your Vista disc into your PC's DVD drive.

   The installation window should appear. (If it doesn't, click My Computer, double-click the DVD drive icon, and then double-click the SETUP file.)

   The installation window provides the following options:

   - Check Compatibility Online takes you to Windows Vista Upgrade Advisor (see the sidebar "The Easy Way to Check," earlier in this lesson).

   - Install Now starts the installation process.

   - What to Know Before Installing Windows provides detailed instructions for the process, as well as steps to take before installing.

   - Transfer Files and Settings from Another Computer closes the installation window and launches the Windows Easy Transfer program, which replaces the Files and Settings Transfer Wizard in Windows XP.

2. Click Install Now.

   The screen displays a pleasant, auroralike background; the Get Important Updates for Installation dialog box; and a thermometer bar at the bottom of the screen, split into two segments.

3. Make sure that your PC is connected to the Internet, and click the first option, which instructs the computer to go online to get the latest updates.

   The Vista setup routine downloads any needed updates and drivers before installation starts so that your operating system is up to date when it first launches the desktop.

4. In the activation dialog box that appears, enter the product key for your copy of Vista; then click Next.

   You'll find the key on a sticker somewhere on the case that your Vista DVD came in.

   It's not uncommon to make a mistake when entering the key, so keep trying until Vista accepts your key.

   TIP ——— Make sure that you keep the product key in a safe place in case you need to reinstall Vista. As a backup, you can write the key on the DVD itself with a permanent marker or put it on a label that you stick on the DVD; that way, you'll still have the product key in case the DVD gets separated from its sleeve.

   The next installation screen asks whether you want to upgrade your existing Windows XP installation (upgrade install) or perform a new Vista installation

   continues on next page

(clean install or full install). The following section shows you how to do a clean install or a full install.

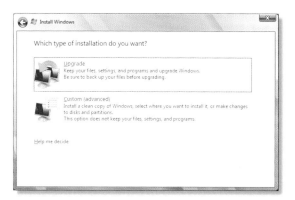

5. Click Upgrade.

A new screen displays a list of drives where Windows can be installed.

6. Because this is an upgrade installation, select the drive that holds your current Windows installation; then click Next.

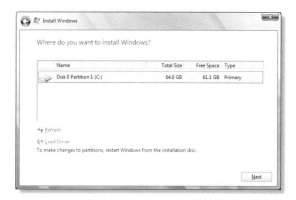

The installer runs a quick check to make sure that key components of your computer will work with Vista. This verification process is not as thorough as the one that Upgrade Advisor does, but it will flag potential problem areas.

7. Click Next in the Compatibility Report screen.

The process of copying and installing files begins.

An upgrade install can take quite a while. Expect this phase to last at least an hour. Note the time warning on the Upgrading Windows screen, and go grab a cup of tea or mug of coffee. But don't go too far. If there is a problem, you may have to intervene, so check back periodically to see whether the installer is asking for more information.

During the process, the computer reboots at least twice, depending on the complexity of your Windows XP setup. When installation is complete, Vista will boot to your upgraded desktop for the first time with your existing wallpaper, desktop icons, and settings intact.

You'll find more detail on the initial desktop experience in Lesson 3.

NOTE —— If there are any problems as a result of the installation, such as incompatible programs or hardware that lacks drivers, Vista notifies you via a pop-up message.

Full or clean install

A *full* install places a pristine installation of Vista on your hard drive, stashing your existing Windows files and folders in a directory called WINDOWS.OLD. You won't be able to run most programs from this directory, but you'll have access to your old files. This type of installation maintains your data files, but they may not be in the locations that your programs expect.

A *clean* install wipes the hard drive clean of any existing operating systems, programs, and data files, and installs a virgin copy of Vista.

Both clean and full installs set up fresh Windows Vista installations. The primary difference is that a full install gives you access to your data and program files from

> ### External Backup Drive
>
> Seagate, Maxtor, and Western Digital all make reasonably priced external USB drives ranging in capacity from a few gigabytes up to a full terabyte. These drives are great ways to back up your files. Since you have to backup anyway, this might be a good time to consider getting one of those drives. You'll use it often.

an older Windows setup (you won't be able to run the programs themselves), whereas a clean install wipes the disk clean and starts from scratch.

Use a full install if you want to keep your files handy on your hard drive, but don't rely on this as your backup! Make copies of your data onto a CD, DVD, another computer on your network or another drive first. Use a clean install if you want to put Vista on a completely clean hard drive.

But be aware that the clean install is not available to users who buy the upgrade version of any Vista edition. You can only do a full install with that version. You can then delete the WINDOWS.OLD folder to save drive space.

Perform either a full or a clean install

1. Make sure that your computer is set to boot first from the DVD drive and then from the C drive.

   Typically, this check is made through the BIOS setting that requires you to press a key when you start Windows. Most modern PCs are set to do this automatically. If yours is not, you'll need to check the manual for your PC or motherboard to see how to change this setting, as different brands have different procedures.

2. Insert your Vista disc into your computer's DVD drive, and restart the PC.

   A screen that says "Press any key to boot from CD or DVD" appears.

NOTE ——— If you're using the upgrade version of the Vista install disc, you won't be able to boot from it. The only way to initiate a clean install is to start it from an existing Windows installation on your hard drive. After your machine reboots and you've entered your product key, you are given a chance to choose an upgrade installation or a clean install.

3. Press any key.

   The installer displays a start screen similar to the one used for an upgrade install (see step 2 in the preceding exercise).

4. Click Install Now.

   A window appears that lets you set your language, numeric formats, and keyboard type.

5. Click Next.

   A window appears that lets you pick the type of installation you want. Because you booted from the DVD, the Upgrade option is dimmed.

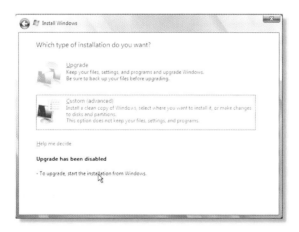

6. Click Custom.

   A window appears that lets you choose where you want to install Vista.

7. Choose the location, and then click Drive Options (Advanced). A list of handy tools appears at the bottom of the screen.

continues on next page

The tools you see are the key to choosing between a clean and a full install:

- **Refresh.** This tool lets you see any changes that have been made to your drives before the installation starts.

- **Load Driver.** If your system requires some special drivers (for a RAID configuration, for example), you can install them before the installation begins.

- **Delete.** This tool allows you to delete the partition. Don't do this unless you want to do a clean install. If you delete the partition, you'll need to create a new one to replace it.

- **Extend.** This tool makes an existing partition on a hard drive larger, if additional room is available on the drive.

- **Format.** This tool formats the drive, removing all data and programs on it. The process is similar to deleting the partition but doesn't require creating a new partition.

- **New.** This tool creates a new partition. If you use this tool on an existing partition, it will split the partition in two at sizes you specify.

If there is a Windows installation on the drive and partition you select, the installer will move all the folders and files into a directory called WINDOWS. OLD. You can access these files, but you can't run the programs. The settings from your existing Windows installation will not be imported.

8. If you don't want to preserve your older files, choose the Format or Delete option first (remember to create a new partition if you delete the old one), and then continue with the installation.

After these choices are made, the installation process begins.

As in an upgrade install, with a clean or full install, you're treated to a progress screen as the installer runs through its paces (see step 7 of the preceding exercise), though notably missing is the warning about the process taking "several hours" to complete. That's because one of the benefits of a clean or full install is that it takes much less time—possibly as little as 20 minutes, depending on the speed of your computer. During this process, your computer will reboot several times.

9. When prompted, make choices about specific settings, including your user name, an optional password, and a representative photo; then click Next.

10. Choose a name for the computer and an image for your background wallpaper; and then click Next.

   If your PC is on a network, pick a name that will identify it as yours. You can choose a different background later, if you want; the options you're shown during setup are only a fraction of the wallpaper options available.

11. The Help Protect Windows Automatically screen includes the settings for automatic updates, which instruct Vista to grab patches, fixes, and new features on its own.

   We advise choosing Use Recommended Settings, which can report problems to Microsoft and alert you when fixes are found.

continues on next page

12. Set your computer's time and date. The installer picks up the time and date from the computer's built-in clock, but you likely will need to set the correct time zone. If your computer is on a network, go to step 13; if it isn't on a network, proceed to step 14.

13. In the Select Your Computer's Current Location window, choose the kind of network your computer is on.

Choose the Home or Work option when you trust the network and those who are on it. These options let you see other computers with the same workgroup name in the Network folder, for example. Choose the Public Location option when you are connecting to the Internet in a public place, such as hopping onto a Wi-Fi network in a coffee shop. You can change these settings later for any given network connection. You may also see this screen again when you finally boot to the desktop.

When you've completed these steps, you'll see a "Thank you" screen.

14. Click Start.

Vista begins a performance check, preparing a system rating that will come in handy later. (We'll discuss this rating in detail in Lesson 3.) Several different screens will appear as Vista runs benchmark tests on various components. The screen may also flicker and go black briefly.

15. When the sign-in screen, finally appears, enter the password you chose in step 9, if you chose one (passwords remain optional despite Vista's emphasis on security).

You'll see several more screens as Vista prepares the desktop, establishes settings for various components, and possibly downloads more updates. When those chores are complete, you'll see your pristine new Windows Vista desktop.

You also will see the Welcome Center, a screen that lists common tasks new Vista users may want to perform, including connecting to the Internet, transferring files from an older PC, adding user accounts, and viewing the computer's details. The bottom half of the Welcome Center displays some marketing offers from Microsoft and/or the PC's manufacturer.

Now that Vista's up and running on your computer, you can begin to get familiar with it.

What You've Learned

■ How to tell if your existing PC can handle Vista

■ The difference between an upgrade, full, and clean install, and which may be best for your situation

■ How to do each type of install

3

GOALS

Learn about the basic
Vista interface

Determine whether
your hardware is up
to speed

Customize the
Vista desktop and
Start menu

Work with folders
and files

Use Windows Help
and Support

Get to Know Vista

Even if you're an old Windows hand, you'll find a lot of new things in Vista. Your knowledge of Windows will help, but as you work through this lesson, you'll notice that some things have changed. We're assuming that you're working on a machine with Vista already installed; if not, refer to Lesson 2.

Starting Out with a Clean Screen

Like Windows XP, Vista starts out with a relatively clean and uncluttered desktop. Assuming that your PC maker hasn't added anything, all you see are the desktop itself, Welcome Center, the Recycle Bin, and the Sidebar with some gadgets.

Over time, your Vista desktop may get cluttered much like our physical desks do, with icons that are placed there either by you or by the software programs you install. For now at least, enjoy the pristine look of your new desktop.

Optimizing Vista's Performance

As with all operating systems, Vista's performance depends in part on your hardware configuration. In Lesson 2, we talked about how to determine whether your machine has the minimum hardware needed to run Vista. Even if your PC does have what it takes, you may be able to improve Vista's performance further by increasing memory, getting a faster hard drive, or upgrading your graphics card.

The Windows Welcome screen provides links to common tasks for new Vista users.

From Welcome Center, you can determine just how well your hardware is performing by viewing the Windows Experience Index base score or the detailed breakdowns on several of your hardware components.

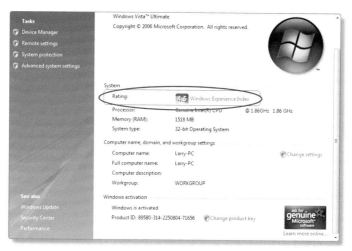

The Windows Experience Index rating gives you the score of your lowest performing component.

The *base score* is determined by examining the performance of your processor (CPU), memory (RAM), graphics adapter, and gaming graphics, as well as the data-transfer rate of your primary hard disk. That score isn't actually a summary or an average of all your components; it's the score of the component that ranks lowest. Microsoft says that some software vendors will use this result to indicate the minimum score you'll need to run their applications.

To determine your Windows Experience Index base score:

1. If Welcome Center isn't already running, run it by typing Welcome in the Search box at the bottom of the Start menu. Don't press Enter; instead, click on Welcome Center when it appears at the top of the Start menu (see "Access applications from the All Programs menu" later in this lesson).

continues on next page

A summary of your hardware configuration displays in the top section of the screen.

2. Click Show More Details in the top-right corner.

    The Windows Experience Index base score appears.

3. For more details, click the Windows Experience Index link just to the right of your score.

The scores for your processor, memory, graphics, gaming graphics, and primary hard disk appear.

NOTE ——— If you change any of your hardware, you can refresh the numbers by clicking Update My Score on the lower right of this screen.

TIP ——— Another (and quicker) way to get to the Performance Index screen is to type `Performance Information` in the Start menu's Search box.

Customizing Your Desktop

When we described Welcome Center in Lesson 1, we pointed out the little Run at Startup check box in the bottom-right corner that lets you decide whether to run Welcome Center at startup. Having Welcome Center on your screen is a great idea when you're getting to know Vista, but after a while, it becomes wasted screen real estate. After you're comfortable with Vista, we suggest that you uncheck the check box so that you don't have to deal with Welcome Center all the time.

NOTE ——— If you ever need Welcome Center again, you can display it by choosing Control Panel > System and Maintenance > Welcome Center or by typing `Welcome Center` in the Start menu's Search box.

With the exception of the Aero interface and the optional Sidebar, the Vista desktop looks a lot like the one in Windows XP. But right-click any unused portion of the desktop, and notice three new options in the shortcut menu that pop up: View, Sort By, and Personalize.

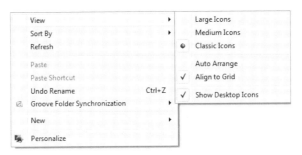

Vista's right-click menu adds some new options.

The View submenu lets you change the size of the icons on your desktop. You may have noticed that in Vista, the icons are larger than they are in XP. If you prefer the old XP size, right-click any blank area of the desktop and choose View > Classic Icons from the shortcut menu. If you end up not liking the smaller icons, you can always reverse the process.

The View submenu also lets you arrange icons automatically. Vista does this by aligning the icons to a grid, which makes the icons line up neatly but maybe not exactly where you want them.

The Sort By option replaces the Arrange By option in XP. The function is still the same: It lets you sort the icons on your desktop by name, size, type, or date modified.

The Personalize option replaces XP's Properties option, which lets you adjust display settings such as themes, desktop icons, wallpaper, screen resolution, and monitor refresh rates.

Customizing the Start Menu

Look at the bottom-left corner of the screen of a Windows XP system, and you'll see the Start button, which you click to display the Start menu. In Vista, you no longer see the word *Start;* instead, you see a large round Start button with the Windows flag. (Microsoft refers to this icon internally as *the Pearl.*)

Vista's newly designed Start button.

Despite this difference, the Start menu and its functions are the same.

View your options and programs

The Start menu has a number of options, depending on the programs you have installed, and it also displays a list of all of your installed programs.

To see your options in the Start menu:

■ Click the Start button. (Your Start menu may look different from the screen shot that follows because you may have different programs installed.) Some of the programs you want to use will be immediately apparent. Don't worry if you don't see the application you want to run; in a moment, we'll show you how to add programs to the Start menu.

To see a list of all installed programs:

■ Click All Programs. It's possible, however, that some installed programs won't show up in this list. If that's the case, see "Run a program that's missing from the Start menu" later in this lesson.

Keyboard Shortcuts

Ctrl+Esc	Displays the Start menu.
Windows key	Also displays the Start menu. The Windows key is on most (but not all) keyboards and typically is located just to the right of the Ctrl key. After you display the Start menu, you can navigate by using either the arrow keys or the mouse.

Add or remove Start menu items

The items that appear in your Start menu by default were placed there by Vista, your PC maker, or by various programs. You can add or remove items at will, however.

To add any icon to the Start menu:

■ Drag it to the menu (Vista adds a shortcut but doesn't actually move the icon), or right-click the icon and choose Pin to Start Menu from the shortcut menu.

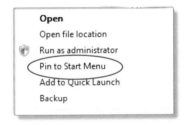

To remove an item from the Start menu:

■ Click the Start button, right-click the application icon, and from the shortcut menu, choose Remove from This List.

Rearrange the Start menu or revert to Classic Style

You can rearrange items in the Start menu by dragging them up or down to a new location. You can also revert to the "classic" Windows Start menu.

We recommend that you experience the benefits of Vista's Start menu before reverting to the old one. But if you've tried it and had enough, you can bring the old Start menu back.

To revert to the classic Start menu:

- Right-click the round Start menu button and choose Properties > Classic Start Menu from the shortcut menu.

Access applications from the All Programs menu

Unlike the Start menu in Windows XP, the Start menu in Vista doesn't have cascading menus. Programs within the All Programs menu are displayed alphabetically, either on their own or within folders.

This list is scrollable, so if you don't see what you're looking for, click the down-arrow button at the bottom of the list or drag the scroll bar to the right.

In some cases, you may have to click a group or folder—such as to run one of the Windows accessories. To run Calculator, for example, you would follow these steps:

1. Click the Start menu button to open the Start menu.

2. Choose All Programs > Accessories > Calculator.

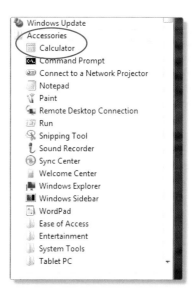

Run a program that's missing from the Start menu

Sometimes, a program doesn't show up in the Start menu or even in the All Programs submenu. If this happens to you, try the following:

1. Type the name of the program in the Search box below All Programs.

    You don't usually need to type in the full name of the program. For example, you can enter word and the search engine will return "Microsoft Office Word" before you press the Enter key. You should consider using this procedure to open all your programs, even if you can find the program via the All Programs menu—it's often faster than navigating menus.

    The name of the program should appear at or near the top of your Start menu. (You may see other items that also meet the search criterion.)

2. Double-click the program name.

    The program should launch. If it doesn't, proceed to step 3.

3. In the right panel of the Start menu, choose Select Computer.

4. Double-click the C-drive icon, and scroll down to Program Files.

5. Open the Program Files folder, and try to locate the folder for your missing program.

6. When you locate the program, open its folder, and look for the executable file (with the file extension .exe).

    NOTE ——— By default, file extensions aren't displayed. To learn how to display them, see the sidebar "Making Extensions Visible" in this section.

7. Double-click the program to run it.

Bringing Back XP's Run Command

For the most part, we agree with Microsoft that the Search box is a better way to launch programs than the old Run command. But unlike the Search box, the Run command kept track of programs you ran previously. If you miss the old Run command, you can bring it back:

1. Right-click the Windows icon and choose Properties from the shortcut menu.

2. Click Customize.

3. Choose Run Command, and then click OK.

Explore with the right pane

The right pane of the Start menu is your gateway to some pretty important functions in Vista, including the help system, Control Panel, Network Places, folders on your computer, and the search system.

The right side of the Start menu takes you to a number of useful places.

Making Extensions Visible

One thing that annoys us about Vista is that by default (like most previous versions of Windows), it hides the extensions for known file types—that is, for most files.

We realize that not including file extensions makes lists less cluttered, but knowing a file extension can be important. Seeing it tells you what type of file it is, which can be very useful, not only for running programs, but also for opening files.

If you have a file named patti.jpg, for example, you know that it's some type of graphic— probably a digital photo. If the filename is patti.gif, you know that it's a different type of image file, such as an uncompressed photo or graphic. But if the filename is just patti, you don't know much about it. The file could be a photo, a document, or even a program. Vista would know, however, so if you double-clicked the file, it would launch in its associated program—assuming that nothing goes wrong. But things *can* go wrong, and even if they don't, sometimes it's nice to know what type of file you have.

Fortunately, you can change the default setting and make extensions visible for known file types. Follow these steps:

1. From the Start menu, choose Computer.

2. Double-click the C-drive icon.

3. Click the Organize tab near the top-left corner.

4. Click Folder and Search Options to open the Folder Options dialog box.

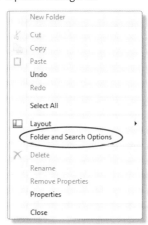

5. Click the View tab.

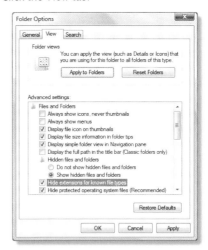

6. Clear the Hide Extensions for Known File Types check box.

7. Click OK.

This pane is similar to its counterpart pane in Windows XP, though there are a couple of name changes. Instead of *My Documents,* for example, you'll see the name of the active user of the computer. Clicking that user name yields access to that person's documents. This feature isn't all that useful if you're the only person who uses your PC, but if you share your machine, it helps you keep track of who the current user is.

You'll also find a Recent Items option, which lists you the documents you've worked on recently, and a Games option, which takes you to both the games that came with Windows and those you installed.

Getting Acquainted with the Taskbar

Just as it is in Windows XP, the taskbar is a horizontal bar along the bottom of the screen. The portion of the taskbar just to the right of the Start icon is the Quick Launch toolbar, which is just another place to put icons for frequently used programs.

The Vista taskbar includes the Quick Launch toolbar.

Thumbnail views

The area immediately to the right of the Quick Launch toolbar stores icons for programs and data files that are currently open. You can switch to one of those files or programs by clicking its icon. Or, if you're running a version of Vista that supports the Aero interface (Lesson 1), you can get a thumbnail view of what's inside a window by holding the mouse pointer over one of the running icons.

Move the mouse over an icon on the task bar to get a preview.

Notification area

The right end of the taskbar contains the notification area. As in XP, this area is where you'll find the clock, volume control, and icons from various programs. It's named the *notification area* because it may also contain messages from some programs. (Occasionally, you may see it referred to as the *system tray.*)

System clock

At the right end of the taskbar is the system time. If you click it, you'll see a newly reformatted clock and calendar.

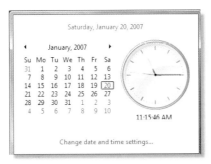

Click on the time in the lower-right corner of the screen to see how
Vista has improved the look of the clock and calendar.

Set the time and date

- Click the time in the taskbar; then click the Change Date and Time Settings link just below the clock and calendar. A screen displays that lets you change the date and time, as well as the time zone.

  TIP —— Be sure you have the correct time zone set; PC makers usually don't adjust the time zone based on where the machine is going.

Synchronize the clock with an Internet time server

1. Click the time in the taskbar; then click the Change Date and Time Settings link.

2. Click the Internet time tab to determine whether your computer is set to synchronize automatically with an Internet time server.

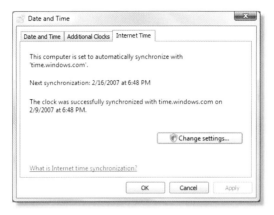

3. If your computer clock is not synchronized, click Change Settings; then
   change the settings so that your computer clock synchronizes with one of the
   online clocks.

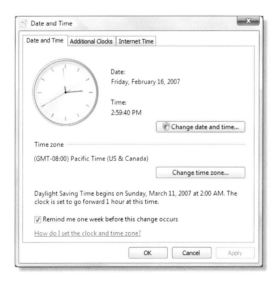

By default, your computer clock synchronizes with time.windows.com.

continues on next page

4. Click Update Now.

    Your clock will be set for the exact time (assuming that you set the correct time zone—see the previous stepped list, "Set the time and date," if you have not).

5. Click OK twice to exit.

    From now on, your clock will be reset automatically on a regular basis.

Exploring Folders and Files

As always, Windows organizes files—which include all your data and all programs—into folders. A folder is basically a collection of files.

You can have many types of folders, including ones you create, ones that are created by programs you install, and folders set up automatically by Vista. We'll start with Vista's automatic data folders; by default, they're the ones that are used to store files you create or download.

Review the primary Vista folders

The mother of all data folders is the one with your name on it (or whatever name you or your PC maker used when setting up the default user account). That folder replaces the My Documents folder in Windows XP.

If you look at the top of the Start menu, you'll notice your user name (or whatever user name the PC manufacturer assigned for the default user). Below it are the names of four other document folders: Documents, Pictures, Music, and Games.

The Start menu lets you select your user name for your master folder or folders for documents, pictures, music, and games.

But you have more folders on your PC than those you see in the Start menu. When you click your user name, the following folders display:

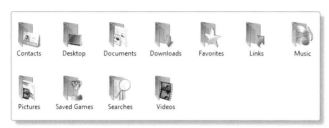

Clicking on your user name displays a handful of folders associated with only you.

Let's say you want to view the files that you've downloaded with your Internet browser. Those files will be in the Downloads folder. Here's how to access them:

1. Click the Start button.

2. Click your user name in the top-right corner of the Start menu.

3. Double-click the folder called Downloads. The downloaded files you want to view are stored there.

Notice the common elements of folders

Every open folder window has common elements that control its behavior. In the top-left corner of each open folder, for example, is a pair of blue buttons that let you navigate backward and forward.

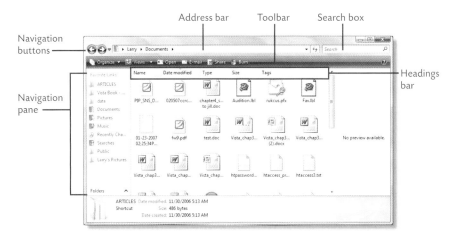

If these buttons are very light in color, no forward or backward direction is available, but when you start navigating, those buttons are active.

Just to the right of the arrows is the address bar, which tells you the actual address or path of your folder. You may have to click it to see the path.

To the right of the address bar is the Search box, which allows you to search for a word or phrase in a file or subfolder within the current folder.

Below the address bar is a toolbar that allows you to perform common tasks, such as changing the view of your folders or burning files to a CD or DVD. As you'll see later, the actual tools may vary depending on the type of files in the folder.

Below the toolbar is the headings bar, which contains items that vary, depending on the type of data in the folder.

The leftmost column of the screen is the Navigation pane, which lets you switch to other folders quickly.

At the bottom of the screen is the Details pane, which tells you common properties associated with the folder, such as the number of items in it.

Living with (or Without) Microsoft's Strategy for Storing Data Files

Windows sets up these standard data folders for a reason. This system not only provides you (and software developers) a logical way to organize files, but also makes life easier if you share the computer, because each user who has an account will have a personal area for documents. Mom and Dad won't have to worry about writing over Susie's files, and if John wants to password-protect his files, he can keep the rest of the family out of his area while giving them access to their own files.

Most users probably will like the way Microsoft set up folders, but you are not required to use this scheme. Some savvy PC users instead create a single folder called Data on the C drive and put all data files in that folder. This approach is most useful if only one person uses the computer, though it's e possible to create separate folders, such as Larry_data and Dwight_data. (But even though we wrote this book together, we don't share a computer, a residence, or even a city.)

One advantage to this approach is that it can make it easier to back up or transfer all your data files. But if you do this, you may have to configure your individual programs so that they place files and look for files in that directory instead of the ones Microsoft created.

Recognize unique elements of folders

Each type of folder has its own characteristics, depending on the type of data it contains. Let's explore some of them:

1. Click the Start button, and then click Music on the Start menu.

2. Notice that the headings, such as Artists, Album, Genre and Rating are specific to music files. You wouldn't expect to see headings like this on a folder full of spreadsheets or photographs.

continues on next page

3. Now go back and check the pictures folder and notice that it differs.

> **NOTE** —— Windows is hard-wired to know about more than just the default folders it sets up. It also can adjust the folder type depending on what types of files you're storing in that folder, even if it's a folder that you created.

Get acquainted with other types of folders

In reading this section, you've become acquainted with your personal folder, the Music folder, and the Pictures folder. By default, Windows also creates Documents, Videos, and Downloads folders. As we mentioned earlier, the Start menu doesn't have a link to video files, contacts, and downloads, but you can find them inside subfolders by opening your personal folder.

The idea is to create a depository of files that you, Microsoft, and software developers can count on. Microsoft Word, for example, will put your Word documents in your Documents folder. Windows Movie Maker and most other video-editing programs will put videos in the Videos folder. Microsoft Internet Explorer 7 will place downloads in the Download folder. You'll find games and game-related files in the Games folder. Also new to Vista is the Contacts folder.

You can access the personal (labeled with your user name), Documents, Pictures, Music, and Games folders directly from the Start menu, and you can access all these special folders from your personal folder.

Change your folder's headings bar

Every folder has items in the headings bar, which are used to sort files and subfolders. But those items can change, depending on what type of folder it is. For example, items may include Name, Date Modified, Type, and Size, but as we've seen earlier, they may be different depending on the type of data that's stored in that folder. The headings that show up by default in any folder are arbitrary—

there are so many more ways to categorize data than what can be displayed on one line—which is why Microsoft allows you to add or remove heading items.

1. Right click anywhere on the headings bar. A pop-up menu displays.

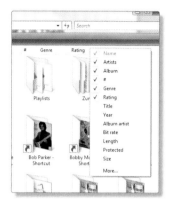

2. Deselect headings to remove them; select headings to add additional ones.

The same process applies to all types of folders, but the options, of course, will differ depending on content.

Change a folder's properties

You can also change the properties of a folder so that it behaves as though it contained other types of documents.

Suppose that you have a folder to store MP3 files that you create for your own use. By default, music folders have headings that are appropriate to music files, such as Name, Artist, Album, Genre, and Rating.

By looking at the headings bar, you can tell when a folder contains music files.

Let's say, however, that you want to look at the files by name, size, and date modified, but not by artist or album. To do this, you would disable Windows' ability to display a music folder with such headings as artists, album, and so on. Here's how:

1. Right-click the folder (or the folder name in the Start menu), and choose Properties from the shortcut menu.

   The Properties dialog box opens.

2. Click the Customize tab.

3. From the drop-down menu, choose All Items.

   This setting changes the properties of the folder so that items in it are no longer displayed as music files, but as more generic files. In our case, the folder now displays files and subfolders by name, date modified, type and size.

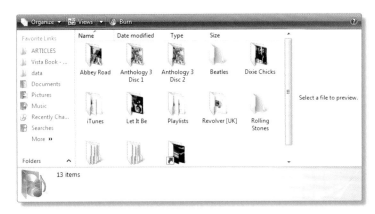

Browse for other folders

You have many more folders than the ones that are listed in the Start menu, and it's easy to find any folder on your machine. In Lesson 5, we talk about how to use the Search function to locate files and folders, but you can also browse for them by using Windows Explorer (not to be confused with Internet Explorer).

To browse files and subfolders using Windows Explorer, do the following:

1. Choose Start > Computer.

   Windows Explorer displays.

2. Double-click the C drive icon.

   All the directories (also called folders) on your C drive display.

3. Double-click any of the folders.

   All the files and subfolders inside that folder display. At this point, you can open a subfolder or work with a file.

Use Windows Explorer to work with files

You can do several things from any Windows Explorer window:

- You can double-click a file or program icon to open it.

- You can right-click a file to copy it or cut it. If you copy or cut the file, you can paste it somewhere else. (If you cut and paste the file instead, you delete it from its current location when the paste is complete.)

- You can move a file to a different folder by dragging it, or you can drag it to a different disk (which copies it).

- You can right-click to delete the file.

Keyboard Shortcuts in Windows Explorer

Alt	Toggles the classic XP menu bar. To display it, press Alt in any Windows Explorer window; to make it disappear, press Alt again.
Alt+up-arrow key	Moves up a level in Windows Explorer
Alt+left-arrow key	Returns to the parent directory
Alt+right-arrow key	Move forward to the directory previously visited
F3	Displays the Search box

Using the Help System

Everyone needs a little help now and then, which is why we wrote this book. But you can also get help from the Windows help system by choosing Start > Help and Support. That displays Windows Help and Support, which is quite extensive and, for the most part, self-explanatory. In fact, it's much better in Vista than in previous versions of Windows; if you're connected to the Internet, it goes online to fetch more detailed information on some topics.

The Windows help system provides answers to many questions.

Browse help topics

You can browse help topics in several ways. The following are just a few of them:

- Windows Basics give you a general overview of computers and Vista, providing details on some of the programs and features of the operating system.

- Table of Contents works pretty much like the table of contents in a book by breaking Vista into logical areas—kind of like chapters.

- Troubleshooting lists various things that can go wrong and includes tips on how to fix them.

Search for help

The most useful part of the help system is the ability to search for help on anything you can think of. If you have a feature you need to look up, simply type its name in the Search box; with luck, you'll get some answers. Windows Help and Support is pretty well stocked with information, so you have a good chance of finding what you're looking for.

To see whether Windows Help and Support can provide information on wireless networking, for example, follow these steps:

1. Choose Start > Help and Support.

   Windows Help and Support opens.

2. Type wireless networking in the Search box.

continues on next page

3. Press Enter (or click the little magnifying glass to the right of the Search box).

You see a table of contents of information on your topic.

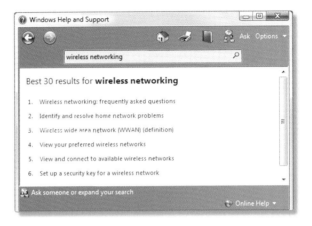

Let someone else help

If you're really stuck, you can enlist another user's help by clicking Ask Someone to Advance Your Search, which appears at the bottom of the Help and Support window when you first access Help and Support. That system gives you access to Windows Remote Assistance, which lets you give someone permission to view your screen and even control your computer remotely via the Internet. This feature can be very handy—almost like having the expert sitting next to you—but use it with caution.

In using Windows Remote Assistance, make sure that you invite only a trusted, knowledgeable person to help you, and be aware the performance at both ends can be quite slow, even if both of you have broadband Internet connections. Still, this feature could get you out of a jam.

What You've Learned

- What the desktop looks like and how to work with it
- How to tell whether your hardware is up to speed by using Windows Experience Index
- How to get rid of Welcome Center if it's no longer welcome
- How to use and modify the Start menu
- How to access programs whether or not they're listed in the Start menu
- How to set the time zone and synchronize your PC's clock via the Internet
- How to work with files and folders
- How to use Windows Help and Support

4

Use Other Programs with Vista

Windows Vista comes with many applications that are built into the operating system, so you can get started immediately with what's included. But at some point, you're going to want to do more, so you'll need to install other software.

This lesson explores the different ways you can obtain new programs and how to install them. It also provides troubleshooting tips you can use when the programs don't work as expected. Because Vista is a new version of Windows, you're likely to run into software that isn't completely compatible with it. But don't despair—we've got some tricks up our sleeves!

Evaluating Existing Program Compatibility

Microsoft works hard to make sure you can run your existing programs when you upgrade to a new version of its operating system. So one of the strengths of the Windows operating system is that most programs written for older versions work with the latest ones. This capability is called *backward compatibility.* Even the simplest software programs are complex under the hood, however, and as anyone who's upgraded an existing Windows-based PC knows, not every program survives the transition.

In the vast majority of cases, if your programs work with Windows XP, they're likely to be compatible with Vista—with a few significant exceptions that we'll delve into later in this lesson. But the older a program is, the more likely it is to encounter problems. Software that is compatible with Windows ME, 98, 95, and 3.1 might work, but don't count on it.

Use the Windows Vista Upgrade Advisor

If you're upgrading to Vista from Windows XP, the Windows Vista Upgrade Advisor (mentioned in Lesson 2) can flag programs that may not work or that could cause problems with Vista. In some cases, Vista's installation routine may actually disable problematic programs if they would interfere with the operating system in some way.

Windows Vista Upgrade Advisor warns you about incompatible programs.

Take the Advisor's recommendations to heart, and if it indicates that a program should be removed or updated, do it before you upgrade to Vista.

Get a sense of what works

Certain programs generally work better than others when you upgrade to a new operating system, and these programs vary by type:

- **Productivity applications.** For the most part, the programs you use at work—word processors, spreadsheets, presentation managers, photo editors, and so on—should be compatible with Vista. Exceptions may include programs that work with modems (such as faxing software) and custom programs created in-house to work under a specific operating system.

- **Network and Internet applications.** Email, Web browsers, chat, and FTP programs should work, but there are exceptions. Some instant-messaging applications, such as AIM Triton, don't work well with Vista. Again, when it comes to custom programs, all bets are off.

- **Music and multimedia applications.** Mainstream programs (such as iTunes and Napster's software) will work, but lesser-known programs may not. Programs that write to CD and DVD drives may have a hard time if they don't get along with Vista's built-in drivers for these devices.

- **Games.** Newer games should also do well, but those designed for Windows 98 or ME are likely to cause problems. (Many of them didn't work even under Windows XP!)

- **System utilities.** Programs in this category are least apt to work; they include antivirus and antispyware programs, disk defragmenters, disk editors, and utilities suites. In most cases, the developers of these programs introduce new versions in conjunction with the release of a new Windows version, so you will need to update to those versions when they become available.

Don't be alarmed if one of your favorite or irreplaceable programs falls into one of the problematic categories. There are plenty of exceptions.

TIP —— When Microsoft released Windows XP, it posted to its Web site a list of programs that worked with it. Unfortunately, the company chose not to do that with Vista. But Windows enthusiasts have come to the rescue. IeXbeta has set up a wiki site on which Vista users post reports about program compatibility. See it at www.iexbeta.com/wiki/index.php/Windows_Vista_RTM_Software_Compatibility_List. If you know something about a program that's not in the list, feel free to contribute your knowledge.

Evaluating Compatibility for New Programs

In the case of retail software, you should be able to tell whether it's compatible with Windows Vista by looking on the box for the software's system requirements. Web sites that offer software should have similar information available, either on the page that features the program you want or via a link. Because Vista's new, not all software that works with it may be listed as such in the system requirements.

If a program that interests you indicates that it works only with Windows XP, use the categories offered earlier in this lesson as a guide. Also check the support area of the software developers' Web pages. If they're doing their job, they should have information about Vista compatibility and available upgrades.

TIP —— Although you'll find a lot of software available online, be very careful about what you download and install on your computer. Some programs that look legitimate may not be; there's quite a racket in antispyware and antivirus programs that in fact place malicious software on your PC.

Before you download a copy of a program you've never used before–and certainly before you pay money for it–enter the title in your favorite search engine, and see what kind of results you get. If you aren't familiar with the product or the Web site that's distributing it, look it up at one of download sites listed in the sidebar "Great Download Sites." These sites work hard to avoid distributing sleazy software.

One benefit of acquiring software online is that many developers offer trial versions of their programs. You can try out these titles for a specified period before you have to pay for them. In some cases, advanced features are disabled until you pay for the full version, or the trial version may be full featured but time out after a fixed number of days or uses. Rarely, trial versions are offered on the honor system—fully functional, with no time-outs and only a request that you pay for the software after a certain amount of time.

This scenario is perfect when you're using a new operating system for which developers may not have updated their programs. If you install a trial version, and it doesn't work, you haven't lost anything but your time.

Great Download Sites

Where can you find software that works under Windows Vista? Lots of reputable Web sites feature thousands of freeware and shareware titles to download, as well as trial versions of commercial programs. Some the better ones include the following:

- **Download.com** (www.download.com). Huge database of software from CNET.

- **Tucows** (www.tucows.com/Windows). One of the oldest and most respected download sites.

- **BetaNews/FileForum** (www.betanews.com). Great source for cutting-edge titles.

- **FilePlanet** (www.fileplanet.com). Good source for game demos.

Installing Programs

The way programs are installed depends on how you acquire them. Retail software usually comes on a CD or DVD; downloaded software is a file that you double-click to launch. Windows Vista reacts a little differently in each case.

Install software from a disc

In previous versions of Windows, installing disc-based software was relatively simple: You'd insert the disc into a CD or DVD drive, wait for the installer to launch, click a few OK buttons, and agree to a license agreement, and you were done.

But because Vista is much more security conscious, you've got a few more hoops to jump through.

Install using AutoPlay

AutoPlay is a feature that causes Windows to take automated action when a disc is put into the CD or DVD drive, or an external drive is connected via the USB port. In most cases, it's turned on by default. Some PC makers, however may disable it. Unless you dig around in Windows' settings, you won't know for sure until you insert a disc or plug in a drive.

1. Insert the installation disc into your PC's CD or DVD drive.

   If AutoPlay is enabled, the AutoPlay dialog box appears.

   If AutoPlay is not enabled on your system, you need to launch the installer manually; see the next stepped instruction, "Launch the Installer Manually."

   NOTE ——— See the Set AutoPlay Defaults in Control Panel link in the AutoPlay dialog box? Clicking it takes you to a screen that lets you determine just what happens when you insert a CD or DVD into your computer's optical drive. You can choose what to do with specific kinds of files. You may want to set music discs to play automatically, for example, but set programs to launch only with your permission. You can also launch the AutoPlay panel by typing `autoplay` in the Start menu's Search box. For more information, see Online Resource A, which deals with the Control Panel. (You can access this and other additional information about Vista by visiting www.peachpit.com/vistalearningseries and registering your copy of this book.)

2. Do one of the following:

   • Click the option below Install or Run Program to start the installer.

   • Click the Open Folder to View Files icon to be taken to the folder that contains the installer. (Do this if you want to look for read-me files or other instructions before installing the software.)

   • Check the box next to Always Do This for Software and Games if you don't want to see this dialog box again.

     Exactly what happens during the installation process can vary from program to program, but some basic steps are common to most software.

3. If you're asked to confirm that you indeed want to install the software, click Yes or OK.

NOTE —— Depending on the type of software being installed, you may see other types of dialog boxes as you begin the installation process. If a program requires administrator access to run it, for example, you may see a request from User Account Control to grant permission to the program. User Account Control is Vista's new security feature, detailed in Lesson 6, that forces you to confirm you want to perform a critical system function.

4. If some kind of licensing agreement appears, click Yes or Agree.

   Some programs require you to scroll to the bottom of the agreement—a de facto indication that you've actually read it—before clicking a button to go to the next step.

5. If you're asked to enter a registration key or serial number, do so, and click OK or Continue to proceed.

6. If applicable, choose an express or simple installation versus a custom install.

   An express or simple installation asks fewer questions; a custom installation may allow you to control which components are included.

7. If applicable, specify where you want to install the program on your hard drive.

   In most cases, you won't want to change the default location. Choose a different location if you want to install the program on a different hard drive or if you prefer to organize your programs in a different structure from Windows' standard setup.

8. When the installation is finished, click OK or Finish to exit the installer.

9. If applicable, choose to reboot the computer or return to what you were doing.

NOTE —— If you opt not to reboot, the program you installed may not work until you do.

If the software goes online to authenticate itself after installation, you may be asked to register. Authentication is often mandatory, but registration is usually voluntary.

TIP —— It's usually a good idea to register software so that you're informed of bugs or upgrades. But make sure that the software company is legitimate and that it has a privacy policy in which the company promises not to spam you or sell your email address to others.

Launch the installer manually

If AutoPlay is not enabled, you need to run your program's installer manually to install the software.

1. Click the Start button and then choose Start > Computer.

2. Right-click the icon for the drive that contains the CD, and choose Install or Run Program from the shortcut menu.

    or

    If you don't see those options in the shortcut menu, double-click the drive icon.

3. Look for a program named SETUP.EXE, INSTALL.EXE, or SETUP.MSI, and double-click it.

    The installation process begins. Exactly what happens during the installation process can vary from program to program, but some basic steps are common to most software.

4. Follow steps 4 through 9 of the previous stepped instruction.

Install software from the Web

The process of installing software from the Web is different at first from installing via disc, but when the installation gets under way, the process is usually identical.

1. Download the program you want to install.

    Vista presents a dialog box asking whether you want to run or save the file.

You have two options: Click Run, which downloads a temporary folder on your computer and launches the program automatically, or save the file to a location first and then launch it when you're ready. Because the latter option gives you a safety net by putting a copy of the file on your hard drive, take that route.

2. Click Save.

   The Save As dialog box appears.

3. From the drop-down menu at the top of the dialog box, choose the location where you'd like to store the program.

   By default, Vista saves downloaded files to a Downloads folder within your user folder. If you'd like to store it somewhere else, click the Browse Folders button at the bottom of the dialog box. The Save As dialog box expands to provide you more choices. From here, you can navigate to almost any folder on your hard drive.

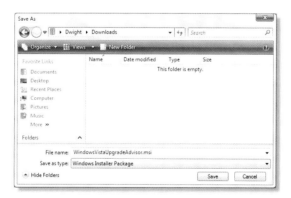

4. Click Save.

5. Navigate to the folder where you just stored the installer, and double-click its icon to start the installation process.

   From here, the installation process should proceed the same way as steps 3 through 8 of "Install using AutoPlay" earlier in this section.

Launching Programs

Traditionally, the most common way to launch programs from Windows has been to click (or double-click) their icons. Vista continues this practice, which applies to both program icons and program shortcuts. The latter are graphical pointers to program files, identified by a small arrow in the bottom-left corner of the icon.

By default, you double-click icons on the desktop or in Windows Explorer, but you single-click icons in the Start menu or the Quick Launch toolbar.

You can also launch programs by quickly searching for them using the Start box in the Start menu, which functions much like an old-fashioned command line from the DOS days.

Programs don't always put shortcuts where you'd like them. You may find that you use a program often enough that you want access right from your desktop, or from the Quick Launch toolbar. We'll show you how to do that, as well as how to organize your icons so that they don't clutter things up.

Add and organize icons on the desktop

Most programs you install will offer to place shortcut icons on a desktop for easy access. Do this often enough, and your desktop can get cluttered. Microsoft encourages users to keep a clean desktop so that when you do a clean install, for example, the only icon that appears on the desktop is the Recycle Bin.

Add icons to the desktop

You can place program shortcuts on the desktop from the Start menu or even from folders on your hard drive by dragging and dropping them, but you'll need to do it a certain way.

1. Right-click a program or shortcut icon, hold down the right mouse button, and drag the icon to the desktop.

If you don't right-click and drag, you could end up moving the program file or shortcut out of its original location. If you do, Vista may warn you that an administrator's approval is required.

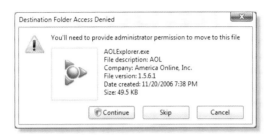

2. From the drop-down menu that appears, choose Create Shortcuts Here.

The program icon is added to the location where you dragged it.

Organize icons on the desktop

Launching programs from the desktop is simple—just double-click and go—but the seductiveness of having your programs that handy can be soured quickly by hunting for them in a crowd. In addition, having lots of icons on the desktop can degrade a PC's performance.

Instead, try organizing desktop icons in folders, which still offers quick access to programs you use frequently. Here's how to create folders and add programs to them:

1. Right-click the desktop, and choose New > Folder from the shortcut menu.

2. Type a name for the folder, such as Games or Utilities.

3. Drag the program items that fit the category into the folder.

continues on next page

4. To customize the icon, right-click it, choose Properties from the shortcut menu, click the Customize tab in the Properties dialog box, and then click the Change Icon button.

5. In the dialog box that appears, select the icon that matches your folder category, and click OK.

Add and delete Quick Launch icons

You can also launch programs from the Quick Launch toolbar. You may recall that we discussed Quick Launch in Lesson 3; it's the toolbar that's integrated into the taskbar, which is located to the right of the Start button.

Add icons to Quick Launch

Adding items to the Quick Launch toolbar is a snap: Just drag the icon you want to add to the toolbar, and release the mouse button. Don't worry about permanently moving the icon from where it was. Unlike when you drag between folders or to the desktop, when you drag to the Quick Launch toolbar or the Start menu, Windows automatically makes a shortcut; it does not move the file.

Delete shortcut icons from Quick Launch

You can also delete shortcuts to programs from the Quick Launch toolbar without actually deleting them from your computer.

1. Right-click any icon you don't want to keep, and choose Delete from the shortcut menu.

   The Delete Shortcut dialog box appears.

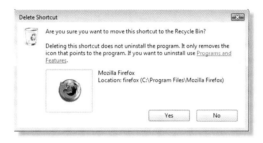

2. Click Yes to confirm and delete the shortcut.

Launch programs from the Start menu

As we discussed in more detail in Lesson 3, almost all your programs will be accessible via the Start menu in one of three ways:

- Clicking one of the icons in the left pane of the Start menu.

- Clicking Programs; then navigating to the icon for the program you want to launch and double-clicking it.

- Typing the name of the program you want to launch in the Search box at the bottom of the Start menu and then pressing Enter or clicking the program name in the search results that appear at the top of the Start menu.

A Solution for an Overcrowded Quick Launch Toolbar

Do you frequently need to click the button that expands the Quick Launch toolbar so that you can see all the icons on it? You can adjust the toolbar so that it shows more icons.

1. Right-click the taskbar, and choose Unlock the Taskbar from the shortcut menu.

2. Do one of the following:

- Click the dotted area that appears next to the Quick Launch button, hold down the mouse button, and drag to the right.

- Click the edge of the taskbar, hold down the mouse button, and drag up slightly. This creates two rows of Quick Launch buttons, as well as two rows of buttons on your taskbar. This method is handy if you run many programs at the same time; it prevents Windows from grouping related buttons from the same programs as quickly.

TIP —— The typing method is often the quickest, especially for programs you don't use often. Don't worry if you don't know the full name of the program; try guessing. Instead of typing Microsoft Excel, for example, you can type Excel.

Setting Default Programs

Double-clicking a document or file launches the program that's associated with that program by default, as you learned in Lesson 3. But when you install new software, it may take over the association for a given type of file. Let's say you have a favorite picture editor, and it launches automatically when you double-click a JPG image file. Then you install a program that manages photos, and it suddenly becomes the program that launches when you double-click a JPG.

Fortunately, in most cases you can control what program is associated with specific file types.

Set default programs at the file level

1. Right-click the file whose association you'd like to change, and choose Open With > [*name of application*] from the shortcut menu.

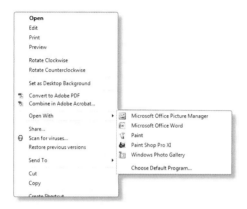

2. From the secondary menu that appears, click Choose Default Program.

   The Open With dialog box appears, displaying several programs in the Recommended Programs list.

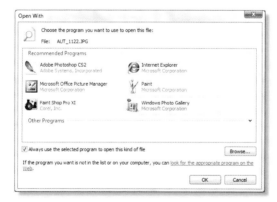

3. Do one of the following:

   • Select the program that you want to associate with this type of file, make sure that the Always Use the Selected Program to Open This Kind of File check box is selected, and click OK. Vista uses the selected program to launch the file with this program now and each time you double-click a file of that type.

continues on next page

- If the program you want to use is not listed in the dialog box, click Browse, and navigate to the executable file's program icon for the program. Click that file, and then click Open. The Open With dialog box reappears, with the program now included in the Recommended Programs list. Select the program, make sure that the check box at the bottom of the dialog box is checked, and click OK.

Set default programs from the Control Panel

You can also change the defaults for some programs in the Set Default Programs module of the Control Panel.

The Set Default Programs module (which exists because of Microsoft's antitrust settlement with the U.S. Department of Justice) features programs that have been involved in legal disputes, including Internet Explorer and other browsers; Windows Media Player and other media players; and Microsoft's Mail, Contacts, and Calendar programs. Microsoft agreed to make it easier for users to set programs other than its own as the defaults for browsing, listening to music, watching video, or reading email.

Suppose that you want Mozilla Firefox to be your default Web browser, so that it launches when you click a link in an email message or a Web page saved to your desktop. Here's how:

1. Click the Start button.

2. In the Start menu's Search box, type `default programs`; then press Enter.

   The Default Programs dialog box appears.

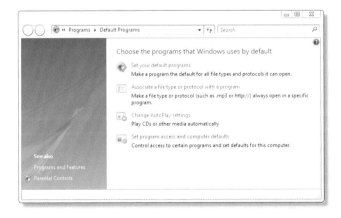

3. Click Set Your Default Programs.

   The Set Default Programs module appears.

4. In the left pane, select the program you would like to set as the default.

   The right pane shows you the program icon, a brief description, and two options.

5. Do one of the following:

   • Click Set This Program as Default to designate the program you've selected as the default program for that activity. If you selected Firefox in the left pane, for example, it will be your default Web browser.

   • Click Choose Defaults for This Program to be taken to another module that lets you choose subcategories of actions the program may perform. Scroll through the list, select the types of files and actions you want the program to control, and then click Save. You're returned to the Set Default Progams Module.

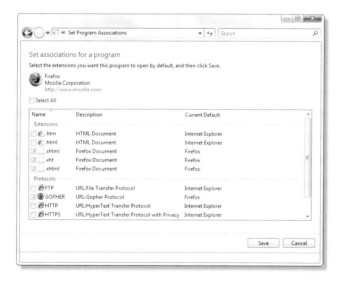

6. In the Set Default Programs module, click OK.

Managing Startup Programs

Vista can launch programs for you when it starts, which can be both a blessing and a curse.

This feature is great for a program that you use regularly, such as your email or instant-messaging software, because that program can launch when Vista boots up, ready to go when you are. On the other hand, programs that you install may set themselves up to launch when the computer starts without asking your permission. This can cause your system to take a long time to boot or to run slowly; in rare cases, it could cause more serious problems.

In this section, you learn how to set up a program to start at launch and how to stop one from doing so.

Launch a program at startup

Many programs have the built-in ability to run at startup. Check the program's settings for an option like Launch When Windows Starts. In AOL Instant Messenger 6, for example, you get to this option by choosing Edit > Settings > Sign In/Sign Out.

AIM's Launch Settings window.

When a program doesn't have this built-in capability, you can still program your PC to launch it when Vista starts. Here's how:

1. Right-click the Start button, and choose Explore from the shortcut menu.

   Windows Explorer opens.

2. In the bottom-left pane of the Explorer window, click the Startup folder (you may have to scroll down).

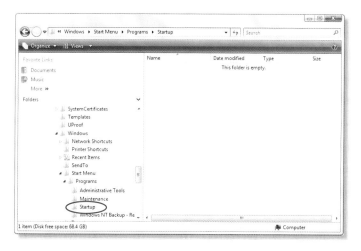

3. Choose Start > All Programs.

4. On the left pane, right-click the shortcut for the program you want to launch at startup; hold down the mouse button; drag the shortcut into the Startup folder of Windows Explorer; and release the mouse button.

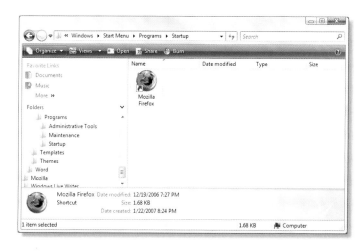

5. From the shortcut menu that appears, choose Copy Here.

Prevent programs from launching at startup

Trying to cut down on the amount of time it takes for your system to boot? Disabling the launch of programs at startup can be an effective strategy, and it's easy to do.

Vista has a program called System Configuration, commonly known as MSCON-FIG, that's been a feature of most versions of Windows since Windows 98. (For some reason, it was not included in Windows 2000.) MSCONFIG provides a list of programs that are slated to start when Vista does and allows you to deselect any of those programs.

Use MSCONFIG cautiously, because it could disable programs that you need to run Vista or your software properly and safely. Write down all the settings before you make any changes. If a problem occurs after you restart your computer, run MSCONFIG again, and undo the changes. If your computer won't start, start it in safe mode (see Lesson 16), undo the changes, and then restart normally.

1. To access MSCONFIG, click the Start button, type `msconfig` in the Search box, and press Enter.

   The System Configuration dialog box appears.

2. Click the Startup tab.

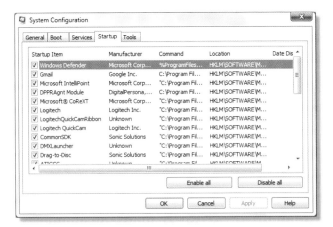

3. Scroll through the items in the list, and uncheck the check boxes next to any programs that you don't want to launch at startup.

4. Click OK.

MSCONFIG has lots of other handy uses, particularly for troubleshooting, and we'll explore more of them in Lesson 16.

What You've Learned

- How to determine whether exiting programs will work with Vista

- How to install software on Vista

- How to download and install software from the Web

- How to control what programs handle which tasks

- How to manage programs that launch when Windows does

5

GOALS

Understand the
benefits of instant
search capability
in Vista

Practice three
methods for searching
documents, email
messages, and
other files

Run advanced searches
to limit or expand
your search

Use the Search box to
search the Internet

Save search criteria so
that you can run the
search again later

Add directories to
your search

Find It with Vista Search

One of the biggest changes Windows Vista delivers is the way it handles searches. Windows XP and previous versions had the ability to search your hard drive, but they did it very slowly, especially if you were trying to locate a file based on its content rather than just its filename. With Vista, searches are very fast—sometimes taking only a couple of seconds to do what used to take several minutes.

The reason for Vista's newfound search speed is that it creates an index to track what is on the drive. The search index is like a book index; it's a lot faster to find a term in an index than it is to scan the entire book. So instead of looking inside every file when you do a search, Vista simply checks the index and locates the file, email message, or contact information.

Microsoft isn't the first company to come up with the idea of indexed search, of course; it's been around for a long time. Several free desktop search products for Windows XP users are available, including offerings from Google; Yahoo; and, yes, Microsoft too. But this is the first version of Windows that includes a fully integrated indexed search as an integral part of the operating system (Apple did it in 2004 when it introduced Spotlight in its OS X operating system), so Vista marks a significant milestone for Windows users.

Another bonus about Vista's integrated search is that because it's available system-wide, developers can incorporate it into their own applications."

We've already seen that with Microsoft Office 2007, which finally has a decent search system.

Conducting an Instant Search

With the new search engine, as you type your search term, Vista instantly starts to display results based on what you've entered so far. The more you type, the more refined your search is.

Let's say you're looking for a file with the name Martin Luther King. If you type only M, the search engine will find all files with that letter—not very useful. But as you continue to type, Vista gets more specific. Typing Mar returns not only *Martin*, but also *Martha, demarcation, market,* and other words containing *mar.* By the time you finish typing Martin, you will have eliminated all files that don't contain that word. You can do even better, however. If you type Martin Luther, Vista returns any files with the name of both the civil-rights leader and the cleric who inspired the Reformation.

Using the Vista interface, you can conduct a search in any of three ways:

- Start searching in the Search box at the bottom of the Start menu.
- Search within folders and subfolders from any Windows folder.
- Select the Search option in the right pane of the Start menu. That brings up the Search Folder, which by default is configured to search all indexed locations.

The method you use depends on the scope of your search.

Search using the Search box

The Search box at the bottom of the Start menu is the best place to search for a program you want to run, a document, a recent email message, or a contact.

Suppose that you want to run Notepad:

1. Click the Start button to open the Start menu.

2. In the Search box, type not.

   As you type, notice that the Notepad icon appears at the top of the Start menu.

3. Click the icon to launch Notepad or keep typing. After you type all of note-pad, press Enter.

You can also use the Search box to find Control Panel items. Try typing Game Controllers; you immediately get access to that particular Control Panel option.

The Search box will also locate email messages and files, but if you're going to use it for either of these purposes, be sure to click See All Results just above the box.

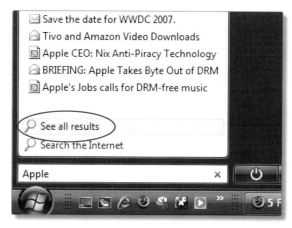

To locate email messages and files, it's best to click See All Results.

Clicking this option displays Windows Explorer, which returns all instances of the word or phrase you typed.

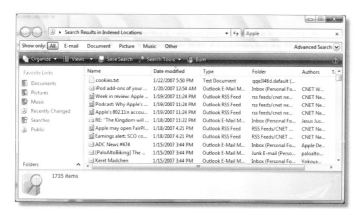

Searching for email messages and files containing the word
Apple yields a long list of results in Windows Explorer.

Search within a folder and its subfolders

If you're sure that the term you're looking for is in a particular folder or one of its subfolders, you can start by displaying the folder in Windows Explorer.

To use this method to search for the term *Vista* in a document, follow these steps:

1. Click the Start button to open the Start menu.

2. Click the Documents folder to open the folder window.

3. Type Vista in the text box in the top-right corner of the folder window.

As you can see, this search yielded only a handful of files: the files containing the word *Vista* that are in the Documents directory or one of its subdirectories.

Search using the Search option

If you use the Search option in the Start menu, you get the same results that you would if you'd typed your search words in the Search box *and* selected See All Results. This searches through all of your *indexed* locations but not necessarily your entire hard drive.

To search all indexed locations from the right panel of the start menu:

1. Choose Start > Search.

2. In Windows Explorer, enter `Vista` to initiate a search of your entire PC.

The search engine looks for all instances in your computer's indexed locations.

Look at the number displayed in the bottom-left corner of the screen. In this example, we found 2,523 instances of the word *Vista* in the indexed locations of our test computer. Many of these hits are from emails; some are from documents and Web sites; still others could be tags associated with music, pictures, or videos. This is where the power of this method becomes apparent. You can start to isolate the results.

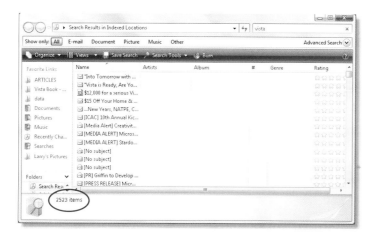

3. In the Show Only bar near the top of Windows Explorer, click Document to filter the results so that only documents containing the word *Vista* are displayed.

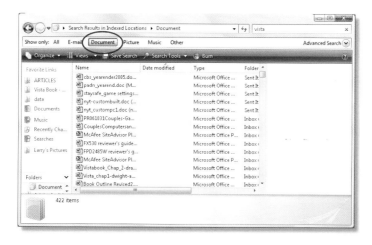

continues on next page

NOTE —— You could filter the results to show only e-mail messages, photographs, songs, and other items by choosing E-Mail, Picture, Music, or Other, respectively.

4. Click Date Modified to get a list of documents containing the word *Vista* displayed in reverse chronological order.

   Now we're down to 522 items—documents (in this case, mostly Microsoft Word files) that contain the word *Vista*. But because the items are sorted chronologically, we can quickly find the most recent documents containing that word.

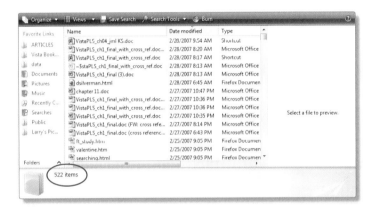

Running an Advanced Search

By default, Vista searches all files in all indexed locations that meet your criteria. If that's not what you want, however, you can expand or limit your search.

Expand or narrow your search

If you're looking for a file that may be in a specific folder, you may want to search beyond the indexed locations. You can do that by following these steps:

1. Choose Start > Search.

2. In Search Folder, click the down arrow beside Advanced Search in the top-right corner.

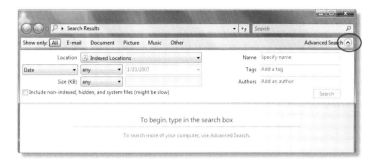

3. From the Location drop-down menu, choose the location where you want to start your search.

   Selecting Local Disk (C:), for example, means that the search engine will search all files on the C drive, regardless of whether they are indexed.

   You could also select Everywhere, which would search any network drives linked to your computer, or Computer to search all of your PC's drives. Alternatively, you can narrow your search by selecting a directory and all its subdirectories.

4. Check the Include Non-Indexed, Hidden, and System Files check box.

5. Type the filename or other search term in the Name text box.

TIP —— You can narrow the search further by specifying the date or all or part of a file's name.

continues on next page

93

6. Click Search.

While you wait for the search to finish, you may see a green thermometer bar near the top of the window indicating the search's progress. This process may take a few minutes.

Use Vista to search the Internet

You can use the Search box at the bottom of the Start menu to search the Internet, too.

- To search the Internet, enter a search term in the Search box, and click the Search the Internet option just above the Search box. Vista displays your default browser and conducts the search using your default search engine.

For more information on configuring your browser and search engine, see Lesson 10.

Saving Your Search Criteria

After you complete a search, but before you close Windows Explorer, you can save the search so that you can perform it again later. If you've created a search for all documents and email messages that contain the words *Windows Vista,* for example, you could save the search to a file that will allow you to conduct that same search easily, with up to-date results, any time. If you get a new email message or create a new document containing that term, those items would show up the next time you used that saved search.

Save a search

When you save a search, keep in mind that what you're saving is the search criteria, not the search results. Here's how to save your search:

1. Conduct a search, using any of the methods described earlier in this lesson.

2. When you have the results, click Save Search in the search folder's toolbar.

3. Accept the proposed file name or give the search file a different name.

4. Click Save.

Your search is saved to that file so that you can recall it later.

Access saved searches

To access the searches that you've saved in your user folder, follow these steps:

1. Near the top of the Start menu, click your name (or the name assigned by the PC manufacturer).

Your personal Windows Explorer folder appears.

2. Click the Searches subfolder.

3. Find the file that corresponds to the saved search you want to perform, and double-click it.

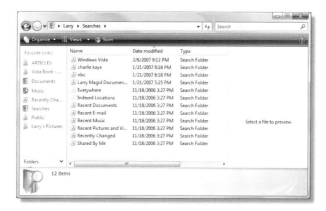

continues on next page

95

<table>
<tr><td colspan="2">What Are Boolean Filters, and How Do You Use Them?</td></tr>
</table>

A *Boolean filter* is another way to contract or expand a search.

If you're looking for *Jim,* for example, you would just type `Jim`. But if you're looking for documents or email messages that contain both *Jim* and *Sally,* you would search for `Jim AND Sally`. If you're looking for a document that contains either *Jim* or *Sally,* you would type `Jim OR Sally`—or `Jim NOT Sally`. And lest you accuse us of shouting by using capital letters for the conjunctions AND and OR, that's because Vista requires its Boolean terms to be in caps.

Following are some Boolean terms that you may find useful to include in your searches:

- AND. Finds files that contain both words (`Jim AND Sally`).
- OR. Finds files that contain either word (`Jim OR Sally`).
- NOT. Finds files that contain one word but not the other (`Jim NOT Sally`).
- Quotation marks. Find files that contain the exact phrase (`"Jim Smith"`).
- Parentheses. Find files that contain both words in either order (`Jim Sally`).

Vista conducts the search again. If there is new information that fits the search criteria (such as new email or documents) it will be included in the results.

NOTE — You can still use Boolean searches even when natural-language search is turned on.

Adding Directories to Your Search

Even though searching an index is a lot faster than searching an entire hard drive, it does take time. The smaller the index, the faster the search. So to make the search process as fast as possible, by default Vista limits indexing to the most common places for storing data files, such as your personal folder and your email files. Vista doesn't index program and system files, because it's very unlikely that you would ever have to search within those files.

You can search for individual program and system files, however, if you know parts of their names. If you store data in folders other than Vista's standard

An Alternative to Boolean Logic

Wouldn't it be nice if you could ask your computer questions the way you would ask a person? Well, that's sort of possible with Vista's natural-language search.

Vista isn't quite as intelligent as a human being when it comes to figuring out what you're asking, but you can configure it to locate files by using a natural-language search instead of the Boolean logic that computers normally respond to. You could enter `e-mail from Charlie sent today` or `music by Bob Dylan`, for example.

To enable natural-language search:

1. Choose Start > Computer.

2. Choose Organize > Folder and Search Options.

3. Click the Search tab.

4. Select Use Natural Language Search.

5. Now try typing the search as though you're just asking a question.

Document folders, for example, you can add the folder to the index. But be careful—add only those directories that you're likely to need to search. Don't add your entire hard drive; doing that would slow your searches.

To add a folder to an index search:

1. Click the Start button to open the Start menu.

2. In the Search box, type `Indexing Options` and press Enter.

3. In the Indexing Options window, click Modify.

continues on next page   **97**

4. In the window that appears, click Show All Locations near the bottom of the window.

5. If User Access Control warning appears, click Continue.

6. Double-click on the drive that contains the directory you want to add.

   All the directories on that drive display.

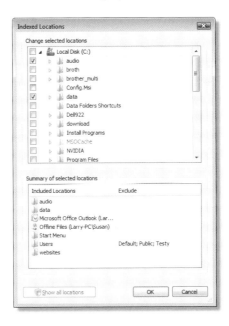

7. Select the directory you wish to add and click OK.

   The directory is added to the search index.

Learning About Other Search Options

To get to know your options and configure the behavior of Vista's search engine, from any Windows Explorer window, do the following:

1. Click Organize in the toolbar, and choose Folder and Search Options from the drop-down menu.

2. In the Folder options window that appears, click the Search tab.

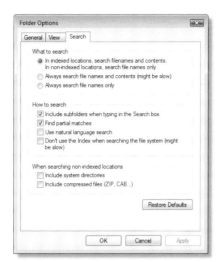

3. Choose the type of searches you want done, how you want the search conducted and how to handle non-indexed locations, by selecting any of the various options in each category.

What You've Learned

- How to search your hard drive quickly for documents, email messages, and other files

- Where to start your search

- How to launch programs and Vista components, such as Control Panel modules, by using the Search box at the bottom of the Start menu

- How to use advanced search functions to limit or expand your search

- How to save search results

- How to use the Search box to search the Internet

- How to use natural-language search

- How to use and configure Vista's search index

6

GOALS

Practice easy ways to
make Vista more secure

Use Vista's built-in
security tools

Set up user accounts
and parental controls

Make Vista Safer and More Secure

Microsoft invested an enormous amount of resources in shoring up some of the security problems of previous versions of Windows. As a result, the company claims that Vista is the safest and most secure version of Windows to date.

We'll have to wait to see just how secure this operating system turns out to be, but one thing we know for sure: It can't be bulletproof. No operating system is 100-percent secure.

We also know that how you interact with Vista has a lot to do with how safe it is. Keeping your information secure is a matter of knowing how to use Vista's built-in security tools, taking advantage of appropriate third-party offerings, and—most important—practicing safe computing.

What Is Safe Computing?

Regardless of which operating system they use, most people get into trouble not so much because of operating-system and software problems, but because of the way they use their computers.

Being careless with passwords, downloading software from unknown sources, and giving out too much information to the wrong places can get you in trouble, regardless of what protections are in place. In some ways, computers are a lot like cars: You can build in seat belts and airbags, but ultimately, safety is a matter of caution and, to a certain extent, luck.

The following are some basic security tips that apply regardless of what type of computer or operating system you use:

- **Keep your personal information private.** Know who you're dealing with before giving out credit card numbers, physical addresses, or any other potentially confidential information. Be extremely careful about your Social Security number: Banks and other financial institutions, insurance companies, employers, and creditors are among the few organizations that have a legitimate right to know it.

- **Watch where you click.** Don't click links in unsolicited email you receive, including mail that may appear to come from a legitimate organization, especially if the message asks for information about one of your accounts. The email may be part of a phishing scheme that takes you to a rogue site designed to steal your information. Sometimes these are obvious scams, but increasingly they're quite realistic looking. If you think the site is legitimate, go to it yourself by typing what you know to be the correct URL in your browser instead of clicking the link in the email.

- **Use strong passwords, and guard them carefully.** Don't use a password that's easy to guess, such as your street or dog's name. If you're protecting something valuable (such as the data on your PC or your online bank account), make up a password that's easy for you to remember but hard for anyone to guess.

How to Create Secure Passwords

Weak passwords, especially words that are in the dictionary, don't offer as much protection as you might think because hackers' toolkits include programs that can often break them. That's why you need a strong and secure password. The following are some tips for creating passwords that keep your data safe:

- Ideally, passwords should contain at least six characters, including one uppercase letter and at least one number. One trick is to make up a phrase that you can't forget, such as I met Sally Jones in 1992, and create an abbreviation using the letters and numbers from the phrase—in this case, ImSJi1992. Another example: I moved to Chicago when I was 12 would be ImtCwIw12.

- Don't use the same password for all occasions.

- Create other passwords—perhaps weaker ones for things like getting a free account on a newspaper site or for logging into sites that you don't know and trust.

Working with User Account Control

User Account Control (UAC) is a new feature in Vista, designed to prevent unauthorized changes to, and activities on, your computer. UAC asks you for permission or, in some cases, to provide an administrator password before you can carry out an action that could damage your computer. The feature is designed to protect your system from malicious software and hackers, as well as actions by standard users who may be unauthorized to carry out certain tasks (see the "Configure User Accounts" section in this lesson).

A built-in warning signal

UAC generally asks you for permission to carry out potentially dangerous tasks, such as changing settings, uninstalling software, making administrative changes, or deleting large amounts of data. UAC warns you by darkening the screen briefly and then displaying a message to ask whether you're certain you want to carry out the task. In essence, this feature reminds you to think twice before pulling the trigger.

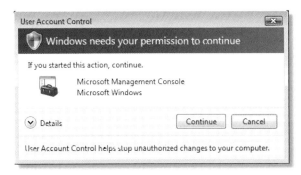

User Account Control pops up quite often in Vista.

In addition to interrupting you when you're issuing a command, UAC can halt a program in midstream to ask whether it's OK for the program to continue (although this situation is rare). UAC can also prevent a standard user from accessing a program that an administrator has blocked from running on your machine or under your account.

Turn off UAC

We don't recommend turning off UAC. Even though we're experienced users, we leave it on for our machines to protect against malicious software and, yes, even our possible mistakes. As annoying as UAC is, it's something we've just gotten used to—kind of like having to put on seat belts when we get behind the wheel of a car.

But if you find that you need to turn off UAC, here's how:

1. Choose Control Panel > User Accounts and Family Safety.

   The User Accounts and Family Safety options display.

2. Click User Accounts.

3. Click Turn User Account Control On or Off.

4. Click Continue when the UAC warning comes up.

5. Deselect Use User Account Control (UAC) to Help Protect Your Computer.

6. Click OK.

   Vista displays a notice that you must restart your computer to apply the changes.

7. Click Restart Now or Restart Later.

Keep in mind that UAC can protect you only if you want to be protected. It's a warning. If UAC is kicked off by a malicious program, clicking Continue without thinking could allow that program to damage your computer or your data. Consider the UAC a big sign with the word *THINK* blinking on it.

Using the Windows Security Center

The best place to start configuring Vista's security settings is the Windows Security Center: a basic control panel that tells you whether your firewall, automatic updating, and "malware protection" (antispyware and antivirus) are installed, up to date, and working properly.

You can get to Security Center in two ways:

1. Choose Start > Control Panel.

2. Click Security.

continues on next page

3. Click Security Center.

or

1. In the Start menu's Search box, type `Security Center`.

2. Press Enter.

The Security Center appears.

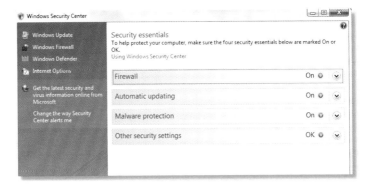

You can get more information on the status of the firewall or other security settings by clicking the down arrow to the right of each listing. In the case of firewall and malware protection, the information includes which program, if any, is currently protecting you. As we discuss later in this lesson, you have a choice of firewall and malware protection software.

Get to know Windows Firewall

Windows Firewall is designed to protect your PC from incoming threats, such as attacks by hackers coming in through the Internet. You can configure it to protect against outgoing threats, too, such as *malware,* which is software that infiltrates your computer and may try to send data from your PC to a remote computer.

Before you rely on Windows Firewall to protect you from outbound threats, however, see the sidebar "Limitations on Windows Firewall." You may find that ensuring that level of protection is more than you bargained for, at least by using the firewall.

Windows Firewall is turned on by default, though you can turn it off or replace it with a firewall from another company. If the firewall isn't turned on, a red button and the word *Off* appear in Security Center's Firewall page.

Security Center warns you of a vulnerability by shading it red.

Turn Windows Firewall on or off

1. On the left side of Security Center, click Windows Firewall.

   The Firewall page displays.

2. Click Change Settings.

3. If a User Access Control warning appears, click Continue.

4. Toggle the firewall off or on by clicking the button in the Firewall bar.

Block incoming connections

You also have the option of blocking all incoming connections, which gives you extra protection by blocking unsolicited attempts to connect to your PC. This option is useful if you're on a public network, such as a Wi-Fi network at a coffee shop or hotel. Microsoft recommends that you also use this option when a high-risk worm is spreading via the Internet.

By default, this option is off, which is OK for home or office use.

To block incoming connections:

1. Make sure Windows Firewall is turned on.

2. Click Change Settings.

3. If a User Access Control warning appears, click Continue.

4. On the General tab of the Windows Firewall Settings window, select Block All Incoming Connections.

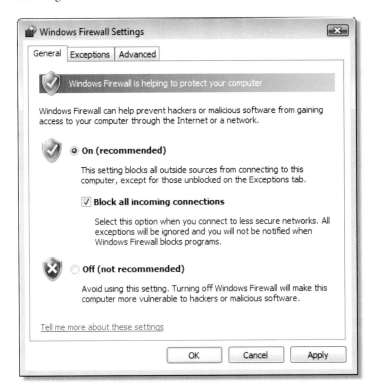

Limitations on Windows Firewall

Like the firewall that comes with Windows XP Service Pack 2, the firewall in Vista is configured to protect you automatically from incoming threats, such as when a hacker or intruder tries to reach into your machine to steal information, plant software, or damage your PC. But what about outgoing protection? Can Windows Firewall do that too? Well, yes, but not by default, and it isn't easy.

The only way to turn on outgoing protection in Windows Firewall is to use something called Windows Firewall with Advanced Security. Even the name is intimidating, and the process doesn't end there. If you display this control tool (type Advanced Security in the Start menu's Search box), you'll soon see that it's very complicated to use. Advanced Security is really designed for system administrators and information technology specialists.

We don't recommend that the average person mess with Advanced Security, and frankly, we don't feel confident about giving instructions here, because a mistake could render parts of your computer unusable. If you feel that you really need outgoing protection, however, you have three choices:

- Ignore our advice and try to configure the control tool yourself.

- Spend a lot of money by hiring a professional to set up Advanced Security.

- Purchase a third-party security product that can provide outgoing protection.

We recommend the third option. See "Bolstering Vista Security" later in this lesson for more information.

5. Click OK.

As we discuss in Lesson 14, when you use Vista's Wi-Fi capability to connect to a wireless network, you have the opportunity to indicate that you're on a public network, which temporarily turns off incoming connections.

Use Windows Update

Bad guys are always looking for ways to exploit holes in Windows, and the most effective way to fight back is to ensure that your system is up to date by downloading the latest patches and updates to help fix bugs and protect you against new threats. Updates also can improve performance and fix bugs in drivers and other software. Microsoft periodically releases these fixes to Windows, traditionally once a month on a Tuesday.

In the short time that Vista has been available, Microsoft has already issued security updates for it. How do you know when they've been issued? The automatic-updating tool, Windows Update, goes online to look for updates or patches for Vista, other Microsoft software, and even hardware drivers. Enabled by default in Vista, Windows Update is a painless way to make sure that your system has the latest security enhancements.

Not always a help

We use automatic updating and recommend that you do, too. Still, we must disclose the slight risk that an update could harm your computer.

In previous versions of Windows, an update caused some type of system instability in a few cases, to the point where Microsoft had to update the update to fix the problem. Still, the chances of that happening are relatively low compared to the greater risk of missing out on an important update that protects you against a serious threat.

Disable Windows Update

Automatic updating can be disabled, but we (and Microsoft) recommend that you leave it on.

To disable Windows Update:

1. On the left side of Security Center, click Windows Update.

   The Windows Update page appears.

2. Click Change Settings.

A screen appears that lets you configure how Windows installs updates.

3. Click Never Check for Updates (Not Recommended); then click OK.

Keep in mind that we recommend the first option, Install Updates Automatically, but you might want a bit more control over what software updates are being installed on your machine, even from Microsoft.

Schedule updates

1. On the left side of Security Center, click Windows Update.

The Windows Update page displays.

2. Click Change Settings.

A screen appears that lets you configure how Windows installs updates.

3. Make sure that Install Updates Automatically is selected.

4. In the Install New Updates section, specify how often to check for new updates by making a choice from the drop-down menu.

continues on next page

We prefer having the system check every day, but you may decide to have it updated once a week on any day you select.

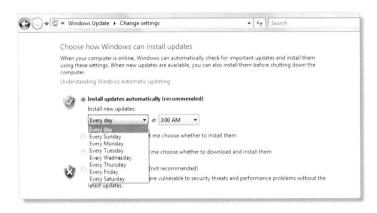

5. Specify the time of day you want the system to check for updates by making a choice from the drop-down time menu.

   Make sure that you choose a time when your PC will be running and connected to the Internet. The checking and the update happen in the background, so they probably won't interfere with what you're doing on the computer, but you may notice that your machine and Internet connection run slowly during the process. If you leave your PC on overnight, selecting a time like 3 a.m. allows the update to take place during your downtime.

Check for and install updates manually

Although you can schedule Windows to update automatically, it's also nice to be able to do it manually when you hear that a new security fix or other patch is available. With manual updates, you instruct the system to go online and check for updates; Windows informs you if it finds any. If so, you have the option to install the updates. (You must be connected to the Internet for this procedure to work.)

To check for and install updates manually:

1. On the left side of Security Center, click Windows Update.

   The Windows Update page displays.

2. In the left side of the screen, click Check for Updates.

   Windows displays a "Checking for updates" message as it checks via the Internet.

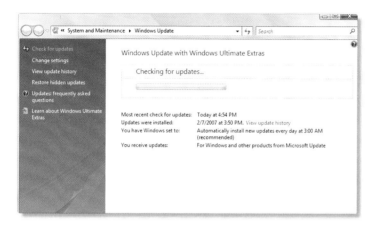

   If Windows finds one or more updates, Security Center displays a page reminding you to download and install the updates.

3. Click View Available Updates to see what updates Windows found.

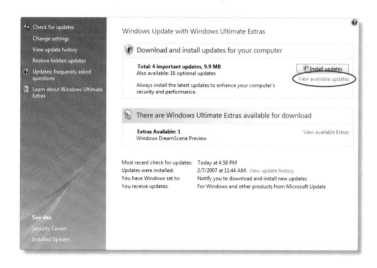

continues on next page

4. Select the updates you want to install, deselect the others, and then click Install at the bottom of the screen.

   Recommended updates are already selected.

5. If a User Access Control warning appears, click Continue.

   Windows downloads the updates via the Internet and installs them for you.

   Occasionally, you'll need to restart Windows for the update to take effect. If this is the case, a message prompts you to restart. Windows closes the programs that are running and reminds you to save any files.

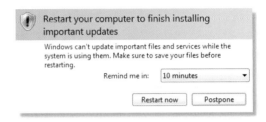

View your update history

You can look at your update history to find updates that you've downloaded manually or automatically:

■ On the Windows Update page of Security Center, click View Update History.

A screen appears with the update history.

Use Windows Defender

Windows Defender is software bundled with Vista that looks for and removes malicious programs, called *spyware*, that can jeopardize your privacy and slow your computer.

Although Defender does a good job of protecting you from common spyware, it does not protect you from all forms of malicious software, so we recommend you purchase antivirus software that provides more comprehensive protection from viruses and other malicious programs. See the next section, "Bolstering Vista Security."

To use or configure Windows Defender:

1. On the left side of Security Center, click Windows Defender.

   The Windows Defender page displays.

   If it's been a while since you've scanned your computer, a warning message displays, telling you that you should scan for spyware and other potentially unwanted software.

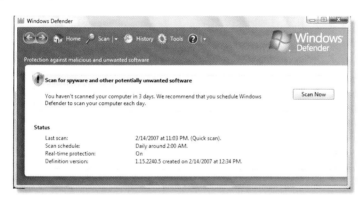

2. Click Scan Now, and wait while Windows scans your PC. The scan can take several minutes.

   When Windows Defender is done, it displays a status report such as "No unwanted or harmful programs. Your computer is running normally."

Bolstering Vista Security

Several products on the market provide virus and malware protection, an inbound and outbound firewall, and robust spyware protection. Products such as ZoneAlarm Internet Security Suite from Check Point, McAfee Internet Security Suite from McAfee, Norton Internet Security from Symantec, and Microsoft's own Windows Live OneCare will protect your PC from a wide variety of threats. Even these products can't guarantee that nothing bad will happen, but they do offer state-of-the-art protection, are easy to configure, and keep up-to-date.

We don't have a strong preference as to which security suite is best. All the ones we list (plus some we may have left out) are from highly reputable companies that spend a great deal of effort keeping their software up to date. Most of these products offer a free trial period, so take advantage of the trial period to figure out which product you like the best.

Whichever product you use, make sure that you turn on the suite's live-update feature so that it always knows about the latest threats. And as with any type of security, don't expect a software vendor to protect you against your own mistakes. You should still practice the safe-computing habits we laid out earlier in this lesson. Remember that you never have a 100-percent guarantee that something bad won't happen.

Watch out for overblocking

Whatever firewall program you use, know how to configure it so that it doesn't overblock. Windows Live OneCare, for example, automatically blocks access to your PC from other PCs on your network, which may or may not be a good thing, depending on your situation. Learn how to use the program's configuration tools so that you can unblock anything you need to access. Configuration tools vary from program to program but are usually covered in a settings option.

Discover the free route to security

When it comes to basic security, antivirus protection is the only major element that isn't covered by the free programs that come with Vista. You can purchase an antivirus program from a variety of vendors, or you can use a very good free program called AVG from Grisoft (http://free.grisoft.com). We've used this program on our PCs and like it for its ease of installation, ease of use, and low impact on system performance.

Configuring User Accounts

Like previous versions of Windows, Vista lets you set up multiple user accounts on your PC so that several people can use it, with each person having different areas for file storage and, in some cases, different privileges. By creating separate accounts, each person can have his or her own desktop background colors and theme, and even a different Start menu.

Vista provides two types of user accounts:

- An *administrator* account, which provides full access to all of Vista's commands all files on the PC.

- A *standard* account, which allows users to perform common tasks and run programs, but not to see other users' files or make system changes.

Vista provides an added feature: You can create accounts with parental controls, and limit such things as the content your kids can see on the Web, the specific times they are allowed to use the PC, what games they can play, and what programs they can run.

Before we get into the details on parental controls, we show you how to create user accounts and administer certain privileges within those accounts, such as whether the users can install software or issue potentially dangerous commands.

Create and administer accounts

With user accounts, it's possible for more than one person to be logged into the same PC at the same time. If more than one person is logged in, you can switch from one account to the other, or the person who is using the PC can log off.

If you installed Vista yourself and are already using it, you already have at least one administrator account; either your PC manufacturer created it for you, or Vista created it for you automatically when you installed or configured the software.

You can tell which user account is active by looking at the top of the Start menu, which displays the user's name and a graphic representing him or her. By default, Windows assigns a graphic to each new user, but as you'll see later in this section, you can assign any graphic, including a photo of the person.

If you're using a new PC, you may have discovered that a generic name has been assigned to you (such as Lenovo User, if you purchased a Lenovo laptop). This section also shows you how to change your user name.

All configuration of user accounts, including adding new users, is done in User Accounts and Family Safety, available via the Control Panel.

Add a user

When you create a new account on your PC, you have to decide whether to give that person an administrator or a standard account. How do you decide?

If the person is a typical user who is not very tech savvy—or if you simply don't want that person installing programs, deleting programs, or doing other things that could harm the PC—by all means assign a standard account. If you want to limit a person's access to other people's data files, assign a standard account.

On the other hand, if you want to give the person full control of the PC, assign an administrative account. Be aware, however, that a person who owns an administrator account can do anything, including deleting *your* account!

To add a new user:

1. Choose Start > Control Panel > User Accounts and Family Safety; then click Add or Remove User Accounts. If a UAC control message displays, click Continue.

   The Manage Accounts window displays.

2. Click Create a New Account, located just below the name(s) of any existing user accounts.

3. In the Create New Account window that appears, type the user name in the name field near the top of the window; then choose whether to make that person a standard user or an administrator by clicking the appropriate radio button.

4. Click Create Account.

   The Manage Accounts screen displays, with the new account name added and a generic graphic assigned to that account.

Change a user's picture

Vista assigns a graphic to each account, but you can substitute any image you want, including a digital photo.

To change a user picture:

1. Choose Start > Control Panel > User Accounts and Family Safety; then click Add or Remove User Accounts. If a UAC control message displays, click Continue.

continues on next page

2. In the Manage Accounts window that appears, click the user name (Larry, in this example).

   The Change an Account window displays.

3. Click Change Picture.

4. In the Change Picture window, click a supplied graphic; then click Change Picture.

   or

   Click Browse to select a digital image from your hard drive, navigate to the folder that contains the picture you want to use, and double-click that picture.

   The picture is assigned to that user. (Yes, that really is Larry!)

Create a user password

If you wish to add a new user to the PC:

1. Make sure that you're logged on to your account, or if you're an administrator, make sure that you're logged in to the account whose password you want to change.

2. Choose Control Panel > User Accounts and Family Safety.

3. In the User Accounts and Family Safety window that appears, click Create a Password for Your Account.

4. In the Create Your Password window, enter a password; then re-enter it on the following line.

   Be aware that passwords are case sensitive. If you use capitals, you'll have to use them any time you sign in.

5. If you want, you can create a password hint that will be displayed on your PC when you log in. It can be anything that triggers your memory, but see the note below about the dangers of password hints.

6. Click Create Password.

   Your password is set and you're returned to the User Accounts window.

Change a user password

If you want to change the password for this account, click Change Your Windows Password.

To change a password:

1. Follow steps 1 and 2 of the preceding exercise.

2. Click Change Your Password.

3. In the Change Your Password window, enter your current password, type the new password, and re-enter the new password on the following line.

   Be aware that passwords are case sensitive. If you use capitals, you'll have to use them any time you sign in.

continues on next page

4. If you want, you can create a password hint that will be displayed on your PC when you log in.

5. Click Change Password.

Your new password is set and you're returned to the User Accounts window.

TIP ——— In addition to creating a password you can remember and writing it down in a safe place, two reminder tools in Vista can help you if you forget your password. You can read more about them at www.peachpit.com/vistalearningseries.

Set up parental controls

Vista is the first version of Windows to include parental controls that can be assigned to any standard user account. You cannot put controls on an administrator account, so if you feel that you need to place controls on such an account, you need to change it to a standard one. At least one administrator account must remain on your PC, however.

These controls are designed to help parents accomplish the following:

- Set time limits on children's computer use, including specific hours when they can log on
- Prevent children from playing games based on age rating levels, content, or specific game titles
- Restrict the Web sites that your children can visit
- Prevent your children from running programs you don't want them to use

Configure parental controls

1. Do one of the following to access parental controls:

    • Type Parental Controls in the Start menu's Search box, and press Enter.

    or

    • Choose Start > Control Panel > User Accounts and Family Safety > Parental Controls.

2. If a UAC warning displays, click Continue.

3. In the Parental Controls window, click the icon of the user for whom you want to establish controls.

    If that person doesn't already have a user account, set one up as described in "Add a user" earlier in this lesson.

4. In the Parental Controls area of the User Control window, select On, Enforce Current Settings, but do not click OK.

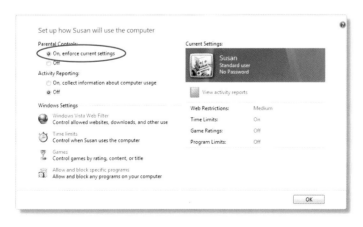

continues on next page

5. If you want to be able to run activity reports about the user, in the Activity Reporting section, select On, Collect Information About Computer Usage.

6. In the Windows Settings section, click Windows Vista Web Filter.

   The Web Restrictions window displays.

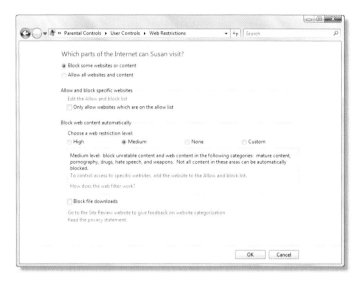

7. Choose the Web-filtering level you want to use: High, Medium, None, or Custom.

   • **High** blocks all Web sites except those specifically approved for children. This option is extremely restrictive, so if you choose it, you should be pre-pared to add Web sites that your kids can visit. We don't recommend using this option except for very young children.

   • **Medium** blocks unrated content as well as content that is considered to be mature or that pertains to pornography, drug advocacy, hate speech, or weapons.

   • **None**, of course, means that no sites are blocked, but you can manually add sites (see the next exercise).

   • **Custom** lets you block sites that focus on other types of potentially inap-propriate content, such as hate speech, bomb making, drugs, alcohol, and gambling, among others. Allow or block specific Web sites.

Manually allow or block a single Web site

Whichever Web-filtering option you choose, you can also block or allow specific Web sites.

We found that www.breastcancer.com, for example, was blocked by Vista's default (Medium) filter setting at this writing. If a parent wanted his or her child to be able to visit that site, that parent could specifically allow access.

To block or allow a specific Web site:

1. Follow steps 1 through 3 of the previous exercise.

2. In the Windows Settings area of the User Control window, click Windows Vista Web Filter.

    The Web Restrictions window displays.

3. Just below the Web restriction levels, click To Control Access to Specific Web Sites.

    The Allow or Block Specific Web Sites window displays.

4. Enter the full name of the site you want to block or allow; then click either Allow or Block.

5. Click OK.

    The site is added to the allowed list or the blocked list.

Remove Web sites from blocked or allowed lists

You may want to remove Web sites from the blocked or allowed list.

1. Follow steps 1 through 3 of the previous exercise.

2. Select the site in the Allowed Web Sites box that you want to remove from the list.

continues on next page

125

3. Click Remove.

The site is removed from the list.

Create and view activity reports

If you decided to create an activity report for a user, you can view it at any time to see what that user has been doing. By clicking around, you can get quite a bit of detail, including what sites the child visited and what sites he tried to visit but was blocked from. You can also find out what applications and games the child ran, what email was sent and received, and details about instant-messaging and media use.

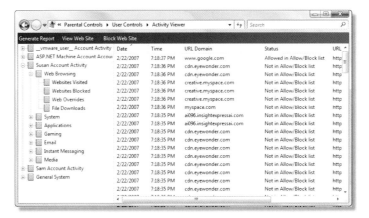

An activity report showing which Web sites were visited.

If you have activity reports turned on, you'll be prompted to review them when you log in to an administrator account.

If you did not enable activity reports when you set up parental controls, you can still add them:

1. Follow steps 1 through 3 of "Set up parental controls" earlier in this section.

2. In the Activity Reporting area of the User Control window, select On, Collect Information About Computer Usage.

3. Click OK.

Activity reports are now enabled. You can view them at any time; If you're an administrator, you'll be prompted to review them when you log in.

Set time limits

Vista lets you control when your child can and cannot use the computer. With this setting, you can block the child from signing on to the PC during certain hours of specific days. If the PC is running, and the time comes when the child is blocked, he or she will get a notice and will be given time to sign off.

To set time limits:

1. Follow steps 1 through 3 of "Set up parental controls" earlier in this section.

2. On the right side of the User Control window, click Time Limits.

   The time-limits grid is displayed.

3. Use your mouse or pointing device to select the hours you want to block.

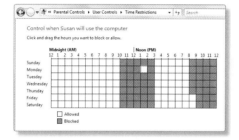

   Notice that you can choose different hours for different days of the week. The periods that are blocked will be in blue; time allowed will be in white.

4. Click OK.

   The User Control window displays again, this time with the time controls set.

Use game ratings to control game access

Vista allows you to determine whether a child can play games, and, if so, what ratings you will permit your child to play.

Windows takes advantage of the Entertainment Software Rating Board (ESRB) ratings to empower children to block games that may not be age-appropriate.

You also have the option to load in ratings from other organizations. Ratings are divided into six age groups: Early Childhood (C), Everyone (E), Everyone 10+, Teen (T), Mature (M), and Adults Only (A).

Vista can determine what a game's rating is and allow or disallow play based on criteria set by the parent.

To control the ratings of games your child can play:

1. Follow steps 1 through 3 of "Set up parental controls" earlier in this section.

2. In the Windows Settings area of the User Control window, click Games.

3. In the Game Controls window that displays, select whether the child can play games.

   If you select No, all games will be blocked; click OK. If you select Yes, follow the remaining steps.

4. To block or allow games by rating, click Set Game Ratings.

5. In the Game Restrictions window, select whether to allow or block games with no ratings.

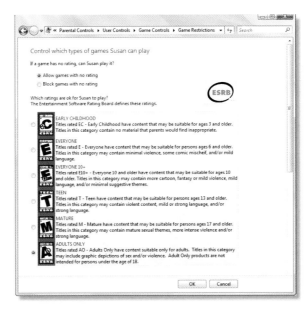

Be aware that it's quite possible for age-appropriate games to be unrated; it is also possible for inappropriate games to lack a rating.

6. Select the maximum rating you will allow.

   Everything below that rating on the chart will be blocked. If you select EVERYONE 10+, for example, you will be allowing games for that age group and everything before it on the chart, but not games for Teen, Mature, or Adults Only.

7. If you want, you can set additional criteria based on a wide range of content, including blood and gore, cartoon violence, and nudity, by selecting the check boxes at the bottom of the window. Go through the list to decide which, if any, types of games you want to block based on their content.

8. When you are finished, click OK.

Block specific games

You can also use parental controls to block all games or certain games.

1. Follow steps 1 and 2 of the previous exercise.

2. In the Games Controls window that displays, click Block or Allow Specific Games.

   Vista displays the games that are installed on your PC. In most cases, you'll also see the ratings. Note that if you have turned on ratings, Vista displays your ratings by default, but you can block or allow any specific games.

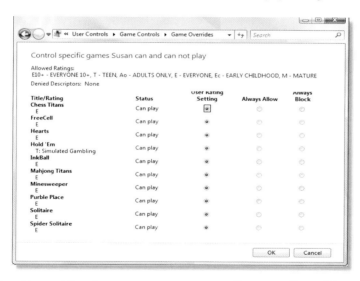

3. Select Always Allow for any games you want to allow, regardless of their ratings; select Always Block for any games you specifically want to block or allow.

Block file downloads

Vista allows you to prevent children from downloading files. This setting is a good way to help protect against viruses, spyware, and other malicious software, as well as files that could contain pornography or material that may violate copyright laws.

Should You Place Controls on Your Children's Computer Use?

The decision as to which, if any, controls to place on a child's computer is up to the parents. Some parents may feel no need to put any software controls on their PC, either because they don't think controls are necessary or they prefer establishing verbal rules that they trust their children will follow. Other parents take a different approach, either because they feel that their children need external controls or because they want to be sure that their kids don't accidentally stumble onto appropriate Web sites.

As parents ourselves, we both opted not to use controls. (Vista's controls are the first built into Windows, but third-party parental-control software programs have been around for more than a decade.) Parenting isn't an exact science, however, and one size definitely doesn't fit all families and children, which is why we're very glad that Microsoft decided to make these controls available.

If you do decide to use controls, we recommend that you discuss them with your kids. Don't try to hide the controls; your children will catch on soon and probably will resent the controls if you don't discuss the situation with them in advance.

Consider the age-appropriateness of the controls. As every parent knows, what's appropriate for a 12-year-old may not be so for an older teen. Remember that teenagers can be very resourceful and may find a way around such controls.

Also remember that any controls you put on your family PC work only on that machine. They don't work at your child's friend's house; on public computers; and on other devices your children have access to, including Web-enabled cell phones.

Finally, be aware that with or without controls, parenting is a teaching process. Regardless of what you do, children ultimately grow up and start making their own decisions, not only about what Web sites they visit and games they play, but also about other things—such as drinking, drug use, and whether to get into a car with someone who may be intoxicated. At the end of the day, what you want to do is teach your children critical-thinking skills so that they can make good choices. If you feel that parental controls can help, by all means use them. But remember that the most effective controls aren't the ones that run on your PC, but the ones that run inside your child's head.

1. Follow steps 1 through 3 of "Set up parental controls" earlier in this section.

2. In the Windows Settings area of the User Control window, click Windows Vista Web Filter.

   The Web Restrictions window displays.

3. At the bottom of the screen, select Block File Downloads.

4. Click OK.

Join the Discussion About Internet Safety

Co-author Larry Magid maintains three Web sites designed to help parents protect their children on the Internet while also protecting free speech:

- www.safekids.com (advice for parents of preteens)

- www.safeteens.com (advice for teens and parents of teens)

- www.ConnectSafely.org (co-directed by Anne Collier; an interactive forum where parents can ask questions, discuss issues, and get expert advice)

If your kids are using MySpace, check out *MySpace Unraveled* (Peachpit Press, 2007), by Larry Magid and Anne Collier.

Give Microsoft feedback on Web-site categories

As we said earlier in this lesson, no filtering system is perfect, but user feedback can make it better. At the bottom of the Windows Web Filter screen is a link labeled "Go to the Site Review Web site to give feedback on Web site categorization." That link lets you tell Microsoft what you think.

What You've Learned

- How to practice safe computing, regardless of what operating system and software you use

- How to use Vista's built-in security features

- How to use Windows Update to make sure that Vista has the latest security fixes

- Whether to consider using a third-party security program

- How to set up and manage user accounts

- How to set up and manage parental controls on Web use, PC use, and game play

- How User Account Control works and how to turn it off

7

GOALS

Understand the differences among Windows Vista's backup and restore options

Back up and restore individual files and folders

Do a full system recovery

Consider other options for backing up Windows Vista

Backing Up Is (Not) Hard to Do

Like going to the dentist, doing your taxes, or changing the oil in a car, backing up the data and programs on a computer's hard drive is a chore no one likes to do, but it will come back to bite those who don't. It's tedious but very, very necessary; just ask anyone who's had a hard drive die with no backup.

Earlier versions of Windows included programs for backing up data and software, but they were rudimentary and limited, the interface was unfriendly, and restoring from a full backup still required users to reinstall the operating system.

The backup in Windows Vista fixes these problems—for some users. Those who run the Home Basic or Home Premium edition may still find themselves frustrated when trying to accomplish some tasks. And even those who opt for the higher-end versions—particularly Business and Ultimate—may long for a more complete, third-party option that provides more flexibility.

In this lesson, you discover what Windows Vista can—and can't—do when backing up your PC. We'll also offer some alternatives.

Understanding Backup Concepts

Unfortunately, doing a backup on a PC is a bit more complicated than just saying, "Hey, computer, save my important stuff." So many programs are available, generating so many types of data files and documents, that making sure you're saving what's really important can be nerve-wracking.

Understanding the concepts behind backups can help clear up the confusion. The basic idea is simple: Backing up makes a copy of information stored on a hard drive and puts it somewhere other than that drive. The key differences are in what you back up and where you put the copies.

Back up files and folders

The most basic type of backup involves copying files—and, in some cases, whole folders containing files—to a remote drive or location. Within this general approach, you can use several strategies:

- Make a complete copy of each file, which is called a *full backup*

- Copy only the files that have been changed since the last backup, which is known as an *incremental backup*

- Copy only the files that have changed since the last *full* backup, also known as a *differential backup*.

Vista's file backup system uses a variant of incremental backup. Only the portion of the file that has changed is saved, which means that the backup data file is small. If you add six rows to a Microsoft Excel spreadsheet since your last backup, for example, only those six rows are backed up.

Back up the entire hard drive

The most comprehensive form of backup copies the entire hard drive, including the operating system, applications, and any documents or data files that may be present. It also preserves the directory structure and, in some cases, the information the computer uses when it starts up.

An entire-drive backup may simply make copies of what's on the drive, but it also may make what's called an *image* of the drive—a snapshot of the drive that's essentially a perfect copy.

Some backup programs can use the same type of backup strategies—full, incremental and differential—for regular complete-drive backups.

Backing Up with Vista

In previous versions of Windows, users could select specific files and folders by using an application called NTBackup. This application, which used a Windows Explorer-like interface, offered full, incremental, and differential backup capabilities. But it couldn't do image-based backups and scheduled backups.

Vista's new backup application, Backup and Restore Center, simplifies the process, but at a cost. Yes, users of the Business and Ultimate editions can do timed backups (users of the Basic and Home Premium editions cannot), but none of the editions allows users to choose the specific files and folders that get backed up. Backup and Restore Center searches your drive for known document and data file types and backs them up.

Microsoft says this method makes backups more complete and reliable, because the operating system searches for and finds only those common file types that need backing up. But those users who have unusual system configurations and arcane file types may want to rely on a third-party backup solution. In addition, the program backs up all files of common types that it finds. If a program has a folder full of, say, .bmp files used as buttons for its interface, Vista's backup program will save all those .bmp files.

Create your first full backup

The first full backup you create will take a little longer than usual, since all files will be backed up.

1. Choose Start > Control Panel.

2. If you're in Classic view, click Backup and Restore Center.

   or

   If you're in Home view, click Back up Your Computer.

continues on next page

Backup and Restore Center launches.

TIP ——— You can get to Backup and Restore Center even faster by clicking the Start button, typing **backup and restore** in the Search box, and pressing Enter.

3. Click the Back up Files button. If a User Account Control window appears, click Continue.

   Vista searches for a place to store backup files. After it determines at least one potential location, the Back up Files window appears.

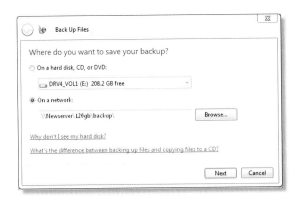

4. Choose where you want to put your backed-up files.

   For the purposes of this exercise, select On a Network.

TIP ——— If your PC is on a network, putting your backup on the hard drive of another computer is a good idea. Another good solution is using a different hard drive on the same PC. Use removable media if you want to store your files offline, but keep in mind that if you have lots of files to back up, you may need multiple writeable CDs or DVDs. Another option is to use a USB 2.0 external hard drive.

5. Click Browse.

6. In the navigation window that appears, choose a folder in which to save your backup file, and click OK.

7. Click Next in the Back up Files window.

    Depending on the security settings on the destination computer, you may also be asked to supply a login and password.

    A window appears that lets you choose which files Vista will include in the backup. You aren't given the option of choosing specific files or folders. The choices are generic: Pictures, Music, Videos, Documents, and so on.

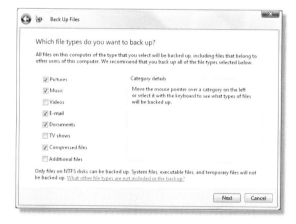

8. Clear the check boxes of the file types you don't want to include in the backup, and click Next.

TIP ——— If you want more detail on the file types, place your mouse pointer over each one to see a tooltip with more information.

    Because you're backing up your PC for the first time, the next window asks how often you want to back up your files, on which day, and at what time.

continues on next page

9. Make your choices; then click Save Settings and Start Backup.

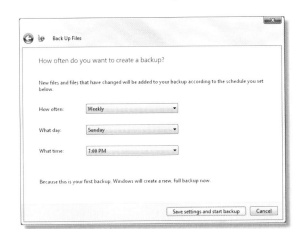

The backup process begins, and Vista displays a progress window. You can close the window if you don't want to leave it onscreen; the backup will proceed. To abort the process, click Stop Backup.

Because you're making your first full backup, all files will be backed up. When Vista performs subsequent backups at the times you specified in step 10, only new and changed files will be backed up, saving both time and disk space.

Back up your entire computer

One of the new features in Vista's backup program lets you create a snapshot or image of your PC's hard drive. In the event of a drive crash, you can restore from this backup, which makes recovery much easier. You can save this image file to another hard drive on your own computer, an external USB drive, or a DVD; you cannot save it to a networked computer.

You should create this snapshot when you set up a new Vista-based PC or when you upgrade your existing PC to Vista. When you have your system configured the way you like it, do a complete backup. If your hard disk dies later, you'll be glad that you have this backup!

To back up your entire computer:

1. Choose Start > Control Panel.

2. If you're in Classic view, click Backup and Restore Center.

   or

   If you're in Home view, click Back up Your Computer.

   Backup and Restore Center launches.

3. Click Back up Computer. If a User Account Control window appears, click Continue.

   As in step 3 of the full-file backup exercise, Vista searches for a place to store the backup. After it determines at least one potential location, the Back Up Files window appears. Unlike the full-file backup, however, a computer backup gives you fewer options for where to store the backup.

4. Choose another hard drive (if your PC has more than one) or a DVD to store your backup, because you can't save to a network PC or to a CD.

   For this exercise, choose a DVD.

5. Click Next.

   If you have more than one drive in your PC, a window displays, letting you choose which drives to back up. (You won't see this window if you have just one drive.) If you are saving the image to a hard drive on your PC, that drive will not be one of your choices. If you are saving to DVDs, including additional drives will increase the number of blank DVDs that you'll need to shovel into your burner.

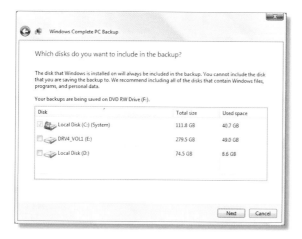

continues on next page

6. Choose the drive(s), and click Next.

   The next screen confirms your backup source and destination.

7. Click the Start Backup button to begin the backup.

   If your backup requires more than one DVD—and chances are that it will—you'll be prompted when a new disc is required. Label the discs and number them. Click OK to get past each new disc prompt.

   When the backup is complete, store your DVDs in a safe place.

   TIP —— Some PCs come with a disc you can use to restore the system to the state it was in the first time you booted it up. Other brands have an image of this disc in a separate partition on the hard drive. You won't need to make a full-disk image in this case unless you want to after adding your favorite software applications and tweaking settings to your liking.

Restoring Files and Systems

Your backup files are like insurance. Ideally, you'll never need them (or this section of the lesson). But if you do, those files will be ready when you are to recover from a problem.

Fortunately, Vista's recovery options give you more flexibility than its backup options do. You can specify files and folders to restore, and by using the full-drive image, you can restore a crashed drive to a usable state.

Recover files and folders

Vista's backup system allows you to recover specific files and folders.

1. From Backup and Recovery Center in the Control Panel, click the Restore Files button.

   NOTE —— Below the Restore Files button in Backup and Recovery Center is an Advanced Restore link. If you click that link, you can expand the scope of a restore to include backups made from a different Windows Vista PC.

2. In the Restore Files window that appears, do one of the following:

- Select Files From an Older Backup if you want to restore from an older backup. A list of available backup sets appears. Choose the one you want, and click Next.

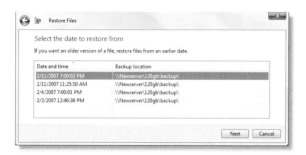

- Select Files From the Latest Backup if you want to restore from the most recent backup. Click Next.

Whichever option you choose, a window appears that lets you select files or folders to restore. You can also search for a specific file to restore.

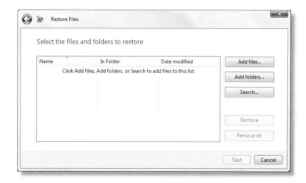

3. Click Add Files to select files, or click Add Folders to work from the folder level.

   Clicking either of these buttons produces a standard Windows Explorer navigation window.

4. Select the file or folder you want, and click Add.

   NOTE —— When you're finding files, you can Ctrl+click and Shift+click to select multiple files. When you're selecting folders, however, you can select only one at a time.

continues on next page

5. When you finish selecting the files and folders to be restored, click Next.

   In the next window, you choose where to restore your files.

6. Choose In the Original Location to put the files back where they came from.

   or

   Choose In the Following Location to put them someplace new.

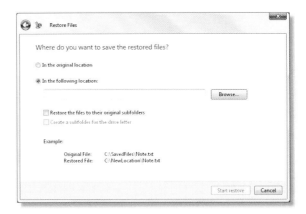

NOTE — If you choose the latter option, you activate a check box that allows you to preserve the original folder structure and designate the original drive letter in the folder path.

7. Click the Start Restore button to begin the process.

   When the recovery is complete, a message box appears.

8. Click Finish.

Restore a complete system backup

You shouldn't have to do a complete system backup unless your lose access to your Windows installation, either through major corruption or a hard-drive crash.

You can follow either of two approaches, depending on the configuration of your system and how much damage has been done:

- In "Back up your entire computer" earlier in this lesson, we mention that some PC vendors place a recovery partition with an image of the drive as it came from the factory. Check your PC's manual to see whether that's the case.

Recover Older Versions of Files

What if you've got a file on your system that you've overwritten, and what you really need to recover is that previous version? All is not lost, One of Vista's new features, Shadow Copies, retains copies of older versions of files you've changed.

To recover a Shadow Copy:

1. Find the file from which you want an older version, right-click it, and choose Restore Previous Versions from the shortcut menu.

You'll see a list of older versions of the file.

2. Select the version you want, and click one of the following buttons:

- **Open** to examine it
- **Copy** to make a copy of it as a new file
- **Restore** to set the older version as the current version

■ If your system does not have a recovery partition, you'll need to use the Vista system disc that came with the PC or the one you bought to upgrade your existing PC.

Restore from a recovery partition

Restoring from a recovery partition means you don't have to insert a system disc. A complete restore image of Vista is already on the hard drive.

1. Turn your computer on, and repeatedly tap the F8 key just before Vista actually begins to load.

If you see Vista start to boot, you'll need to restart and try again.

2. In the white-text-on-black screen that appears, press your down-arrow key to highlight Repair Your Computer; then press Enter.

Vista's installation routine begins.

continues on next page

3. In the next screen, select a keyboard layout appropriate for your country, and click Next.

4. If you set up a password on your computer, enter that password, and click OK.

   The System Recovery Options menu appears.

5. Choose Windows Complete PC Restore.

6. Follow the step-by-step instructions.

7. When you're prompted, put the last DVD from your complete backup set into your DVD drive.

   As more discs are needed, you'll be prompted for those until the restoration is complete.

Restore from an installation DVD

How you proceed depends on how much damage has been done to your Vista installation. If you've lost everything on your hard drive, you'll need to reinstall Vista first, using the install processes outlined in Lesson 2, because the recovery program works by seeing a Windows installation. After you've done that, or if you still have a Windows folder on your drive, go on to the following steps.

To restore from an installation DVD:

1. Follow the instructions in Lesson 2 to boot from the Vista DVD.

2. Choose your language, and click Next.

   The Vista Installation screen appears.

3. Click Repair Your Computer.

   Vista locates your existing Windows setup.

4. Select your setup, and click Next.

The Recovery Options window appears.

5. Insert the last DVD of your backup set into the DVD drive, and click Windows Complete PC Restore.

NOTE ——— Oooh, don't the other options look intriguing? Don't worry—we'll deal with some of them in Lesson 16.

Vista looks first on any hard drives on your PC for the backup and then scans your DVD drive, where it will find the backup.

6. Click Next to confirm the backup location.

7. Insert additional discs into your DVD drive as prompted.

Considering the Alternatives

You don't have to use Vista's built-in backup application, of course. You can also use the following:

- Any backup program that's compatible with Vista
- A service that lets you back up your PC to a remote server on the Internet
- A simple program normally used for copying and compressing files
- Email (send important files to yourself)

> ## What About System Restore?
>
> You may have seen references to System Restore in some of the screen shots in this lesson. This feature—the same one included in Windows XP—lets you restore from changes made to Windows system settings and files. Although System Restore is similar to Vista's backup and recovery tools, it's really designed more to troubleshoot problems, so we discuss it in depth in Lesson 16.

Pick a third-party program

Developers of backup software, knowing the limitations of Vista's built-in backup system, have been rushing to get Vista-compatible versions of their products out the door. Products that are available at this writing include the following:

- **Acronis True Image 10 Home** (www.acronis.com). Primarily used to back up an entire system, this application can also be used to back up music, video, digital photos, and Microsoft Outlook e-mail and contacts.

- **Backup4all** (www.backup4all.com). This simple, powerful backup tool has features that novices will appreciate, as well as those that power users need. One feature it lacks is the ability to create a full, bootable restoration disk.

- **NovaBACKUP** (www.novastor.com). NovaBACKUP does both file/folder and full-system backups. It also allows you to back up any computer your PC can see on a home or small-business network.

Back up online

If something physically damages your computer at your home or business—say, a fire, flood, or tornado—having a backup of your data in a remote location can be a lifesaver.

Whether you can do this smoothly depends on your broadband Internet connection. Most high-speed connections offer much faster downloads than uploads. Check with the backup service to see what speeds it recommends for uploading to its servers. Also, check pricing carefully; if you have a lot of data to upload, the service can get expensive. Many services offer free trials.

Your choices include the following:

- **Xdrive** (www.xdrive.com). Your 5 GB of storage is free at this AOL-owned service, but if you've got a lot of digital music, photos, and videos, that space goes fast. A fee-based service is available after you pass 5 GB.

- **FirstBackup** (www.firstbackup.com). FirstBackup charges based on what its compressed backups hold, not on the uncompressed size of your data, so its pricing is actually better than it looks. The site offers a pricing calculator that lets you see what the service will cost, based on your data.

- **Email.** Although backing up files one at a time is no way to back up your entire PC, it's not a bad idea when you've created a document that you just can't live without. You could, for example, set up a free Gmail account (www. gmail.com) and send yourself a copy of some of your important data files. That way, if anything were to happen to your PC, you would have a backup on one of Gmail's servers.

Back up on the cheap

Need something quick, simple, and inexpensive? PC veterans have been using WinZip for years as a poor-man's backup program. WinZip's new Pro edition allows you to drag and drop files into .zip files you create. Version 11, however, which is Vista-compatible, has some features normally offered in backup programs, including:

- Capability to burn .zip files directly on a CD or DVD
- Scheduled copying of files
- FTP and email capability
- Capability to span multiple CDs or DVDs with large .zip files
- Encryption (128-bit and 256-bit)

You can download a trial version of WinZip at www.winzip.com.

What You've Learned

- How to back up files and folders and then restore them
- How to back up your entire PC and restore it in case of a hard-disk failure
- How to use other options for backing up and restoring your PC, including third-party offerings and online backup

8

GOALS

Understand the
concepts and benefits
behind gadgets and RSS

Customize the
Windows Sidebar

Configure and
customize gadgets

Find and install
additional gadgets

Determine what it
takes to build your own
gadgets

Manage Information Using Gadgets

The good news about Windows Vista is that the operating system makes it very easy to connect to the Internet and drink from its fire hose of knowledge. The bad news is that Vista is indeed a fire hose of knowledge, so it's easy to drown in a flood of information. Fortunately, Vista offers some tools to help you manage the flow.

Vista's desktop features a shaded area that's home to miniprograms (or applets) called gadgets. These applets are new to a Microsoft operating system but not to personal computing; you may have heard them called widgets. Whatever the name, gadgets present specific bits of information in a simple, attractive way.

In the cases where gadgets get their information from the Internet, they most often use RSS (Really Simple Syndication)—a method for distributing and acquiring content. The ability to use RSS is built into Vista. Developers will be taking advantage of RSS as time goes on, and you'll be seeing powerful and useful applications in the future. This lesson provides a glimpse of the current possibilities of Vista's gadgets.

Gadget Basics

You can think of Vista's gadgets as information specialists. In most cases, each gadget presents details about one thing, such as the weather, family photos, the time, a calendar, news headlines, or your PC's performance. You choose exactly what you want to know, and the gadget keeps an eye on it for you.

Gadgets have a venerable history in personal computing. Variations have appeared as far back as the Apple II and Commodore 64/128 computers. These applets are best known in the PC world through the Yahoo Widgets program (originally called Konfabulator) and in Apple's Mac OS X as Dashboard widgets.

Gadgets can get their information from different sources:

- **From the Internet** (usually via an RSS feed). This information can range from weather and stock data to news headlines and multimedia.

- **From information on your computer.** The possibilities include text, photos, audio, and video.

- **From information about your computer.** You can track your PC's available hard drive space, memory usage, and CPU load. If you've got a notebook, a gadget can tell you the strength of a Wi-Fi connection and how much battery life is left.

Vista comes with a dozen preinstalled gadgets. But as you see later in this lesson, lots more gadgets are available, and you can even roll your own!

Vista includes a set of gadgets to get you started, but you can download more.

What is the Sidebar?

In Vista, gadgets start out docked to the *Windows Sidebar,* a shaded area on the right side of the screen. But gadgets don't have to stay there; they can be moved off to sit anywhere on your desktop. In fact, when they are undocked, gadgets sometimes expand to present more details about the information they contain or provide a larger view.

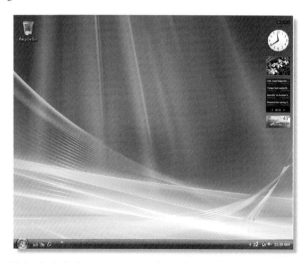

The Sidebar's default position is on the right-hand side of your desktop.

The Sidebar gives you better control of how your gadgets display and how they're organized. You can put the Sidebar itself in different places on your desktop, too, and if you've got a multiple-monitor setup, you can position it on either side of any monitor's screen.

What is RSS?

RSS is a way of getting information from one place to another across the Internet, using a method of structuring data called *XML* (Extended Markup Language). The key word to remember in the acronym *RSS* is *syndication.* When you syndicate something, you offer it up for others to access. RSS simplifies that process.

Chances are that if you use the Internet and the World Wide Web, you encounter RSS every day. If you have a customized page with news headlines at a portal such as Google, MSN, AOL, or Yahoo, you're using RSS; the headlines and other bits of information on those pages are delivered that way.

The ability to grab information via RSS is part of the plumbing within Vista. Gadgets are one manifestation of this ability; so are the Web feeds in Internet Explorer, which we discuss more in Lesson 9.

Configuring the Sidebar

When Vista first launches, the Sidebar appears on the right side of your desktop. If you have more than one monitor, the Sidebar is on the right side of your primary desktop—usually, your leftmost monitor.

Launch the Sidebar manually

If the Sidebar doesn't launch automatically, you can launch it manually:

1. Click the Start menu button.

2. Type Sidebar in the Search box.

3. Windows Sidebar should be the first result entry; if so, press Enter.

   Notice three gadgets are displayed by default: a clock, a photo slideshow, and a headline reader.

Now that the Sidebar is active, you can begin to customize it.

Put the Sidebar in its place

Don't want the Sidebar where it is? It can be docked to the left or right edge of any screen. Let's say you have two monitors, with the left one being the primary display, and you want the Sidebar to dock on the right side of the secondary monitor.

1. Right-click an open area of the Sidebar (not a gadget), and choose Properties from the shortcut menu.

   The Windows Sidebar Properties dialog box opens.

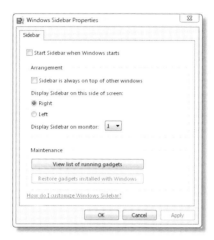

2. In the Display Sidebar on This Side of Screen section, click the Left radio button.

3. From the Display Sidebar on Monitor drop-down menu, choose 2.

   NOTE ——— This menu appears even if you have just one monitor.

4. Click Apply; and then click OK.

Control the Sidebar's behavior

Want the Sidebar to start whenever Vista does or to always be on top of other open windows?

- Open the Windows Sidebar Properties dialog box (see step 1 of the preceding exercise).

- Check the Start Sidebar When Windows Starts check box.

- Check the Sidebar Is Always on Top of Other Windows check box.

- Click Apply; then click OK.

Getting Your Gadgets Going

Now that you have the Sidebar where you want it, you can configure, add, and remove gadgets. We also show you where you can get some more and how you can learn to create your own.

Vista's gadgets start out on the Sidebar, but you can put them anywhere on your desktop. You can also change the order in which they appear in the Sidebar.

Set your gadgets free

1. Put your mouse pointer over the gadget you want to undock.

2. Click and hold the mouse button; then drag the gadget to the desired position on your desktop.

3. Release the mouse button.

To return a gadget to the Sidebar, simply drag it back.

> **NOTE** —— When your mouse pointer hovers over a gadget, a small, icon-based menu appears above and to the right of the gadget. The icon looks like a small grid but is actually a handle of sorts; you can click and hold this icon to drag a gadget as well. Some gadgets (such as the Stocks gadget that comes with Vista) require that you use the handle to move them, but most do not.

Some gadgets expand to provide more information. The Weather gadget, for example, shows current conditions, the location, and the temperature when it's in the Sidebar.

But when you drag this gadget off the Sidebar, it opens to show a three-day forecast, as well as today's high and low temperatures.

Some gadgets display more information when they're undocked; others don't. Experiment to see what each gadget has to offer when it's set free.

Add gadgets to the Sidebar or desktop

1. Right-click the Sidebar, and choose Add Gadgets from the shortcut menu.

    or

    Click the plus sign (+) at the top of the Sidebar.

    The gallery of gadgets appears (refer to the first screen shot in this lesson).

2. Right-click the gadget you want, and choose Add from the shortcut menu.

    or

    Drag the gadget you want to the Sidebar or desktop.

Configure and organize your gadgets

You can place gadgets in any order on the Sidebar simply by dragging them into position. Whether gadgets are on or off the Sidebar, you can tweak their options easily (if they have options—not all gadgets do). This time, we'll use the Clock as an example.

1. Right-click the clock (either on the Sidebar or off; it doesn't matter), and choose Options from the shortcut menu.

    or

    Hover your mouse pointer over the clock, and click the wrench icon from the small menu that appears to the top-right of the clock.

TIP ——— You can tell whether a gadget has changeable options by hovering your mouse pointer over it. If you don't see the wrench icon, you can't change anything about the gadget.

continues on next page

The Clock properties window appears.

2. To change the appearance of the clock, click either of the arrows below the clock's image until you find the look you like.

3. To change the time zone, make a choice from the Time Zone drop-down menu.

4. To give a clock a specific name, type it in the Clock Name box.

   This name will appear on the clock's face.

   TIP ———— You can have multiple clocks on the desktop or the Sidebar, each with its own time zone, appearance, and name. If you change the Clock gadget's Time Zone setting, you won't affect your computer's time setting–though the properties window provides a link that lets you change it.

Among the other options you can change for the included gadgets are:

- The locale for the Weather widget
- The paper color, font type, and size of the sticky notes
- The folder location for the slideshow's photos, as well as how long to show each picture and the transition between pictures
- The feeds for the headline reader, as well as how many recent headlines cycle through the display

Getting More Gadgets

Although Microsoft has given you a dozen gadgets to start with, you'll want to explore what others are available—and you'll find plenty. The structure of gadgets is relatively simple, and those who like to tinker with such things have been hard at work.

Microsoft has created a Web page for available gadgets, and you'll find a link to it in the bottom-right corner of the Gadget Gallery in Vista. Click Get More Gadgets Online, which takes you to the Personalize Windows Vista Sidebar page (http://vista.gallery.microsoft.com/vista/SideBar.aspx).

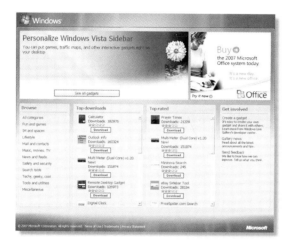

At this writing, the page is broken into general categories, most-downloaded gadgets, and top-rated gadgets. The page also provides a See All Gadgets button.

Download and install gadgets

1. When you find a gadget on the Personalize Windows Vista Sidebar page that you want, click its Download button.

   A message warns you to "Only install applications from developers you trust."

continues on next page

2. Click OK to clear the warning.

3. Click Save on the dialog box that appears to save the file to your hard drive.

> **TIP** —— If you want to run the gadget program but not save it, click Open instead.

The installer launches, and you get a window that lets you place the file in the location of your choice.

4. For this exercise, choose the Desktop; then click Save.

The gadget install file downloads to your desktop.

5. Double-click the file icon on your desktop to launch the gadget.

The Windows Sidebar-Security Warning dialog box appears.

6. Click Install.

The new gadget appears in your Sidebar, as well as in Vista's Gadget Gallery.

> **NOTE** —— The Microsoft site has two kinds of gadgets: gadgets for Vista, and gadgets for Live.com (a portal page) and Windows Live Spaces (a social-networking site). The Web gadgets and the Vista gadgets are not compatible, so pay close attention as you browse the collection of gadgets to get the type you want.

Roll your own gadgets

If you enjoy tinkering with software, you may want to experiment with building your own gadgets. A gadget is basically a small Web page with some special features. It consists of a few components packaged together:

- An XML file called the Gadget Manifest, which establishes how the gadget will look and behave, including such basics as the name and description

- A simple HTML file that includes the gadget's code

- A separate settings file for the HTML

- Scripts, graphics, and Cascading Style Sheets (like Web pages, gadgets can feature these elements)

- An icon to represent the gadget in the Gadget Gallery

Microsoft has good documentation on how to build and fine-tune gadgets at http://gallery.live.com/devcenter.aspx. The site also tells you how to build Microsoft's other types of widgets.

When you finish making your own gadgets, you can test them with other developers in forums on this site and then submit them to be included in Microsoft's online gallery.

Keyboard Shortcuts

Window key+spacebar	Bring all gadgets forward
Windows key+G	Step through the gadgets

What You've Learned

- How to position and customize the Vista Sidebar

- How to manage and configure gadgets

- Where to get more gadgets

- Where to find detailed help for building your own gadgets

9

GOALS

Find your way around
Internet Explorer 7's
new layout

Take full advantage of
tabbed browsing

Keep up with
frequently updated
Web sites via RSS

Surf the Web more
safely and securely

Get better printing
out of IE7

Discover Internet Explorer 7

When it released Internet Explorer 6 in 2001, Microsoft clearly had won the hard-fought browser wars, rendering the previous champ, Netscape, irrelevant. By its earlier bundling of the browser with its Windows operating system, the company made it unnecessary to use anything else.

The move may have served as a knockout blow, but it had unintended consequences. Microsoft was sued by state and federal officials, accused of violating antitrust laws by the initial bundling in Windows 98. And because Internet Explorer (IE) had deep hooks into the guts of Windows, it became a target for authors of malicious software who sought to damage or gain control of Internet-connected PCs. In Windows XP, IE6 became the attack vector of choice for the bad guys.

In addition, Mozilla Firefox (a direct descendant of the Netscape browser) has gained a foothold among Web surfers, eroding IE's market share. It includes features that are absent in IE6, such as tabbed browsing, and is more secure.

So Microsoft has a lot riding on its latest version, Internet Explorer 7, which comes with Vista and is also available for XP. IE7 plays catch-up in some ways; it has tabbed browsing, for example. It also has enhanced security and is less tied to the operating system. As you'll see, IE7 is a distinct improvement over IE6, though you may still want to consider alternatives.

What's New in IE7?

So much is new in Internet Explorer 7 that it may be helpful to give you a quick overview of the major ways in which it differs from IE6:

- **Simpler interface.** The most obvious change is the look of IE7, with fewer buttons and menu items visible. Key buttons such as Home and Print have been moved. In keeping with the overall design of Vista, the familiar menu bar (which includes commands such as File, Edit, and View) is hidden.

- **Tabbed browsing.** Tabbed browsing lets you see multiple Web pages in a single window. You can even open multiple pages at the same time by using Tab Groups or have multiple home pages that launch with each browser window.

- **Built-in search.** The ability to access your favorite search engine is now built into IE7 in an area to the right of the address field. The default is Windows Live Search, but you can change it to whatever you like.

- **RSS support.** You can subscribe to and read RSS feeds within IE7.

- **Improved security.** By default, IE7 runs with very low system permissions; it can't talk to other parts of the operating system and flags users when programs are trying to make changes. It is more selective about how it parses Web addresses. Also, IE7 includes a phishing filter that checks a database of known malicious sites, and it looks for suspicious behavior by sites.

- **Smarter printing.** IE7 can resize a Web page for printing, no longer chopping off the right side of a page that's too wide. It also lets you prevent headers and footers from printing, and it lets you print only part of a Web page's content.

IE7 has many other changes and tweaks, but these are the major ones. Next, we'll dive into the details.

Launching Internet Explorer

Actually, maybe we should title this section "Find Internet Explorer," because finding IE isn't as easy as it used to be.

In Windows XP, IE's icon was everywhere—on the desktop, in the Quick Launch toolbar, at the top of the Start menu, in the program groups. But when Vista is first installed, IE7 is not on the desktop. This situation is largely fallout from Microsoft's battles with state and federal governments over the bundling of Internet Explorer.

IE's not far away, however. Here's how to get to it:

1. Click the Start button.

2. Click the Internet Explorer icon at the top of the Start menu.

    or

    Click the IE7 icon in the Quick Launch toolbar, if that feature is enabled.

    IE7 launches, with MSN.com as the default home page.

TIP ———— As we mention in earlier chapters of this book, the Search box at the bottom of the Start menu is useful for typing the name of a program to launch it. And yes, you can type `Internet Explorer` and press Enter to launch IE7 with your home page loaded. But another option yields slightly different results. Type `IE` and press Enter; the browser launches, but what loads instead is the Windows Marketplace page for IE add-ons. We talk more about add-ons later in this lesson.

Exploring IE7's Prettier Face

Beauty is in the eye of the beholder, and at first glance, users either love or hate Internet Explorer 7's facelift. Those who don't like it often complain that they can't find the easily accessible menus from the previous version, but those menus aren't gone—they've just been moved around.

If you find that you can't live with IE7's new look, you can restore part of the original interface. We show you how at the end of this section.

First, we give you a tour of the top part of IE7.

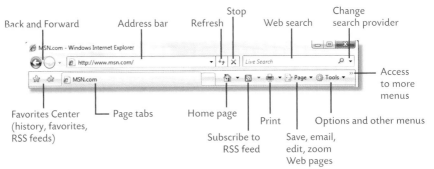

The layout has changed in these major ways:

- Two of most commonly used task buttons—**Home** and **Print**—have been moved from the area right of the Back and Forward browser buttons to the bottom-right corner of IE7's toolbar, in an area called the **command bar**.

- Two more often-used buttons—**Refresh** and **Stop**—are to the right of the address bar.

- Only one drop-down menu is associated with the **Back and Forward** buttons, rather than a drop-down menu for each direction. Clicking this menu shows your most recently viewed pages and a link to your browsing history.

- The **menu bar**—which holds the File, Edit, View, Favorites, Tools, and Help menus—is hidden.

- Buttons for adding and accessing favorites have been moved to the left of the page tabs and dubbed the **Favorites Center**. This area is also where you see your history and RSS feeds.

- A field for **searching Web pages** has been added to the right of the address bar.

- The **Tools menu** gets its own button in the command bar. If you're frustrated because you can't figure out how to do something in IE7, look here first.

- New to IE7 is a **Page button**, which handles many tasks listed in the File menu in IE6.

- Another new feature is an **RSS button** that "lights up" when a site offers an RSS feed.

Customize the toolbar

As in IE6, you can customize the toolbar, though your choices are a bit more limited. You can't move the address bar to different levels of the toolbar anymore, for example. But here's what you can do:

1. Right-click the toolbar to display the shortcut menu.

2. Click Menu Bar or Links to add those items to the toolbar.

   If you've installed other software that can be added to IE's toolbar, such as Google or Adobe Acrobat, those items are available too.

3. To increase the size of IE's icons, click Use Large Icons.

4. Put your mouse pointer over the Customize Command Bar option to display a submenu, and choose Add or Remove Commands.

   The Customize Toolbar dialog box appears.

continues on next page

165

5. To add a button to the Command Bar, click it in the left pane and then click Add; to remove a button, click it in the right pane and then click Remove.

6. To change the order of the buttons, select the one you want to move and then click the Move Up or Move Down button.

Bring back the menu bar

New IE7 users often complain that the menu bar is no longer available to them. This situation matches the overall design of Vista; you'll note that the menu bar is also absent from the top of folders.

But because consistency doesn't always equate to friendliness, here are two ways to restore it:

■ To restore the menu bar temporarily, press the Alt key. The menu bar will be visible until you click elsewhere in the browser window.

or

■ To make the menu permanently viewable, choose Tools > Menu Bar.

Turning On to Tabbed Browsing

After the changes in Internet Explorer 7's interface, the capability to browse multiple pages in a single window—a.k.a *tabbed browsing*—is the next-most-obvious change you'll find. Tabbed browsing is also the new feature you're sure to love the most. Although it's new to Internet Explorer, tabbed browsing will be familiar to anyone who has used alternative Web browsers such as Firefox, Opera, or IE6 add-ons (Maxthon, for example).

The implementation of tabs in IE7 is slightly different from that in other browsers, with some additional features that the other browsers don't have at this writing.

Take a look at the structure of IE7's tab system.

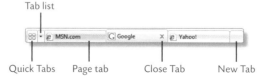

Here's what each part of IE's tab system does:

- **Quick Tabs.** This button shows thumbnails of what's in each tab. Clicking any of the thumbnails brings that page forward in the browser.

- **Tab list**. Click the small arrow to see a drop-down menu of all active tabs, and click any of them to bring that tab forward.

- **Page tab.** When you have multiple tabs active, click any of the tabs to display its page in the browser. You can reorder them by dragging them into position along the tab bar.

- **Close Tab.** Click the small *X* to close an open tab.

- **New Tab.** Click this narrow tab on the far right of the tab bar to launch a new browser tab. By default, the page shows an explanation of tabs, but you can change that behavior, as we show you in the next section.

Configure tabs

IE7's tabs are simple on the surface, but you can change their display and behavior, including what happens when you open a new one. You can even set up tabs so that multiple pages open when you start your browser.

Open with your home page

Be default, IE7 opens a new tab with an explanation of tabs. But you can set it to open with your home page or with nothing loaded at all.

1. In Internet Explorer, choose Tools > Internet Options. The Internet Options dialog box appears.

2. Click the General tab if it's not already selected (it's normally the default).

3. In the Tabs area of the General settings page, click the Settings button.

4. Select Open Home Page for New Tabs Instead of a Blank Page.

5. Click OK.

Open with a blank page

If you'd rather have a blank page open for each new tab, you can do that without configuring the Internet Options dialog box.

1. Click the New Tab stub.

    The page that opens contains an explanation of tabs.

2. Select Don't Show This Page Again near the bottom of the screen.
3. Click Close.

Open multiple tabs at once

You can set up IE7 to open more than one tab at a time, both when the browser first launches, and as a Tab Group.

Have more than one start page

To launch IE7 with multiple start pages:

1. In a browser window, open the sites you want as start pages.
2. Choose Tools > Internet Options. The Internet Options dialog box appears.
3. In the General tab, click the Use Current button.

4. Click Apply and then OK.

Open multiple pages from favorites

You can create *Tab Groups,* which are folders of favorites that can be opened at the same time. Suppose that you want to create a Tab Group of newspaper sites—say, *The New York Times,* the *Los Angeles Times,* the *San Jose Mercury News,* and the *Houston Chronicle.* Here's how you do it:

1. Open the pages you want to join in a Tab Group.

2. On the Command bar, click the Add to Favorites button ⌹.

3. Click Add Tab Group to Favorites.

    The Favorites Center dialog box displays.

4. In the Tab Group Name box, type a name for the group.

5. To store the Tab Group in a specific folder, open the Create In drop-down menu and navigate to that folder.

6. Click Add.

    The pages you have open are saved as a Tab Group.

Once you've created a Tab Group, you can open it in Internet Explorer.

To open a Tab Group in IE7:

1. On the Command bar, click the Favorites Center button ⌹. The Favorites Center appears.

2. Find the Tab Group you want to open, and right-click it. A popup menu appears.

3. Choose Open in New Tab Group.

    All the pages that are part of the Tab Group display in your browser.

NOTE —— You can right-click any folder in your Favorites list and then launch it this way as a Tab Group.

Keyboard Shortcuts

Open links in a new tab in the background	Ctrl+click
Open links in a new tab in the foreground	Ctrl+Shift+click
Open a new tab from the address bar	Alt+Enter
Open Quick Tabs (thumbnail view)	Ctrl+Q
Switch between tabs	Ctrl+Tab/Ctrl+Shift+Tab
Switch to a specific tab number	Ctrl+n (n can be 1–8)
Switch to the last tab	Ctrl+9
Open a new tab in the foreground	Ctrl+T
Close all tabs	Alt+F4
Close current tab	Ctrl+W
Open a new tab from the address bar	Alt+Enter
Close other tabs	Ctrl+Alt+F4

Setting Up Built-In Search

Vista is all about the search, as we explain in Lesson 3, and this philosophy extends to Internet Explorer 7, too.

In past versions of IE, you had to install a third-party program to get a built-in search box in the browser's toolbar. (You could, however, search directly from the address bar—an almost-hidden feature.) In Vista, an Instant Search box has been added to the right of the address bar.

By default, the Instant Search box is set to search Microsoft's own Windows Live Search, but you can configure this feature to use multiple search engines and set your own default.

Add a search provider

To add a search provider to IE7's search box:

1. From Instant Search's drop-down menu, choose Find More Providers.

The Add Search Providers to Internet Explorer 7 page appears.

2. Click the name of the provider you want to add.

3. In the confirmation dialog box that appears, click Add Provider.

   If the provider you want to use isn't listed, use the form on the right side of the Add Search Providers page.

Change the default provider

To choose which search provider is the default:

1. From the Instant Search box's drop-down menu, choose Change Search Defaults,

   The Change Search Defaults dialog box displays.

2. Select the provider you want to set as the default.

3. Click Set Default.

4. Click OK.

Keyboard Shortcuts

Select the Instant Search box	Ctrl+E
View list of search providers	Ctrl+Down arrow
Open search results in new tab	Alt+Enter

Reading RSS Feeds in IE7

In Lesson 8, we talk about RSS and how it's used in Vista's Sidebar gadgets. Now we look at how you can use Internet Explorer 7's built-in feed-reading capabilities to keep up with your favorite information sources. Other browsers (including Firefox and Safari in the Mac OS X) have had this feature for a while, but it's new to Internet Explorer.

Many Web sites that update information frequently—such as news sites, blogs, and technical-support sites—offer RSS feeds. To access them, you need a feed reader that subscribes to them and checks them regularly, downloading new information as it's available.

IE7 makes this process easy. When you visit a Web site that offers an RSS feed, an icon in the Command bar ⊠ turns orange ⊠.

Subscribe to a feed

1. In the toolbar, click the orange RSS icon.

    A page appears, showing you the feed's contents.

2. Use the box on the right side of the page to sort the feed by date, title, author, or category.

3. To subscribe, click Subscribe to This Feed in the yellow box at the top of the page.

4. In the dialog box that appears, you can change the name of the feed and use the Create In drop-down menu to store the feed in a specific folder.

5. Click Subscribe.

   The feed page will change to indicate a successful subscription.

TIP —— Not all pages that have RSS feeds are set up to notify IE7 and other RSS-reading browsers that a feed is available. If you know a site offers RSS, but the command-bar icon isn't lighting up, look for that icon or one similar to it on the page, and click it to display the feed-reading page for that site. Then click Subscribe to This Feed to add it to your list.

View and read feeds

To access the feeds to which you're subscribed:

1. On the toolbar, click the Favorites Center button.

   The Favorites Center displays.

2. Click the Feeds button.

   A list of subscribed feeds appears.

3. Click the feed you want to read.

The articles in feeds may be summaries or complete text. If you see summaries, you can click a headline to go to the page that contains the complete article.

Control feed updates and properties

You can manage many aspects of each subscribed feed, from how often it's checked for new content to how many articles are stored on your computer.

1. Click any feed in the Favorites Center.

2. Click the View Feed Properties link on the right side of the page.

continues on next page

The Feed Properties dialog box appears.

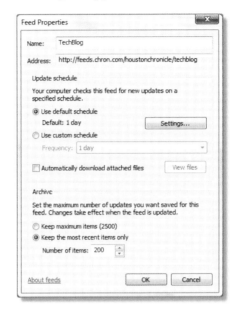

3. Click Settings.

   The Feed Settings dialog box appears.

4. From the Every drop-down menu, choose a frequency ranging from 15 minutes to once a week.

5. If you want IE7 to mark a feed as read automatically when you view it, turn off feed-reading view, or play a sound when something new arrives in the feed, select any of those options.

> ## Common Feed Store in Windows Vista
>
> When you add an RSS feed to the list in Internet Explorer 7, the feed is placed in a component of Vista called the Common Feed Store. No, it's not for selling food for barnyard animals; it's a common location where RSS feeds are kept.
>
> The Common Feed Store allows applications that know about it to access it. If you prefer to use different software to read RSS feeds, and if that software can access the Common Feed Store, the software will stay synchronized with the feeds you add via IE7. Microsoft Outlook 2007 can read RSS feeds, for example, and it can be configured to pull feeds from the Common Feed Store.
>
> As Vista becomes more ubiquitous, look for other applications that take advantage of this feature.

6. Click OK to confirm your changes.

   You return to the Feed Properties dialog box.

7. Check the Automatically Download Attached Files check box to save attachments, such as podcast audio or video files, in the feeds.

8. In the Archive area, set the maximum number of updates you want to save for that feed.

9. When you're finished, click OK to exit.

Keyboard Shortcut

Open feeds	Ctrl+J

Securing Internet Borders

In an effort to make IE7 less of a target for hackers, Microsoft partially decoupled it from the operating system. IE no longer offers a direct pipeline into the guts of Windows, instead behaving in a similar fashion to third-party browsers. Microsoft also added some features that protect against identity theft and that warn you if changes in your IE security settings are leaving you vulnerable.

Run in protected mode

By default, almost all Web sites are displayed in what's known as protected mode, which means that IE7 can write only to very specific folders on your hard drive. IE cannot write to crucial areas of the registry—though it may save basic information there, such as Web addresses visited—and it can't have much impact on the rest of the operating system.

You may want to give some sites more access than others, however. For example, you may want to allow some pages to run add-ons without prompts. You can tweak IE7's security settings for some sites by adding them to a list of trusted sites but do this sparingly and only for sites you really do trust.

To add Web pages to the list of Trust sites:

1. Load the site into your browser.

2. Choose Tools > Internet Options.

   The Internet Options dialog box appears.

3. Click the Security tab.

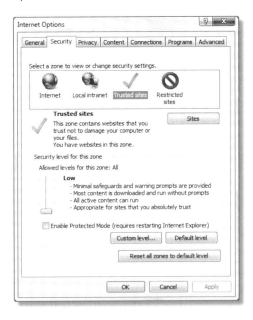

4. Click the Trusted Sites icon.

5. Click the Sites button.

   The Trusted Sites dialog box appears.

6. The site you've loaded into the browser should appear in the Add This Website to the Zone box; if not, enter the site name and then click Add.

7. If a site you're adding doesn't start with *https://,* indicating that it requires server verification, clear the Require Server Verification check box.

8. Click Close.

   You return to the Internet Options dialog box.

9. Click Apply and then click OK.

   NOTE —— When you add a site to your list of trusted sites, it runs in a window separate from sites that are running in protected mode. If you type the address of a trusted site in the address box of an IE7 window displaying a nontrusted site, the trusted site you enter will open in a separate window. You can't run a mix of trusted and untrusted sites in the same IE7 window.

The Security tab on the Internet Options dialog box functions very much as it did in IE6, letting you adjust settings for sites you visit on the Internet, a business intranet, and trusted and restricted sites. Note that you can add sites the Local Intranet and Restricted Sites in the same way you did for trusted sites.

Fending off the phishers

Phishing is the nasty practice of luring unsuspecting computer users to sites that attempt to extract personal information. A common phishing technique is to send an email warning that a bank account is about to be closed unless you rush to a site and input sensitive data, such as your Social Security, bank account, or credit-card numbers. The information is used to steal your money or, worse, your identity.

IE7 has a new feature called Phishing Filter that can alert you when you're about to visit a site that phishers could use.

Enable or disable Phishing Filter

1. In IE7, choose Tools > Phishing Filter. A submenu appears.

2. To turn the filter on, choose Turn on Automatic Website Checking; to turn it off, choose Turn off Automatic Website Checking.

3. If you've turned automatic checking off, you can check sites manually by choosing Tools > Phishing Filter > Check This Web Site.

What happens when IE7 discovers a phishing site?

If you click a link when Phishing Filter is enabled, IE7 checks the link against a known database of phishing sites and does one of two things:

- If it finds a match, the filter blocks access to the site and displays the following page instead.

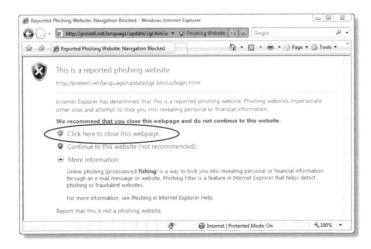

> ## Color-Coded Security
>
> When IE7 displays a page letting you know that the Web site you are trying to access is a possible phishing site, the address bar at the top of the page is tinted red (see the previous screen shot). This feature is part of a color-coding scheme that IE7 uses to indicate the status of a site.
>
> If a site uses High Assurance site certificates, for example, which guarantee and verify the identity of a Web site, the bar is tinted green. Other notifications may also show up in the bar, such as a gold padlock indicating that you've connected to a secure site.

Of course, you want to select Click Here to Close This Webpage. Trust us—you *don't* want to go to the site!

- If the site isn't listed in the database but behaves suspiciously, such as presenting a numeric Internet address while purporting to be a mainstream site, IE7 may block it.

Because IE7 is new, time will tell if the Phishing Filter can reliably protect users from malicious sites. We've noticed that the Phishing Filter can slow down Web browsing at times as it checks sites—Microsoft has already released a patch for IE7 that helps speed the process. We advise you leave it on, but if you do opt to turn it off for a performance boost, be very careful about where you post personal and/or financial information, and consider using the manual phishing check before filling out forms that ask for this kind of data.

Managing IE7

Internet Explorer 7 gives you a set of tools for keeping the browser running smoothly. With this version, it's much easier to identify and, if necessary, remove add-ons. And the process of cleaning up temporary Internet files, cookies and browser history has been moved to a single dialog box and simplified.

Manage add-ons

You can extend Internet Explorer 7's capabilities through the use of *add-ons*—small applications that plug into the browser. But add-ons have been the sources of problems in past versions of IE, ranging from simple software conflicts to spyware infections. In this new version, Microsoft provides the Add-Ons Manager, which makes controlling and disabling these applets easier.

To manage add-ons in Vista:

1. Choose Tools > Manage Add-Ons. A submenu appears.

2. Click Enable or Disable Add-Ons.

   The Manage Add-Ons dialog box appears. The center window displays the add-ons that are currently loaded and active in Internet Explorer.

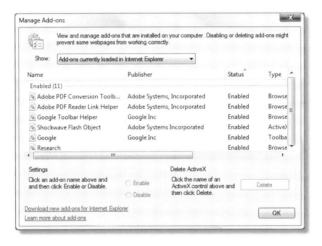

3. If you want to see something different from the active add-ons, make a choice from the Show drop-down menu.

   Options in the Show field include the following:

   • Any add-ons that IE has ever used

   • Add-ons that run without requiring permission

   • Any ActiveX controls that you've downloaded and installed

   • Third-party add-ons that are built into IE7

4. To enable or disable an add-on, select it and then click either the Enable or Disable radio button.

5. To delete an object, select it and then click the Delete button. If a User Account Control warning appears, click Continue.

6. Click OK when you are finished.

Clean up with a click

In previous versions of Internet Explorer, removing cookies, temporary Internet files, browsing history, and other privacy-related data required gaining access to several different places via the Tools > Internet Options command. In IE7, Microsoft provides access to all this information in one handy dialog box containing a clean-it-all button for maximum efficiency.

Delete cookies, temporary files, or data

Keeping your PC in pristine condition by ridding it of cookies, temporary files or other browsing data is much easier with Vista. Here's how:

1. Choose Tools > Delete Browsing History.

    The Delete Browsing History dialog box appears.

    The dialog box contains five categories:

    • **Temporary Internet Files.** Stored images, text, audio and video that can help speed up surfing when you return to the same sites regularly.

continues on next page

- **Cookies.** Small text files placed on your hard drive by Web sites for a variety of reasons, ranging from storing site-specific passwords to tracking what areas of a site you visit. (See more about cookies in the sidebar that follows.)

- **History.** A record of the sites you visit, accessible from the History button in the Favorites Center.

- **Form Data.** If you've enabled this feature, IE7 stores information you've entered in Web forms to save you from having to enter it again and again.

- **Passwords.** Login information stored on your computer separately from passwords stored in cookies.

2. If you want to delete data in any category, click that category's Delete button.

    or

    To delete data in all five categories at the same time, click the Delete All button.

    A delete-confirmation dialog box appears.

3. Check the check box if you want to delete files and settings stored separately by IE add-ons.

    A toolbar may also store passwords or Web-form information, for example.

4. Click Yes to perform the action.

5. Click Close when you are finished.

Remove specific files

The Delete Browsing History dialog box is a rather brute-force method of managing these files. In some cases, such as with cookies, you may want to delete specific files. Here's how:

1. Choose Tools > Internet Options.

    The Internet Options dialog box appears.

continues on Page 184

About Cookies

Mention cookies to some Internet users, and you'll get a horrified reaction. Some users consider them to be a serious threat to privacy and urge others to delete them regularly. But like anything else, cookies have both pros and cons.

Simply put, cookies are text files that contain very specific information. Web sites may place them on your hard drive for a variety of reasons. If you set up login information on a site that requires it, for example, information needed to log in again may be stored in the cookie, saving you from typing a password at each visit. Cookies may also store preferences for a site, such as what features are displayed on an entry page.

In addition, cookies can be used to track what you do on a Web site. Site operators use them most often to determine what pages are getting the most traffic, but they can also use cookies to determine what you're most interested in on a site and then possibly serve up ads related to those interests.

What concerns most privacy advocates are cookies that share information across sites. Some sites are members of networks that track users' browsing habits with an eye toward always showing site ads that interest you. Let's say that you spend lots of time looking at pet accessories at one site that's a member of an advertising network. You may go to another member site that has nothing to do with animals but still see ads for pet accessories.

In most cases, cookies don't identify you by name or other private information. In essence, you're User No. 385577BHx. If, however, you've entered personal data in any forms, that data could be tied to information stored in a cookie.

Regularly deleting cookies is one way to block cross-site tracking, but it also means that you'll have to re-enter information at sites you visit regularly. It's a trade-off, and you'll have to decide which is more important to you: privacy or convenience.

2. In the Browsing History area, click Settings.

The Temporary Internet Files and History Settings dialog box appears.

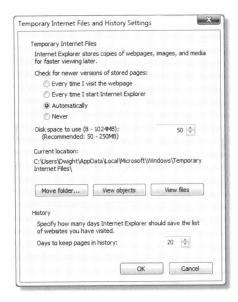

3. Click the Move Folder button to select another location to store temporary internet files; then click OK.

4. Click the View Objects button to see add-ons you've downloaded and delete them manually; then click OK.

5. Click the View Files button to display a window that lets you view and/or delete individual cookie files; then click OK.

6. Click OK to close the Temporary Internet Files and History Settings dialog box.

Improving Your Printing

In the past, printing Web pages from Internet Explorer was a crapshoot. A wide page would often cut off on the right margin unless it was printed in landscape mode. It's become a larger problem as Web designers, taking advantage of monitors with wider resolutions, have made their pages wider. The end result: prettier Web pages, but lots of wasted ink and paper.

But IE7 makes printing more reliable and easier through several new features, including the ability to print a wide page without cutting part of it off.

Preview and print your pages

The best place to start exploring IE7's printing improvements is Print Preview.

1. Load a page you'd like to print.

2. From the Print drop-down menu in the IE7 Command bar, choose Print Preview to see how your page will look when it prints.

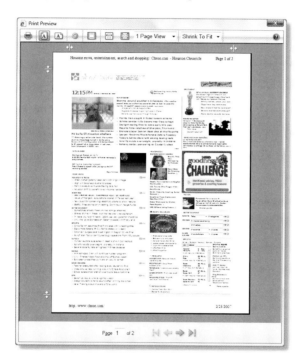

The Print Preview toolbar lets you control how the page is printed and how you preview it.

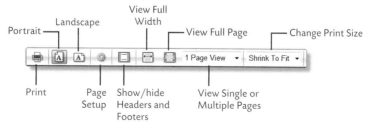

By default, the page is previewed so that the entire page is printed without cutting off any margins.

continues on next page

3. If you want to change the size of the print area, make a choice from the Shrink to Fit drop-down menu.

> **NOTE** —— Be aware that making the print area too large may prevent parts of the page from printing.

By default, headers and footers that show page numbers and the source Web address don't print.

4. Click the Show/Hide Headers and Footers button to display or hide headers and footers.

5. Click the Page Setup button to go the page settings for your printer driver.

The options available depend on your printer type and model. For example, you may be able to change the order of pages printed, print quality, etc.

6. To change the orientation of your printing from vertical (Portrait) to horizontal (Landscape), click the Landscape button.

   or

   To change from horizontal orientation to vertical, click the Portrait button.

7. To adjust the preview settings, click the View Full Width or View Full Page button.

   These settings do not affect how the page will print.

8. To see more than one page at a time, make a choice from the 1 Page View drop-down menu.

9. Click the Print button to begin printing.

Keyboard Shortcut

Print	Ctrl+P

What You've Learned

- How to find your way around IE7's new interface

- How to use and configure tabbed browsing

- How to add or change a search provider in IE7's new Search field

- How to use RSS in IE7 to keep up with your favorite information sources

- How to use IE7's new security features to make browsing safer

- How to manage add-ons and delete cookies and temporary files

- How to take advantage of IE7's improved printing features

10

GOALS

Get pictures on
your PC

Learn to edit, organize,
and share your photos

Work with Images

Vista comes with several tools for working with photos and other graphics. These tools include the new Windows Photo Gallery, the Paint program, and a new Snipping tool that lets you capture screen images and save them as files or paste them into other files.

Vista's file system also has been updated to help you work with images, as we discuss in Lesson 3. And Vista offers new views, including extra large icons that give you a better view of your pictures before you even click them.

Getting Pictures into Your PC

Once you've taken pictures with your digital camera, the next step is to get them onto the PC. This is done by either connecting the camera or the camera's memory card to the PC. Most digital cameras come with a cable that plugs directly into one of your PC's USB ports. Also, most cameras store photos on removable memory cards—typically, SD or Compact Flash. Some PCs have built-in readers for those cards, or you can purchase an external card reader that plugs into a USB port.

Windows XP had a Scanner and Camera wizard but that's no longer with us. Instead, Vista has an Import Pictures wizard that is supposed to come up automatically when you plug in a digital camera or insert a memory card with digital images into a card reader. We say "supposed to come up" because AutoPlay could be turned off or configured to perform a different function, as we explain in Lesson 4.

The easy way to import photos into your PC

You can use Windows Photo Gallery to import pictures from your camera or scanner to your PC, as we explain later in this lesson. But even if Photo Gallery isn't running, Vista will prompt you (by default) to import pictures as soon as you plug your camera or memory card into your PC.

Here's how to import images simply by plugging in your camera or card reader:

1. Plug your digital camera cable into your PC's USB port, or insert your camera's memory card into a card reader.

   When Vista recognizes the camera or memory card for the first time, an AutoPlay dialog box pops up, asking you to choose what to do with the media you just inserted.

2. Choose what you want to do with the pictures.

   For the purposes of this exercise, double-click Import Pictures Using Windows.

   Vista pauses to ask you to tag the pictures. It puts a tag in the file that is readable by Windows Photo Gallery and most graphics programs.

3. Type a tag for your photos.

   Use a tag that applies to all pictures you're importing, such as the month when the pictures were taken or perhaps an event such as European Vacation. As we explain in this lesson, you can add tags to individual photos later—to identify who is in them, for example.

4. Click Import.

   Your photos are copied from your camera or memory card to your PC, and Windows Photo Gallery launches automatically with your newly imported pictures on display.

   NOTE —— If AutoPlay isn't working, the feature may not be configured properly. See the AutoPlay section in Lesson 4 for more information.

Other ways to get images onto your PC

In addition to importing from a digital camera, you can copy photos to your PC from a CD, thumb drive, or other device; or you can scan them by using a scanner. Copying images to your PC from media is no different from copying any other type of file.

Copy an image

To copy images from a disc or thumb drive:

1. Insert the disc or thumb drive that contains the images you want to download.

2. If the disc or drive doesn't open automatically, access it by choosing Start > Computer and then double-clicking the drive.

   All the files and folders on the drive should be visible.

3. To display your Pictures folder, click Pictures in the right pane of the Start menu.

continues on next page

TIP —— Before proceeding to the next step, you may want to create a directory in the Pictures folder for the pictures you're about to copy.

4. Select the files you want to copy from the source drive, and drag them to the Pictures folder or the new directory you just created.

Scan an image

If you have a scanner and want to create digital images from regular photos, follow the directions that came with the device. Most scanners come with their own software for scanning pictures, but you can also import scanned images from within Photo Gallery, as you'll learn later in this lesson.

Exploring Windows Photo Gallery

The rest of this lesson focuses on Windows Photo Gallery, a new program included with Vista that lets you organize, edit, and view your pictures. Although Microsoft probably wouldn't admit it, Photo Gallery is somewhat similar to the excellent iPhoto that comes with Mac OS X. We have no complaints; by emulating what Apple did right, Microsoft is bringing easy photo organizing and editing "to the rest of us."

Photo Gallery isn't intended to compete with full-featured photo-editing programs like Adobe Photoshop and Corel Paint Shop Pro, but it may be all you need for basic photo editing, resizing, cropping, and removing red eye. It's also a good tool for viewing slideshows; getting photos ready to send by email; and, of course, printing. It can't create a slideshow that you can upload to the Internet, but as you see later in this lesson, it can pass photos on to Windows Movie Maker, which can create slideshows for the Internet and DVDs.

Even if you have a more elaborate photo-editing program, you may still find yourself using Photo Gallery for basic tasks because it's so easy to use.

Launch Photo Gallery

If Gallery isn't already running, here's how to launch it:

■ Choose Start > All Programs, and select Windows Photo Gallery from the Start menu's All Programs list.

or

In the Search box at the bottom of the Start menu, type Photo Gallery.

If you haven't yet imported any graphics, all you'll see are the sample pictures that Microsoft was nice enough to load on your PC just to get you started.

If you have already imported photos, you'll see your own photos, listed in reverse chronological order from the dates when they were taken.

Add photo tags

One of the first things you may want to do in Photo Gallery is tag your photos. Tagging is enormously helpful because it enables you to quickly find photos of certain people, places or events. Earlier in this lesson, we mentioned bulk-tagging them as you import them from the camera or memory card, but you can add as many tags as you want to identify each picture individually. You might tag all your photos from your recent trip to Europe as European Vacation, for example, but you also may want to tag some with the individual names of the people in the pictures or perhaps the cities you were in when the pictures were taken.

Tag an individual photo

You can use anything you want as a tag. Here's how to do it:

1. In Photo Gallery, select the photo you want to tag, and click Add Tags in the pane on the right.

2. In the text box that displays, type a name for the tag, and press Enter.

    The photo will acquire that tag.

3. If you want to add another tag to the same picture, repeat step 2.

    Notice that the tags you've created are listed alphabetically in the left column.

Tag a group of photos

You can tag several photos at the same time by selecting them and applying a tag to all selected pictures. Here's how:

1. Select the first photo in the group that you want to tag.

2. Move your mouse down the list to the last photo in the group, press and hold the Shift key, and select the photo.

    or

    If you want to select photos that aren't in sequence, Ctrl+click each photo you want to be part of the group.

    All the photos in the group are selected.

Capture Images From Your PC Screen

Sometimes, you want to capture something on your PC's screen. Vista comes with a simple program called the Snipping Tool that lets you capture any portion of the screen. Here's how to use it:

1. Run the program by typing `Snipping Tool` in the Start menu or choosing Start > All Programs and then double-clicking Snipping Tool in the Accessories program group.

   When the program loads, your screen will turn translucent white. You'll see whatever was on display before, but it will be much lighter.

2. Click and drag the mouse over whatever portion of the screen you want to capture; then release the mouse button.

   The Snipping Tool copies the portion of the screen that you highlighted and pastes it into the Windows clipboard.

3. Do one of the following:

   - To copy the screen shot into any program that accepts graphics, such as Paint, open the program and paste the screen shot into the program by pressing Ctrl+V. The portion of the screen you highlighted is copied into that program.

   - To save the graphic as a file, click the disk icon or choose File > Save As and give the file a name.

---

3. In the right column, click Add Tag, and in the text box that appears, type a tag name for the group. Press Enter.

   The tags are added to the photos.

Use tags to find your photos

After you've tagged some photos, you see the tag names in the left column. This is where the fun starts. When you want to find photos with a particular tag, all you do is click the tag name; Photo Gallery displays the photos.

After pictures have been tagged, you can find them by searching within Photo Gallery or by using Windows Search (see Lesson 5).

To Search within Photo Gallery:

1. Click the search box near the top of the screen.

2. Type your search term (typically a tag).

   Photos with that term are displayed as you type.

Manage images in Photo Gallery

As we said earlier, Photo Gallery offers basic editing tools. They're not the most sophisticated in the world, but they are quite useful for everyday photos.

Rotate images

Even before you open a picture for editing, you can right-click it to perform several actions, including adding a tag, previewing, rotating, changing the time taken, copying, deleting, renaming, and inspecting properties.

- Right-click any image, and choose Rotate Clockwise or Rotate Counterclockwise from the shortcut menu.

NOTE ——— Unlike the rotation process in Windows XP, this process will not cause any degradation in the quality of your photos.

Change the time stamp on a picture

If the clock in your digital camera is set correctly when you take a picture, it should date and time stamp it. That information stays with the photo when you copy it to the PC and is used by Photo Gallery to help you sort or find your pictures by date.

It's really a great way to help find photos. If, however, your camera's clock wasn't set correctly, you might want to change whatever date is on the photos.

To change the date and time on a photo:

1. Click the image and notice the date and time on the info pane on the upper right side of the screen.

2. Click the date.

    The date is highlighted.

3. If you wish to select the date from a calendar you can click the down arrow to the right of the date.

    A calendar pops up.

4. Change the date as necessary.

5. Click the time just to the right of the date and make changes as needed.

    The date and time are changed.

Rename an image filename

1. Right-click the photo, and choose Rename from the shortcut menu.

    The filename of the photo is highlighted in the info pane in the top-right corner of the screen.

2. Type the new name, and press Enter.

    Don't worry about the extension (such as .jpg or .tif); Photo Gallery will take care of that for you.

    The new name is displayed in the info pane.

Open the image using a different program

Photo Gallery works well with other programs. You can use Photo Gallery to organize your photos and then open the photo in another photo editor to edit it.

1. Right-click the photo or photos you want to edit, and choose Open With from the shortcut menu.

continues on next page

A list of graphic programs is displayed.

2. Click the program you wish to use.

The picture appears in that program's editor for you to edit.

Import pictures from a camera, scanner, or external disc

Earlier in this lesson, we describe how to use Vista's AutoPlay feature to import photos and other media. But sometimes you might just want to import a photo from within Photo Gallery either because it's more convenient or because Autoplay might not have worked correctly.

1. In Photo Gallery, choose File > Import from Camera or Scanner.

2. Select the device or drive that you want to import from.

A list of connected scanners and cameras is displayed.

If you select a device, Vista launches the import or scanning software associated with that device. If you select a drive, Photo Gallery imports the photos as discussed earlier in this lesson.

Edit photos in Photo Gallery

Photo Gallery's editing options may be limited, but the program does a very good job of helping you perform the most common photo-editing tasks. Many people will probably never feel a need for another program.

Zoom a photo

Even before you do any editing, you can zoom in on a picture. Here's how:

1. Double-click the thumbnail of the image in Photo Gallery.

    The full-sized photo is displayed.

2. If you have a mouse with a scroll wheel, click anywhere on the photo and scroll up to zoom in and down to zoom out.

    or

    Click the Change Display Size tool, which is located just below the photo.

    A slider bar displays; you can use this bar to zoom up or down.

    TIP —— The icon at the bottom of the screen just to the right of the Change Display Size tool can be used to toggle the picture between actual size and fit to window.

Optimize your photo

Photo Gallery has only five functions for fixing pictures, but they're the ones that people will use most of the time.

You access all the photo-editing features by clicking Fix on the menu bar near the top of the screen.

1. Double-click the photo in Photo Gallery.

    Photo Gallery's editor displays the photo full size.

2. Choose Fix in the taskbar.

continues on next page

Where's the File Menu?

If you're accustomed to other photo editing programs, you might find yourself looking for the file menu so you can save whatever changes you've made. It's not there. Photo Gallery automatically saves your files as soon as you're done editing them. If you're not happy with any changes, you can press Undo as many times as necessary while you're editing. Later, you can revert to a the original version of the picture by selecting the file again and clicking Revert to Original from the File Menu which takes you back to the original picture.

3. Select one of the options in the right pane:

- **Auto Adjust** tries to improve both the contrast and brightness. The software takes its best guess about how to improve the picture, but it's not an exact science. Try it, but if you're not happy, click Undo at the bottom of the right pane. If you like what you see, do nothing. If you prefer the way the picture looked before you clicked Auto Adjust, click Undo at the bottom of the screen.

NOTE —— Don't worry about saving your pictures. Photo Gallery automatically saves all your changes and saves copies of your original, should you want to restore it later (see the side-bar "Where's the File Menu?"

TIP —— The Undo button at the bottom of the info panel undoes your last command. If you keep clicking the button, it keeps undoing previous commands.

- **Adjust Exposure** gives you a slider that lets you adjust the brightness and the contrast. Brightness can shed more or less light on a subject, and contrast adjusts the difference between the brightest and darkest parts of the picture. The two elements go hand in hand, so you may have to experiment with each to get it right. If you're not happy, you can always click Undo.

- **Adjust Color** allows you to adult the color temperature, tint and saturation. How to do this is pretty obvious. Just click Adjust Color and you'll see three slider bars. The color temperature is really the mixture of red and blue making the picture feel "warmer" or "cooler." Play with it until you have a nice skin tones and are happy with the rest of the pictures colors. Tint controls the amount of green in the picture—again you need to experiment to see what this does. Saturation controls how dense the colors are.

- **Crop Picture** allows you to select the parts of the photo you want to keep and delete the rest. When you click Crop Picture, Photo Gallery automatically draws a box around the central part of the picture. You can click anywhere in the box to drag it to a different location or grab any of the little square handles on each corner and in the middle of each side to change the size of the box. When you have things just the way you want them, click Apply to crop the picture.

Before   After

- **Fix Red Eye** (covered separately; see the next exercise).

Repair red eyes

The Fix Red Eye option removes the red-eye effect that sometimes happens when you take a flash picture. What's nice about Photo Gallery's red-eye reduction feature is that you don't have to be precise about highlighting the center of the eye. You can simply highlight the entire eye or even both eyes, and Vista will probably fix the red eye without distorting the picture. Because of the Undo command (and the fact that you can always revert to the original), it's worth just trying this feature to see what happens. Chances are that you'll be happy with the result.

To use Fix Red Eye:

1. Open the picture by double-clicking it in Photo Gallery.

2. Click Fix Red Eye.

   Instructions in the right pane tell you to drag the mouse pointer to draw a rectangle around the eye you want to fix.

3. Use the mouse to draw a box around the eyes.

   That's right—contrary to what the onscreen instructions say, you can fix both eyes at the same time.

4. Release the mouse button.

Sharing Photos

For many people, a PC is the roach motel of photography. Photos go in but they never come out. Thanks to sharing tools you can liberate your photos by sharing them with friends and loved ones. There are a variety of ways to share—you can print them, you can have them professionally printed, and you can exchange electronic photos for people to enjoy on screen or print themselves. The choice is yours, but the tools are all there.

Print your photos

You can print from Photo Gallery in two ways: You can print to a printer attached to your PC or network, or you can order prints via the Internet.

The obvious advantage of printing photos yourself is that you get them right away, but don't assume that doing it yourself is less expensive than using a commercial printing service. By the time you add up the cost of ink and paper, it may be cheaper to have the printing done for you.

Professional services use a wet glossy process in which the photos look like they came out of an old-fashioned darkroom. If the service messes up, you don't pay, and you don't have to worry about printer jams or wasted supplies. Typically, 4 x 6 inch photos cost as little as 19 cents each (and sometimes less). Larger photos and wallet-size photos often cost more to print professionally than they do at home.

If you want to forge ahead and print a photo yourself, here's how to do it:

1. Select the photo in Photo Gallery.

    The photo is highlighted in blue.

2. In the main menu, choose Print > Print.

    The Print Pictures window is displayed.

3. Select printer, paper size, quality, paper type, and number of copies.

    Check the options on the right side of the screen for number of photos per page. Be sure to scroll down. Sizes range from a single print on one sheet to a contact sheet, which typically has 35 pictures per page.

If you have more than one printer, pay attention to the Printer drop-down menu near the top of the page. Also pay attention to paper size, and be sure that you have your printer properly configured for the type of paper and the print quality you want to use.

1. Select a picture, and click Print.

   The How Do You Want to Print Your Pictures page displays with four drop down menus: Printer (to select your printer), Paper size, Quality, and Paper type.

2. If you have more than one printer, click the down arrow to the right of the Printer to select the printer you want to use.

   A dropdown menu appears with a list of printers.

3. Click the printer you wish to use.

   The printer's name is displayed and the rest of the options adjust based on the characteristics of that printer.

4. Click the down arrow to the right of Paper Size to select the size of the paper you will print on.

5. In the dropdown menu that appears, click the paper size you wish to use.

6. Click Quality to select the print quality in terms of dots per inch.

7. Click Paper type to select the type of paper you plan to use.

8. In the dropdown menu that appears, click the paper type you wish to use.

   Once you've set all the parameters, you're ready to print.

9. Click Print.

   The picture is printed.

Order prints from a service

You can order prints from online services, which include retail outlets such as CVS, Ritz, and Walgreens. You can have the pictures delivered to a nearby store or to a store near a friend or relative with whom you want to share the photos.

1. Select the pictures you want printed.

2. Click Print near the top of the screen.

3. Select Order Prints.

   The Order Prints dialog box displays.

4. Pick a company to order from and click Send Pictures.

5. Follow the instructions on the screen to sign in to your account with that company. If you don't have an account, you can set one up as part of this process.

   Depending on the company you order from, you'll either be able to pick up your prints or they will be sent to you.

Copy photos to the desktop

Photo Gallery is very well integrated into the operating system. It shows not just views of images, but actual files. If you drag an image from Photo Gallery to the desktop, for example, you're actually moving the file from whatever folder it's in to the desktop. So if you want to put a file on the desktop, you may be better off copying it as follows:

1. Right-click a photo in Photo Gallery and don't let go of right the mouse button.

continues on next page

2. Drag the photo to the desktop or to the folder you want to copy it to.

3. When you let go of the mouse button, select Copy Here.

Email photos from Photo Gallery

You can use Photo Gallery to send a photo through the email program that you have registered as the default program for Vista (see Lesson 4).

1. Select the photo(s) you want to email.

   To select more than one, hold down the Ctrl key while you click each photo you want; to select a sequence of photos, click the first photo, hold down the Shift key, and click the last photo.

2. Click Email in the bar near the top of the screen.

   The Attach Files dialog box displays.

3. If you want to change the size of the pictures you're sending, make a different choice from the Picture Size drop-down menu.

4. Click Attach.

   Vista sends the pictures to your default email program.

5. Address the email to the person you wish to send it to, type your message and send it.

   NOTE —— Sending large photos by email can be time consuming for both you and the person receiving them. It's not polite to send large attachments to someone who isn't expecting them, particularly if that person has a dial-up Internet connection; a large attachment could tie up the recipient's email program and PC while the photos are being downloaded. Photo Gallery lets you send smaller files because they take less time to transmit.

Burn CDs

Photo Gallery is well integrated into two other companion programs: Windows DVD Maker and Windows Movie Maker. You can copy photos directly to a CD.

To burn photos to a CD:

1. Select the photos you want to copy to the CD.

2. Click Burn in the taskbar.

   A menu pops up giving a choice between a data disk and a Video DVD.

3. Click Data Disc.

   Vista asks you to insert a blank disc in your CD burner.

4. Insert a blank disc.

   Vista proposes a title for the disc (usually, the date).

5. Leave the suggested title as it is or change it.

6. Follow the instructions on screen to burn the image to your disc.

Windows DVD Maker lets you turn your photos into a DVD slideshow that can be played on a regular DVD player—the kind that most people have connected to their TV sets. You also have the option of adding an audio soundtrack. You would use this option only if you wanted to create a DVD. We'll cover this in the next lesson.

Windows Movie Maker also creates DVDs but it's more versatile in that it can also create movies that can be viewed on a PC, uploaded to video services like YouTube, or sent by email. This, too, will be discussed in the next lesson.

What You've Learned

- How to import photos to your PC
- How to use Vista's Photo Gallery to edit and share pictures via print, online, or on CDs

11

GOALS

Play audio and video
using Windows
Media Player

Create and edit
video projects using
Windows Movie Maker

Record audio using
Sound Recorder

Burn a DVD using
Windows DVD Maker

Consume and Create Media

Like Windows XP, Vista has tools for both consuming and creating media. All versions of Vista come with Windows Media Player for playing audio and video; Windows Movie Maker for creating and editing video projects; and Sound Recorder, a rudimentary tool for recording audio. The Home Premium and Ultimate editions also come with Media Center, which allows you to play audio and video, display photos, and watch and record television if your PC has a TV tuner installed. Home Premium and Ultimate also come with Windows DVD Maker for burning your own video projects to DVD.

A growing number of people are using PCs to create audio and video for podcasts, uploading movies to YouTube and other purposes, but just about everyone uses a PC to consume media from time to time. So we'll start with Media Player, and move on to video- and audio-creation tools. This book's Web site (www.peachpit.com/vistalearningseries) has a lesson devoted to the Media Center, which you can access by registering your copy of this book when you visit the site.

Media Player or Media Center?

Before we start, let's distinguish between Windows Media Player and Windows Media Center, two programs with similar names and somewhat overlapping functions.

Windows Media Player is designed to play music and video, view pictures, copy (rip) music files from a CD, and also create CDs (burn) from music on your computer. You can also use it to copy music from your PC to portable digital music players and to maintain and organize your library of media files.

Windows Media Center is designed to play music, video, and TV, as well as to display photos and record live TV. The main difference is that Media Center was designed to work on a TV set as well as a PC screen. In fact, some machines come with a remote control, so you can sit back and use Media Center to change channels, load video, or play music from your easy chair. You can think of Media Center as turning your PC into a TiVo-like digital video recorder (DVR) that also plays content from your PC. Information about the Media Center can be found online at this book's Web site (www.peachpit.com/vistalearningseries).

Exploring Windows Media Player

Windows Media Player in Vista has been updated with a new look. If you have a lot of music, you may notice the improved album art. If you accept the defaults when installing Media Player, it attempts to grab album covers for your music from the Internet, helping create a more pleasant and more useful visual impact for the program.

Media Player also has a simpler navigation system, with a taskbar at the top offering five simple choices and an easier-to-use navigation pane in the leftmost column.

In addition, as with other aspects of Vista, Media Player makes it easier to find your music because of an improved search function. Although the software maintains its ability to display video and photos, it is, at its heart, an electronic jukebox for acquiring, playing, and organizing music.

What is Digital Rights Management?

As you work with Media Player and Media Center you may come across music or video files that are in some ways encoded with Digital Rights Management (DRM) software to limit how you can use the file. The various DRM technologies can be used to control a great many things you may want to do with your music or view, including:

- How many times you view or listen to a file

- How much time can go by before the file will no longer play

- How many times you can copy the file and to which devices

- Whether you can burn the file to a CD or DVD or copy it to a digital music player

One problem with DRM is that it is sometimes platform specific. Some DRM works only with files designed to play with Apple's iTunes, for example, whereas other technologies work with files that will be played by Windows Media Player, Media Center, or other Windows-based media software.

The good news for Windows users is that most DRM technologies that work with Windows work with a variety of Windows software programs, as well as with Windows-compatible devices such as portable media players that support Microsoft's PlaysForSure standards. These devices are certified by their manufacturers to work with media files designed to play on Windows Media Player. But DRM can still limit what you can do or require you to make a payment or subscribe to a service before you can enjoy the media you've downloaded.

If all this seems confusing, it's not just you. DRM is one of those things that a lot of people complain about. Even Steve Jobs, whose iTunes Store is the most popular place to buy protected music, has called for the elimination of DRM, and we're starting to see companies talk about selling music without DRM. But for the foreseeable future, DRM is likely to remain with us to some degree, so we have to figure out how to work with it.

To start Windows Media Player:

1. Click Start.

2. Choose All Programs > Windows Media Player.

   or

   Type Media Player in the Search box, and press Enter.

   If this is the first time you've run Media Player, an initial setup screen displays. You'll see it only once.

3. Choose the settings you want for Media Player. Most users will probably be happy with Express Settings, but if you want to learn more about your installation options, see the "Media Center Setup Options" sidebar in this section.

   Windows Media Player launches with sample music that comes with Vista.

Media Player Setup Options

You'll most likely be fine choosing Express Settings in Windows Media Player startup screen, but you may want to consider your options.

If you select Custom Settings, a screen displays that lets you choose different installation options:

- **Display Media Information from the Internet applies to your CDs and DVDs.** This option determines whether Media Center will attempt to display the cover art that it gathers from the Internet about your CDs and DVDs.

- **Update Music Files by Retrieving Media Information from the Internet** pertains to the *metadata* that is stored with each of your songs, such as the track name, album name, and artist. If any data is missing, Media Center will attempt to fill it in by getting that information online.

- **Download Usage Rights Automatically When I Play a File** authorizes Media Center to download usage rights automatically when you play a file. Media Player is capable of playing songs and movies that have been encoded with Digital Rights Management (DRM). When this option is checked, the software can automatically try to determine whether you have the right to use that particular media file. If this option is not checked, you may be asked each time you try to play the file. This setting has no bearing on MP3 files, media files you create yourself, and other unprotected media.

- **Send Unique Player ID to Content Providers**, which is deselected by default, identifies your player and provides information about your setup. Fortunately, most content providers don't require that this option be selected; however, it's possible you may come across some who do.

- **I Want to Help Make Microsoft Software and Services Even Better by Sending Player Usage Data to Microsoft** lets you be a nice person and help Microsoft out by sending unique player user data to the company. By selecting this option, you are joining what Microsoft calls the Customer Experience Improvement Program—which, the company says, "helps to improve the quality, reliability, and performance of Microsoft software and services." Microsoft also says that the information you send is anonymous. Whether you want to enable this option is totally up to you, but it's off by default.

- **Save the File and URL History in the Player**, which is checked by default, displays your most recently played files in the File menu. This setting makes it more convenient to replay media that you recently played, but it also means that others who have access to your computer can find out what you've played.

Hide Media You've Played

If you choose Express Settings when you're using Media Player for the first time, Save the File and URL History in the Player is selected by default.

If you want to remove the list of files you've played, follow these steps:

1. On the Media Player taskbar, hover your mouse pointer over the Now Playing tab, and click the down arrow to open a menu.

2. Choose More Options.

3. In the Options window that appears, click the Privacy tab.

The Privacy options are displayed.

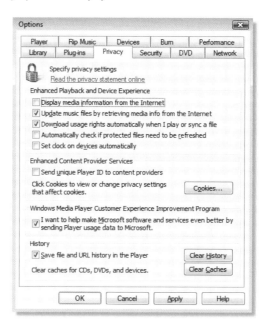

4. Click the Clear History button; then click OK.

The history of the files you've viewed or listened to is deleted.

Get to know the face of Media Player

After the program is configured, the first thing you see when you start Media Player is the library, which typically displays the album art for your music. Media Player may not find art for all of your music automatically, though you can add art later.

The **Now Playing** tab in the Media Player taskbar shows whatever visual is associated with content that is playing. For a movie or TV show, that visual is the actual video. For music, the visual is *visualization*—computer-generated shapes, colors, and patterns that change and move depending on the music playing.

The Media Player taskbar.

The remaining tabs on the taskbar are your keys to all that Media Player can do:

- **Rip** lets you copy music from a CD.

- **Burn** lets you copy music from the PC to a CD.

- **Sync** copies music and media from the PC to a portable digital player.

- **URGE** connects you to the same-named digital music store operated by Microsoft and MTV.

The **back and forward arrow buttons** at the left end of the taskbar let you move ahead or backward to retrace your steps.

Choose the media you want to view

Just below the taskbar is the **Category button,** which lets you choose among various types of media: music, pictures, video, recorded TV, and other media. By default, the category is set to music.

To choose a different medium:

- Click the Category button, and choose another category from the drop-down menu.

continues on next page

215

When you use this button to change categories, you also change the menu options to the right of the button. The icon changes depending on the category. If you're looking at music, for example, the icon will be a musical note.

Sort your media

The left column of the display is the navigation pane, which changes depending on the category of media you're working with. You can use this pane to sort your display according to the categories displayed in it. In the case of music, for example, those categories include Recently Added, Artist, Album, Songs, Genre, Year, and Rating.

To sort your music (or any media you selected by clicking the Category button):

■ Click one of the headings in the library section of the navigation pane.

Because we selected Artist in the left column, music in the center pane is sorted alphabetically by artist name.

If you have even a modest-size library, of course, you have far more artists and titles than can fit on one screen, so you can use the scroll bars on the right side of the window to scroll to look at additional artists and titles.

Change your view

Even though it's nice to see album art, sometimes that view can get a bit overwhelming. Because the albums take up so much space, you see fewer items on the screen, which makes it harder to find what you're looking for, especially if you have a large collection.

If you blink, you may miss two of Media Player's most important icons. Just to the left of the search box is the **View Options** icon, and to the left of that icon is the **Layout Options** icon. Both icons let you alter your view of your media.

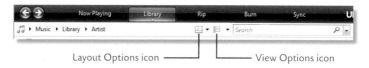

The View Options and Layout Options icons are located on the taskbar.

The View Options icon lets you change the display from Icon (album art, in the case of music) to Tile (album art with a little more detail) to details, which is basically a listing of the artists, songs, and albums.

To change the view of how your music is displayed:

■ Click the down arrow next to the View Options icon, and choose Icon, Tile, or Details from the drop-down menu.

For the purposes of this exercise, we chose Details, which isn't as pretty as the other two options but can be very useful if you have a lot of information onscreen.

Layout Options lets you configure the look of Media Player.

The Layout Options drop-down menu lets you hide or display the navigation pane and list pane, as well as classic menus.

By default, the navigation pane is displayed, and the list pane and classic menus are hidden. We recommend that you display all three elements, at least for now. Classic menus gives you back the old familiar File, View, Play, Tools, and Help menus, which can be very useful. The list pane lets you create lists of things to do, such as a list of media to play. You can add items to the list pane by dragging them into the pane, and you can mix different types of media, such as playing a song followed by playing a video. We give you more information on those topics when we talk about creating playlists later in this lesson.

Get music into Windows Media Player

You have three ways to get music into Windows Media Player:

- If the music files are already on your computer, you can add them to your library by monitoring the folders where they are stored.

- You can copy (rip) music from CDs to your PC and to Media Player's library.

- You can purchase or subscribe to music by using Media Player or another compatible program from the URGE music store, or by shopping at other online music stores.

Add music by monitoring folders

Media Player monitors certain folders on your PC for any media files they contain. If it finds files that are compatible, it automatically adds them to your library. By default, Media Player looks for media files in your Music, Video, and Pictures folders, but you can add or remove folders.

To add a folder for Media Player to monitor:

1. On the Media Player taskbar, click Library.

2. Select Add to Library.

   The Add to Library dialog box is displayed.

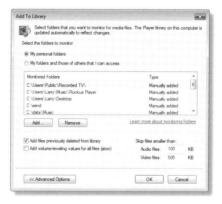

3. Select either My Personal Folders or My Folders and Those of Others That I Can Access.

For this exercise, select My Personal Folders.

Media Player scans folders on your hard drive for compatible media files and, while it's scanning, displays its progress by showing you a screen with a moving green bar, as well as the number of files it's found and the files it's added. If Media Player doesn't find any new files, it displays 0 in the Files Added section.

NOTE —— The My Personal Folders option in the Add to Library dialog box refers to the folders on your PC that are associated with your account and that contain media files, as well as any public folders on your machine. The option My Folders and Those of Others That I Can Access refers to those folders and folders that another person has shared with you.

4. When the scan is complete, click Close.

    Alternatively, you can close the dialog box at any time and let the search continue in the background, albeit a bit slower.

    Any new media files found are added to your library, and because you are monitoring these folders, any new files that are added to those folders are automatically added to your library.

Add folders to monitor

You may want to keep some of your media files in folders other than the standard ones used by Vista. If so, you can add those folders to the list of the ones that are monitored for music and video.

1. On the Media Player taskbar, click Library, and choose Add to Library from the drop-down menu.

    The Add to Library dialog box appears.

2. Click Add.

    The Add Folder dialog box appears.

3. Browse for the folder you want to add.

4. Select the folder you want, and click OK.

Add album art

If you have albums whose art Media Player can't find, it displays the image of a blank CD with the note "Paste Art Here."

If you find the album art, you can copy it to the clipboard and paste it in that spot, but before you do that, try letting Media Player find it for you on the Internet:

1. Right-click the blank CD, and choose Find Album Info from the shortcut menu.

   Media Player searches for album info and displays the Find Album Information window.

2. If you find the album cover, click it.

   Media Player updates the tracks in the album with the information it found online.

3. Close the Find Album Information window by clicking the red X in the right corner.

   The library should display the proper album art for your album.

   NOTE —— Don't forget that you can click the down arrow next to the View Options icon in the taskbar and choose Icon, Tile, or Details from the drop-down menu to alter the level of detail you see about the album (see "Change your view" earlier in this lesson).

Search music

You can search for an artist, album, song, or any text that shows up in the name of a song, artist, or album (sorry—Media Player doesn't search lyrics).

If you're programming music for a birthday party, for example, you could look for any songs that include the word *birthday* in the title. Here's how:

1. Click the Start button, and type `birthday` in the Start menu's Search box.

    Media Player automatically starts searching for the item, based on what you've typed so far; you don't need to press Enter. Media Player finds all listings and presents the matches from your library and those from the URGE music store.

2. Click the matches from your library.

    Media Player displays the songs or the cover art for the albums that contain songs with the word *birthday*.

3. Click any of the items to play them, or drag them to the list pane to create a playlist, which we show you how to do in the next section.

Create and use playlists

Remember those old "mix tapes" from the 1980s? Back in the day, people would get out their stack of albums or CDs and make tapes with selected tracks from different albums. The process was extremely time consuming, but the result was a musical collage that was tailored to an individual. Media Player's playlist function makes this process very quick.

You can create a list of songs or videos or a mixture of songs and videos that are played back in a specific order any time you want. You can not only play these songs and videos on your PC, but also copy a playlist to a portable digital music player or burn it to a CD to create an on-demand custom listening experience.

Make a new playlist

Creating a playlist is very simple:

1. In the navigation pane on the left side of Media Player, click Create Playlist.

The text in that box changes from Create Playlist to New Playlist.

2. Type the name of your playlist, and press Enter.

    The new playlist is listed in the playlist area of the navigation pane. Now all you need to do is add music to it. You do this by dragging songs or albums to the list, but you have to be very careful, because it's very easy to drag is to the wrong location. In the next steps, we show you the most reliable way.

3. Right-click the song, artist, album, video, or other item you want to add, and choose Add To from the shortcut menu.

4. In the Add To submenu, click the appropriate playlist.

    The item is added to the playlist.

Use another method to create a playlist

There's an easy way to create a playlist and add music to it at the same time by using the list pane on the right side of the screen. (If you don't see the list pane, see "Change your view" earlier in this lesson.)

1. Select the item you want to add to a playlist, and drag it into the list pane.

    All the individual song titles for whatever item you dragged appear in the list pane. If you dragged an artist, for example, all that artist's songs are included.

2. Repeat this process for all items you want to add to the playlist.

3. Click Save Playlist at the bottom of the screen.

    The words `Untitled Playlist` are highlighted in the box at the top of the list pane.

4. Replace that text with whatever you want to call your playlist, and press Enter.

    The playlist is created and added to the playlists in the navigation pane on the left side of the screen.

Rip music from CDs

You can take that stack of CDs you have and turn the songs into digital music to play on your PC and on portable digital players. The process is called *ripping*.

To rip a CD:

1. Insert the CD into the computer's CD or DVD drive.

    Vista may automatically ask whether you want to copy the music from the CD, depending on whether AutoPlay is configured for this task. If so, whether this feature actually works is sometimes a hit-or-miss proposition. For this exercise, assume that the feature isn't working.

2. With the CD in the drive and Media Player running, click Rip in the taskbar.

    Media Player starts to copy the music from the CD. As it works, you see its progress in the Rip Status column. If Media Player doesn't start ripping on its own, click Start Rip in the bottom-right corner of the screen.

continues on next page

When Media Player finishes the rip, the songs from that CD appear in your library.

3. After all songs have been ripped, remove the CD from the drive.

Change the format of the music you rip

By default, Media Player saves your ripped music as .wma (Windows Media Audio) files. This format is actually a good one, because it uses a fairly good compression system that gives you the maximum quality of sound for the amount of disk space used.

Not all music players can play .wma files, however. If you want to play the music on an Apple iPod, for example, you're going to want your files compressed in the MP3 format, a nonproprietary, standards-based format supported by virtually all portable music players and all music software. Fortunately, Media Player gives you a choice of formats.

To rip in MP3 format:

1. Move your mouse pointer over the Rip tab on the taskbar, and click the down arrow next to it to open a drop-down menu.

2. Choose Format from the drop down menu and then select MP3 from the submenu that pops up.

From now on, all music files you rip will be saved in MP3 format.

TIP —— Explore other options in the Rip drop-down menu, including Bit Rate, which lets you adjust the quality of the ripped music files. A higher bit rate gives you better-quality sound but also takes up more disk space. Before you permanently change from the default, try different bit rates. You may find that you're unable to distinguish between a higher bit rate and a lower one.

Burn digital music to a CD

Media Player can copy digital music to a CD for use in standard CD audio players, and it can also copy the files to a CD that can be played in computers and CD players that are capable of playing .mp3 or .wma files.

1. Start by inserting a blank CD into the CD/DVD burner.

   Vista may ask whether you want to burn an audio CD or burn files to disc, but as with ripping, this AutoPlay feature isn't 100-percent reliable. If it does work, it takes you to Media Player. Either way, proceed to step 2.

2. With the disc in the burner and Media Player running, click the down arrow below the Burn tab on the taskbar, and choose Audio CD from the drop-down menu.

   Media Player brings up a blank burn list on the right side of the screen.

3. Select the artists, albums, songs, or playlists you want to burn to CD, and drag them to the burn list on the right side of the screen.

   The only restrictions are that these items need to be either unprotected files or files you have permission to burn to CD (see the "What is Digital Rights Management?" sidebar earlier in this lesson) and that you have sufficient space on the CD for the selected files.

4. Below the burn list, click Start Burn.

   Media Player starts to burn the CD and keeps you updated with its progress. The disc will be ejected when the burn is done.

Synchronize your digital music player

Although many digital music players come with their own synchronization software, you can use Media Player to synchronize music for any device that uses Windows DRM. That list includes most music players on the market, with two notable exceptions: the Apple iPod and, ironically, Microsoft's own Zune music player. Microsoft ships separate synchronization software for the Zune.

To synchronize to a compatible digital music player:

1. Insert one end of the USB cable into the music player and the other into a USB port on your PC.

   If Plug and Play is working correctly, Vista recognizes your device and asks whether you want to sync digital media files to this device. If this feature works, click Yes; when Vista launches Media Player, skip to step 3. If the feature doesn't work, proceed to step 2.

continues on next page

2. If Vista didn't launch the Sync feature automatically, click the Sync tab in the Media Player taskbar.

   Media Player displays the Device Setup screen with the name of your device.

3. Follow the onscreen instructions, which vary depending on your device.

   Media Player takes you back to your library.

4. Select the songs, albums, artists, or playlists that you want to sync to your device, and drag them to the sync-list area on the right side of the screen.

   As you do this, keep an eye on the amount of space that's available, which should be displayed near the top of the screen.

5. When you're ready to start synchronizing, click Start Sync near the bottom of the screen.

   Media Player starts synchronizing and updates you along the way.

Watch movies

Next to listening to music, the most popular use of Media Player is watching movies on DVD. Watching DVD movies is especially popular with owners of laptop computers, because they can use their laptops to watch movies on a plane, in a hotel room, or in a small dorm room.

The easiest way to use Media Player to watch a DVD is simply to insert the DVD into the drive and hope that AutoPlay recognizes the disc and starts Media Player (or displays a dialog box offering to start it for you). If that works, you may have nothing else to do other than click Play.

If Media Player doesn't launch automatically, here's how to get started with the movie:

1. With the DVD inserted in the drive, launch Media Player.

automatically, double-click the movie's

| Memoirs of a Geis... |

see the movie's menu.

ou can right-click the screen to display a shortcut
he video in full screen or resize the video.

ng Windows

o consume media, but Vista also lets you
pretty good tools for creating and editing
dimental tool for recording audio.

Make movies with Movie Maker

The explosion of YouTube and other online video-sharing services has generated
a lot of interest in desktop moviemaking. Movie Maker isn't likely to help most of
us win an Academy Award, but we bet that it could help some people win one of
the new YouTube awards.

Windows Movie Maker allows you to capture video from a digital camcorder or
import video that's already on your PC. It also lets you work with audio files and
photographs that you can import from your hard drive or, in the case of photos,
directly from Windows Photo Gallery.

When media has been loaded into Movie Maker, it's possible to edit clips, cut out
unwanted material, add transitions, insert audio and still photos, and arrange the
movie as you want.

Movie Maker is also a whiz when it comes to creating slideshows. When you've
imported photos, you can not only sequence them in the order you want, but
also add transitions and special effects that make them look almost like movie
clips. You can even add an audio soundtrack, making it possible to create your
own audio slideshow that you can burn to a DVD or CD, email to friends, or post
on a video-sharing site for public or private access.

The exercises in this section show you how to import video from a DV camcorder into Movie Maker, edit the video, and create a project for use on the Web or on a DVD.

Import your video

1. Run Movie Maker by choosing it from the All Programs menu or typing Movie Maker in the Start menu's Search box.

2. In the Import section in the left pane of Movie Maker, click From Digital Video Camera.

3. Connect the DV camera to your PC by plugging it into the FireWire port.

   The Import Video dialog box appears.

4. Type a name for the videotape you will capture.

   For now, accept the default setting: VideoTape.

5. Leave all other settings at their default, and click Next.

   The next screen asks you whether you want to import the entire video or only parts of it.

6. For the purposes of this exercise, choose to import only parts of it; then click Next.

   Movie Maker starts the import process by showing you whatever frame the videotape is currently on. It displays the tape position in terms of hours, minutes, and seconds from the start of the tape.

7. Use the tape controls to play, pause, stop, rewind, fast forward, or go to the previous or next frame.

   To rewind, click the Play button, followed by the Rewind button. That way, you can view the video as it rewinds. When the tape gets to the part where you want to start capturing, click the Stop button. It's better to go a little too far back in the tape than not far enough; you can always trim, as you see later in this lesson.

   Movie Maker rewinds the tape as you watch and then stops it where you clicked the Stop button.

8. When you've reached the appropriate starting place on the tape, click Start Video Import.

   Movie Maker plays the tape and captures the video to your PC in real time. You can see the video playing and also see the progress in terms of how much of the video has been imported, how many megabytes of disk space it's taken up so far, and how much space you have remaining on your PC.

continues on next page

9. When you have captured as much as you want, click Stop Video Import and then click Finish.

   Movie Maker takes you to its main screen, where the newly captured video clips are displayed.

Preview and add more clips

Chances are that Movie Maker divided your video into two or more clips. Movie Maker does this by making its best guess as to where a scene begins and ends, but of course, it's not likely to be all that accurate. This is where you come in. You can preview the clips and then trim and rearrange them as you want.

To preview and edit a clip:

1. Click the clip.

   The first frame of the clip displays in the preview window on the right side of the screen.

2. Click the Play button (below the preview window) to watch and listen to that clip, and do the same for any other clips you have.

   The clip plays in the preview window, and the audio comes out of your speakers or headphones.

3. If you want to use any of the clips in your movie, copy the clips to the storyboard by dragging them to the area of the storyboard that says Drag Media Here.

   You can drag as many clips as you want, but for now, just drag over the first clip.

> ### Storyboard and Timeline Views
>
> Movie Maker gives you two ways of editing movies: the timeline and the storyboard. The storyboard, which is the default view, lets you look at your movie clips and still images in sequence. You can move them around to change the sequence as needed, and you can drag video transitions between clips or add effects to clips.
>
> The timeline allows you to make adjustments to your clips—trim video, for example, or change the duration of a transition. The timeline is really the fine-tuning area of Movie Maker, and it's where a lot of the power is.
>
> To switch between the timeline and the storyboard, click the down arrow to the right of the word Storyboard or Timeline to select the other option.

Split a clip

Now the real editing starts. In this section, you're going to be doing some cutting, but don't worry—you're not cutting the original source material. All you're cutting is the clip that you're using to create the final product. The clips you imported will remain intact, so you can always go back later and access material that you've removed from your movie. I think they used to call that "the cutting room floor."

Movie Maker's split function allows you to turn one clip into two or many clips. You can use this as a way of trimming material from the front or end of a clip; however, as you'll see in the Trimming a Clip section, there's an easier way to do that. Still, spitting can be a handy way to trim away material that you might want to use later.

To split a clip:

1. Click the clip in your storyboard or timeline.

2. When you see the clip in the preview window, click the Play button or press the spacebar (which toggles between Play and Pause).

3. Stop the clip at the place where you to split it by pressing the Pause button or pressing the spacebar.

    The clip stops playing.

continues on next page

The Secret to Video Editing

Editing video is unlike editing words, pictures, or audio, because you can't just highlight a piece of a video clip and lop it off, as you can with other media. But a simple concept makes this process a lot easier. Although you can't just highlight and delete video, you can take a trim a video clip at either end or split it into pieces and discard pieces you don't need.

4. If you want to fine-tune where the clip stops, move the slider below the preview window forward or backward until the clip is at exactly the point where you want the movie to start.

   Now you're ready to split the clip.

5. Split the clip into two clips by clicking Split in the bottom-right corner of the screen.

   NOTE —— You can discard the portion you don't want. Remember that you're not really deleting the source material–just what you will use in this particular movie.

   Now you have two clips on the storyboard. The one on the left is the material from before the split, and the one on the left is the material after the split.

If you wish to discard either clip:

1. Watch and listen to both clips to be sure you know which one you want to discard.

2. When you're sure, click the one you want to discard, and press the Delete key.

   You have one clip with the material you want.

Trim a Clip

Although you can use the split feature to remove the beginning and end of a clip, another way to trim the front or end of a clip is to use the trimming tool. This lets you quickly trim the start or end of a clip.

1. If Storyboard is selected, switch to the Timeline view by clicking the down arrow next to storyboard and selecting Timeline.

2. If you haven't already done so, drag a clip into the timeline and select that clip.

3. In the main menu bar, choose Clip > Trim Beginning.

    The beginning point is set and material prior to that point is trimmed away.

4. If you wish to trim the end, in the main menu bar, choose > Clip > Trim End.

    The end point is set and material beyond that point is trimmed.

5. With the clip selected, press Play to make sure it's the way you want it. If not, you can Clear the trim points to undo what you did just did.

Undo a trim

If you change your mind about a trim to a clip, you undo it:

1. In the timeline, click on the clip where you wish to remove the trim.

    The clip is selected.

2. Choose Clip > Clear Trim Points.

    The trims are removed and the clip is restored to the way it was before you trimmed it.

NOTE —— Don't worry about the fact that the video may be a little choppy. Later in this lesson, you add transitions to smooth it out.

Add transitions and special effects

Movie Maker has both transitions and effects that can make your movie look smoother and more professional and add a bit of flair. As with any special effects, you have to be careful not to overuse them, but they can certainly help smooth transitions between clips.

You can add transitions and special effects in either Storyboard or Timeline view. In some ways, using Storyboard view is easier, because you can see more clearly where the transition or effect is being applied.

Add a transition between clips

Begin fine-tuning your video by adding a transition.

1. Click the clip after where you want to add the transition.

2. Choose Tools > Transitions.

    Movie Maker displays optional transitions. They're labeled, but the only way you can really know what they do is to try them and see which ones you like.

continues on next page

3. Pick a transition you want to try, and drag it to the clip (or, if you're in the storyboard, to the space just before the clip) where you want to apply it.

   Movie Maker applies the transition.

4. Click the clip just before where you applied the transition, and watch the first and second clips to observe how the transition looks.

5. If you want to try a different transition, drag a different one to the clip.

   You can't have more than one transition, so the new one replaces the old one.

6. Repeat steps 4 and 5 until you are happy with the transition you picked.

   NOTE —— A transition takes place between scenes or still photos. It controls the way the movie looks as you make that transition. An effect is applied to a scene or photo and affects how that scene or photo looks while it is playing. You can have only one transition between each scene or photo, but you can apply multiple effects to a scene or photo.

Apply effects

You can apply several effects to scenes and photos. You can make them look like old film, for example, or you can fade in from black or white, or change the color spectrum of the clip. Be judicious in how you use effects, but play around to see which ones you like.

If you're doing a family history, for example, you may want to make part of the film look old—perhaps as though it were shot in the 1950s. You can do that by selecting a clip and applying the Film Age Old effect.

To apply an effect to a clip:

1. In the timeline or storyboard, right-click the clip where you want to apply the effect and select Effects.

   The Add or Remove Effects dialog box displays.

2. Select an effect, and click Add.

The effect is added to the Displayed Effects column.

3. Repeat step 2 until you're done selecting effects; then click OK.

The effects are applied to the clip.

4. View the clip (as well as the ones before and after it) to see how you like the effects.

5. If you don't like some effects, right-click the place in the clip that contains the effect to display the Add or Remove Effects dialog box; select the effect you don't want; click Remove; and then click OK.

TIP —— Although you can add multiple effects at the same time, it's usually best to add one at a time so that you can see the impact of that effect.

Add and edit titles

Movie Maker lets you place titles at the beginning and end of a movie or during a clip, as you often see on TV news broadcasts.

To place a title at the beginning of the movie:

1. Choose Tools > Titles and Credits.

The Add Title screen is displayed.

2. Click Title at the Beginning.

3. In the window that tells you to enter text for the title, type the title of the movie.

continues on next page

The title is displayed in the right pane as it will appear in your movie.

4. Click Add Title.

   A title clip is added to the movie.

   Now that you've created a title, you can change how long it will be on the screen from within Timeline view.

5. If you're not in Timeline view (which means that you are in storyboard view), click the down arrow next to the word Storyboard, and choose Timeline.

6. Place your mouse pointer near the right edge of the title clip so that the pointer becomes a two-headed red arrow.

7. Drag the pointer to the right to increase the amount of time the title is onscreen or to the left to decrease the time.

You now have a title at the beginning of your movie which that will run for the specified amount of time.

Create a slideshow

As we mention in Lesson 10, Movie Maker works with Photo Gallery to allow you to create slideshows based on digital photos in your collection. You can select photos in Photo Gallery and click Make a Movie, which launches Movie Maker with those photos ready to use.

Alternatively, you can start with Movie Maker and either drag the photos from Photo Gallery into Movie Maker or drag them from their directory on the hard drive. Another option is to use Movie Maker's tools to import your photos. We show you how to use the latter method here.

1. If Movie Maker isn't running, launch it.

If you don't see import options on the left side of the screen, you're not in task mode. To get to task mode, choose View > Tasks.

You see Import Tasks on the left side of the screen.

2. Click Pictures to import pictures.

    Movie Maker brings up a window that lets you browse for pictures.

3. Select the pictures you want to import, and click Import.

    Now you have your pictures available to drag into the storyboard or timeline. The process is the same as with video.

4. Drag the pictures to the storyboard in the order in which you want them to appear.

    You can change the order later, if you want to.

    The pictures are imported into Movie Maker and displayed onscreen.

5. To add narration, switch to timeline mode, and choose Tools > Narrate Timeline.

    The Narrate Timeline screen displays.

continues on next page

6. Talk into your PC's microphone, checking the input level meter onscreen, and when you're satisfied with the level, click Start Narration and start speaking your narration as you watch the video.

7. When you're finished, click Stop Narration.

   A box comes up where you can save the audio narration file.

8. Type in a file name and click Save.

   The narration is saved as a file and then placed in the Audio/Music section of the timeline.

   TIP —— You can change the position of the audio relative to the pictures by dragging it to the left or right.

   TIP —— You can also adjust how long each picture stays onscreen in Timeline view by clicking the right side of the picture, so that the mouse pointer changes to a red arrow, and dragging it. If you drag to the left, the picture stays onscreen longer. Dragging to the right causes the picture to be onscreen for a shorter time.

Publish your movie

When you have your movie just the way you want it, your next task is sharing it with others.

1. Choose File > Publish Movie.

   The Publish Movie page displays.

2. Select how you want the movie to be published, based on the criteria discussed in the sidebar "Choose a Publishing Format" in this section.

Choosing a Publishing Format

Movie Maker gives you several optional formats for publishing your movie. The main difference among them is the level of compression, which determines the quality of the movie and the size of the file. File sizes can be a very important issue, especially if you plan to send the movie by email or post it on the Internet. If the file is too long, it could take a great of time for you to upload and for potential viewers to download.

On the other hand, if you plan to burn the movie to a DVD or (in the case of a short movie) to a CD, size may not matter much, so you may as well get optimum quality. That's why you have the choice of DVD or Recordable CD. The same things goes if you plan to use Movie Maker to create digital video for your camcorder. If you select Digital Video Camera, Movie Maker configures your video camera to record the movie at optimum quality.

If you select This Computer, Movie Maker lets you choose a name for the movie and where to publish it. By default, Movie Maker publishes to the Videos directory, but you can change that behavior by clicking Browse next to the Publish To line and browsing for a different directory.

3. Click Next.

The Choose the Settings for Your Movie dialog box displays.

continues on next page

4. Select the quality you desire for your movie.

    The default is Best Quality for Playback on My Computer (Recommended), but you can choose the option below that to change the compression, or choose More Settings and choose a different format and compression ratio from the drop-down menu. For the purposes of this exercise, accept the default.

5. Click Publish.

    A window displays, letting you know how much time remains until your movie is ready to be shared.

Movie Maker works with Windows DVD Maker to burn your movie to a DVD. When you select DVD, you see a message telling you that Movie Maker will save your project and take you to Windows DVD Maker to burn your DVD. Then you are asked to enter a name for the project. When you click Save, Movie Maker saves your project and opens DVD Maker.

Making DVDs Using DVD Maker

DVD Maker lets you copy videos and photos to a DVD that can be played in any standard DVD player—the kind most people have connected to their TV sets. In addition to copying the files, DVD Makers allows you to create professional-looking menus, just like the DVDs you get from the studios.

To run DVD Maker:

1. Click the Start button, and type *dvd maker* in the Start menu's Search box.

    You see a screen that invites you to choose photos and videos to make a DVD.

2. Click Choose Photos and Videos.

    DVD Maker displays a screen where you can add items. Start by adding a video from your hard drive.

3. Click Add Items.

    DVD Maker displays a browsing tool to let you find video on your hard drive.

4. Navigate to any video item, and select it.

    You see a little preview window with a Play button that you can use to preview that clip.

5. If you want to use that clip, double-click the clip.

    You return to DVD Maker with that item in the list of items to be burned to the DVD. In the bottom-left corner of the screen, you see how many minutes of video you have added and how many minutes you have on the disc.

6. Continue this process with all media items you want to include on your DVD; then click Next.

    DVD Maker displays a screen for laying out the DVD menu. Notice the various options on the right side of the screen.

7. Click each of the formatting options until you find the one you like.

    The new format is previewed onscreen.

continues on next page

8. When you're happy with the menu, make sure that you have a blank DVD in the DVD burner, and click Burn.

   The clip is burned to the disc.

9. When the disc is fully burned, remove it from the PC.

10. If you have a regular DVD player and TV set handy, play the DVD in that DVD player to make sure it will work in a standard player.

What You've Learned

- How to get music into your PC

- How to listen to music and watch videos in Windows Media Player

- How to find music

- How to create and use Media Player playlists

- How to copy music from CDs to a PC and from a PC to CDs

- How to synchronize music to a digital music player

- How to create movies using Windows Movie Maker

- How to burn DVDs

NOTE —— You can learn how to use Windows Media Center by visiting this book's Web site (www.peachpit.com/vistalearningseries). There you can register your copy of this book and access additional chapters on the Windows Vista Media Center, the Vista Control Panel, and more.

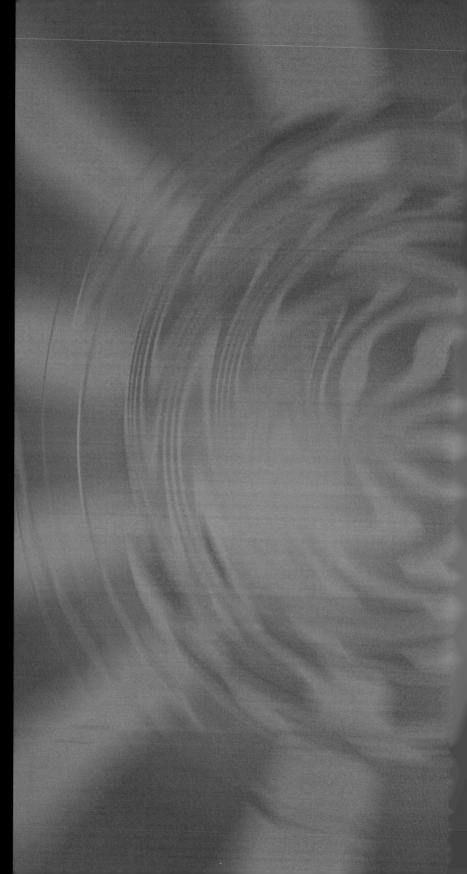

12

GOALS

Configure and use
Windows Mail to
create, receive, and
reply to messages;
protect against spam
and phishing attacks;
and create rules for
processing your mail.

Use Windows Contacts
to keep track of people

Use Windows Calendar
to track your schedule
and tasks

Enhance Your Productivity

As you've probably figured out by now, Windows Vista is far more than just a computer operating system; it's also a library of software that includes some pretty powerful productivity tools. These tools include a replacement for the old Outlook Express email program, along with new calendar and contact management software.

Although email, calendaring, and contact management function as separate programs, they are integrated so that they form a well-oiled personal information management system. Although they don't have quite as many features as Microsoft Outlook, and they're certainly not aimed at the "enterprise-level" requirements of large corporations or agencies, these tools do have everything that most individuals and even some professionals and small businesses need. And unlike Outlook, the tools are bundled with Vista, so there's nothing else to buy.

Using Windows Mail

Vista does basically the same things as the old Outlook Express, but it has enhanced security features, including improved spam filters and tools to help protect you from phishing attacks that weren't even around when Outlook Express was last updated.

A phishing email may look official—it may appear to come from a bank or other legitimate source—and attempt to lure you into providing personal or financial information. The email usually directs you a bogus site that masquerades as the site for the real institution.

Probably the biggest change in Windows Mail is a vastly improved search function that piggybacks on the search engine built into Vista, which we cover in Lesson 5. It also has under-the-hood improvements, such as the ability to handle large attachments more reliably.

Like Outlook Express, Windows Mail can be used to access Usenet newsgroups—forums where people ask and answer questions and discuss issues. Newsgroups, which predate the World Wide Web, were once very popular but don't get as much attention these days as Web sites, including blogs and social-networking sites.

Run and configure Mail

To launch Windows Mail:

1. Click Start > Windows Mail.

    or

    Type windows mail in the Start menu's Search box.

    When Windows Mail launches for the first time, a window appears, asking for your display name. This window begins the process of setting up your mail account.

2. If you want to skip this process, click Cancel.

   or

   Gather the information you need to configure your e-mail account.

   Mail asks a series of questions about your email account, such as your email address, the type of mail server you use, and the names of your incoming and outgoing servers. If you're not sure of the answers to these questions, check with your email service or Internet service provider (ISP), or just look at the settings from whatever email program you were using before.

3. Type the name you want to associate with this account (it can be anything you want), and click Next.

   The next window asks for your Internet email address.

4. Type your address, and click Next.

   The next window asks for information about your server.

5. Select your incoming server type from the drop-down menu or accept the default if you have a POP3 account, which is typical for consumer email accounts.

   TIP —— You need to know what type of mail server you're using, as well as the names of both the incoming and outgoing servers. This information is available from your email host, your ISP, or (if it's a company account) your IT department. Most consumer email services use POP3. Many corporate servers use IMAP, so if you're accessing mail from work, check with your IT department for all your server information.

6. Enter the information on your incoming mail server (POP3 or IMAP) provided by your email host.

   continues on next page

7. If necessary, select Outgoing Server Requires Authentication. Click Next when you're finished.

   Setting this option usually is necessary, because it's the way that outgoing servers validate who is using them to be sure unauthorized people aren't using the servers to send spam.

   The next window asks for your Internet mail logon information.

8. Enter your email user name.

   In some cases, this must include @*mailhost.com*; in other cases, you can get away with just the first part of the user name. If in doubt, check with your email provider, or try it both ways until you get it to work. (Later in this lesson, we tell you how to correct any mistakes.)

9. Type your password and click Next.

   For security reasons, the password is not displayed as you type. Most passwords are case sensitive, so if there's a capital letter, be sure to type it that way.

   Finally, the Congratulations Page window signals that you have entered all the information requires to set up your account. That may or may not be true, however; Mail hasn't yet verified that the information you typed is correct.

10. In most cases, you want to leave the Do Not Download My E-Mail at This Time checkbox deselected; check it only if you want to skip downloading email. Click Finished.

    If all goes well, you'll see a message that Mail is authorizing your information; this message quickly changes to "Checking for new messages on [*name of server*]."

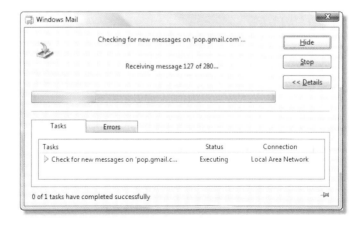

Change your Mail settings

Quite often, all doesn't go so well, because email can be a bit more complicated than the initial setup screens suggest. Sometimes, you have to deal with other parameters.

Windows Mail sometimes assumes, for example, that your incoming and outgoing email servers are using standard ports, which are 25 for outgoing mail and 110 for incoming mail. A port is a pathway between your computer and the Internet. It also assumes that you are not using a secure connection for your mail. Increasingly, email servers are using different ports and different security settings, which is why you need to check with your mail provider or network administrator for all your configuration settings.

If a problem occurs, check everything you've entered; then, using the instructions below, check the Advanced settings to make sure they are correct. Google's Gmail service, for example, requires that you set your outgoing mail server to 465 and your incoming server to 995. It also requires that This Server Requires a Secure Connection (SSL) is selected.

If your email doesn't work, you probably need to change the settings by following these steps:

1. In Windows Mail, choose Tools > Accounts.

    The Internet Accounts setup screen appears, displaying the names of any accounts that are already set up.

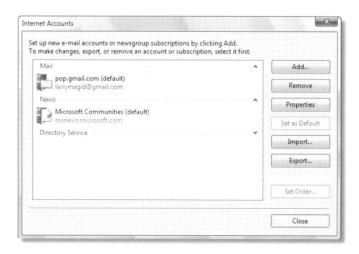

continues on next page

2. Select the new account you just configured and then click Properties.

   The Properties dialog box for that account is displayed.

3. Click the Advanced tab.

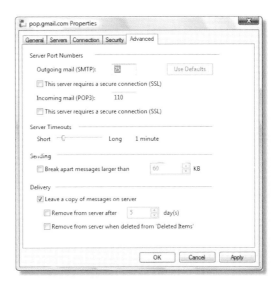

4. Enter the correct configuration information for your servers.

5. If you want mail deleted from the server after you check your mail, clear the Leave a Copy of Message on Server check box.

   or

   If you want mail saved to the server, check this check box.

6. When you're finished configuring the settings on the Advanced tab, click OK.

   Your new settings are saved, and you return to the Internet Accounts dialog box.

7. Click Close.

Create and send a message

When your mail is set up properly, try sending yourself a message.

1. Click Create Mail.

A New Message window displays.

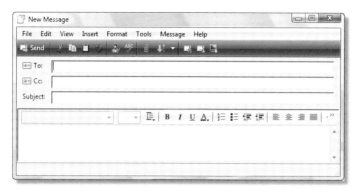

2. In the To field, enter the email address of the recipient.

   or

   If you have entered contacts or imported contacts from another program (see "Using Windows Contacts" later in this lesson), you can enter just part of the person's name and then click the Check Names icon 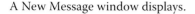 to let Mail look up the person's email address from his or her contact information. When the correct name appears, press Enter or the Tab key.

3. If you want to copy anyone on the message, enter that person's address in the Cc field.

4. Type the subject of your mail in the Subject box.

5. In the body of the New Message window, type your message.

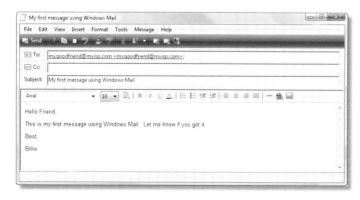

continues on next page

6. When you are finished, click Send.

The message is sent, and you return to the main Mail window.

Send and receive mail

By default, Windows Mail automatically checks for new messages as soon as you click Send. But you can easily check for new mail at any time by clicking Send/Receive in the taskbar. This action also sends any unsent mail you may have in your outbox.

Read and reply to mail

To read and respond to your mail:

1. In the main Mail window, click Inbox in the left pane (in the Local Folders section).

The inbox is displayed, with your unread mail marked in bold. Mail you've already read is in plain text. By default, Mail displays information about the messages in three fields: From (who the messages are from), Subject, and Received (date and time each message was received in your mailbox).

2. Double-click any message you want to read.

The message is displayed.

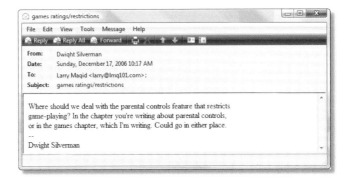

3. After you read the message, you can do any of the following:

   • Click Reply to reply to the sender.

   • Click Reply All to reply to the sender and everyone else listed in the To or Cc field.

   • Click Forward to forward it to someone else.

   • Click the Print icon to print it.

   • Click the red X to delete it.

   • Click the up arrow to read the preceding message.

   • Click the down arrow to read next message.

   • Right-click the From field (the sender's name and email address) to add the person to your contact list.

To respond to a message:

1. Click Respond.

   A new window appears, with the original message displayed farther down the screen.

2. Write your reply.

3. Click Send.

Deal with junk mail

Just about everyone gets too much unwanted email, which is why Windows Mail has a spam filter. Although it's not perfect, the filter seems to be better than the one in Outlook Express. In our tests, we found relatively few false positives (legitimate mail incorrectly marked as spam) and reasonably few false negatives (spam that was not blocked).

We found some cases of both, however, which is why it's important to check the Junk E-Mail folder for false positives and your inbox for spam that slipped through. If you find spam that wasn't caught or legitimate mail that was marked as spam, Windows Mail lets you report the message as Junk or Not Junk. Doing so not only moves the message to the appropriate folder, but also, over time, trains Windows Mail to be more accurate.

Mark a message as junk

Marking junk messages as such gets them out of your inbox and, over time, trains Windows Mail to better recognize your idea of good and bad mail. Marking a message as junk is very easy to do:

1. In the inbox, right-click any field (such as From, Subject, or Received) of the message, and choose Junk E-Mail > Add Sender to Blocked Senders List from the shortcut menu.

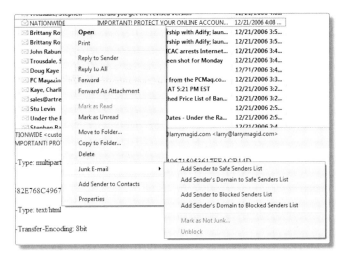

A window appears, notifying you that the sender has been added to your Blocked Senders list and that the message has been moved to the Junk E-mail folder.

2. Click OK.

Mark a message as not junk

As we said earlier in this lesson, you should check your Junk E-Mail folder regularly to look for false positives. Doing this is especially important when you start using Windows Mail, as it takes a while to train the program to distinguish between junk and legitimate mail.

To instruct Mail that a message is not junk:

1. Open the Junk E-Mail folder, and select a message that you do not consider to be junk mail.

2. Click Not Junk in the taskbar.

   The message is moved to your inbox.

NOTE —— Future mail from that sender may again be classified as junk, so check the Junk E-Mail folder frequently.

Prevent future mail from being classified as junk

Marking a message as not junk doesn't necessarily prevent future messages from that person from being caught by the junk mail filter. To do that, you need to tell Widows Mail to add that sender to the "safe senders list."

- Right-click a message from the sender whose messages you don't want to be considered junk mail, and choose Junk E-Mail > Add Sender to Safe Senders List from the shortcut menu.

   The sender is added to your Safe Senders list.

NOTE —— You can also add the sender's domain to the Safe Senders list. Do that if the sender is from a company you trust; that way, any mail from that company will be considered safe. Don't do it for senders from public email services such as Gmail, Hotmail, or Yahoo Mail; many spammers use those services as their return address, even if they're not really sending mail from one of those services.

Protect yourself against phishing

Security experts have long warned users to avoid clicking links in messages because of the risk that they could take you to a rogue site that tries to trick you into disclosing confidential information or, in some cases, attempts to plant malicious software on your machine.

That advice still stands, but now it's easier to avoid acting on the links, because Vista has a way to warn you about messages that might be phishing expeditions. As mail arrives, code within Windows Mail analyzes each message to determine whether it looks suspicious; if so, Mail displays a pop-up warning and places the message in your Junk E-Mail folder.

Like spam filters, phishing messages are not always accurate. In some cases, you get a warning about a message that's perfectly legitimate, and there's always the possibility that a phishing message could slip by the filter. So it's still up to you to practice safe computing and use your judgment before clicking any links. Our advice is that you avoid clicking links in mail that appears to be from a financial institution; if you think the mail may be legitimate, open your Web browser and type the institution's URL in the address bar to go to the site.

As with spam, there is the possibility of a false positive. If you believe that the message is legitimate, you can move the message from your junk folder to your inbox:

1. Click Unblock in the warning message.

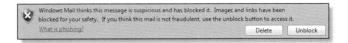

The phishing warning disappears, but the message is still in your Junk E-Mail folder.

2. To remove the message from the folder, click Not Junk on the taskbar.

The message is sent to your inbox.

Create and use signatures

Windows Mail lets you automatically "sign" your outgoing messages with anything you want your recipients to see. A lot of people use this feature to enter their names, work titles, phone numbers, Web addresses, and other information that they want people to know.

To create a signature:

1. Choose Tools > Options.

The Options dialog box displays.

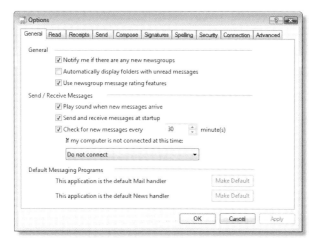

2. Click the Signatures tab.

   The Signature dialog box appears.

3. Click New.

   The cursor moves to the Edit Signature text box.

4. Type your signature, and include any other information you want people to see at the bottom of your messages.

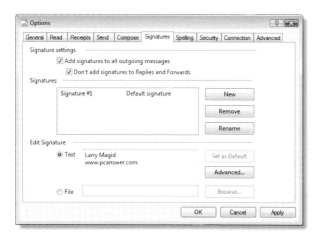

5. Click OK when you're finished.

   Subsequent outgoing email messages will have your signature at the bottom.

A message pops up that says, "Applying rules to messages." This process can take a while if you have a lot of messages in your inbox. When it's done, you see a message confirming that your rules have been applied.

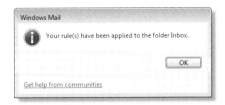

13. Click OK to acknowledge that message.

You return to the Apply Mail Rules Now dialog box.

14. Click OK to exit the dialog box.

15. Look at your invoice to confirm that the rules have been applied.

Messages from the people you selected in step 4 should appear in red.

Access newsgroups

As we said earlier in this lesson, you can use Windows Mail to access news-groups. But frankly, aside from the fact that most people no longer use newsgroups (they were really popular back in the 1990s), you can access news-groups in ways that we think are easier. If you want to access newsgroups, the easiest way is to use Google Groups at http://groups.google.com. There, you can access any content in any group by using Google's incredibly fast search engine.

If you want to use Windows Mail to access newsgroups, first you must contact your ISP to find the parameters of its newsgroup server. After you've done that, you need to add that news-server account.

1. Choose Tools > Accounts.

The Internet Accounts dialog box appears.

2. Click Add.

3. Select Newsgroup Account.

4. Follow the onscreen instructions for the remaining steps.

Using Windows Contacts

With Vista, Microsoft has changed the way you track Contacts. Instead of the old Windows Address Book, you now use the Contacts Explorer. It's the same database that Windows Mail uses when you send mail. In fact, the new contact management system can be integrated into other programs, and we expect third-party programs to use this new contact system.

You manage contacts through the Contacts Explorer, which looks a lot like other Vista Explorer windows.

To access the Contact Explorer:

■ Type windows contacts in the Start menu's Search box, and press Enter.

The Contacts Explorer appears.

At this point, you can perform several functions, including importing your contacts from another program or file, creating a new contact, searching for a contact, or exporting the contact list for use in another program.

Enter a new contact

Now that you have a way to track your contacts, you can start entering them, assuming you haven't imported them from another program (which is a better idea if you can). But, aside from the tedious act of typing, entering contacts is easy to do.

To add people to your contact list:

1. Click New Contact in the taskbar.

A contact form appears.

2. Enter the appropriate information.

Be sure to click the various tabs that allow you to enter the person's name, email address, and contact information at home and work. You can also enter

continues on next page

details about the person's family members, as well as add notes and digital IDs. (*A digital ID* is a way of certifying that a message really came from the person who claims to have sent it.)

3. Click Add when you're finished adding the person's information; then click OK.

   The contact is added.

Find a contact

Because of its tight integration with Windows search, finding contacts is easy and fast, using the same basic process as any other type of Windows search

■ In the Search box in the top-right corner of the Contact Explorer, type the person's name, workplace, city, or any other text that appears in the contact record.

   As with other search functions in Vista, the results appear as you type.

Create contact groups

Contact groups allow you to send email to several people at a time by grouping them. If you have a dozen people in your bridge club, you could create a group called Bridge Club and add each person's contact info to the group. Then, when you want to use Windows Mail to send a message to the entire group, you could enter Bridge Club in the To field so that everyone in the group gets the message.

To create a contact group:

1. Click New Contract Group in the taskbar.

   The Properties dialog box appears.

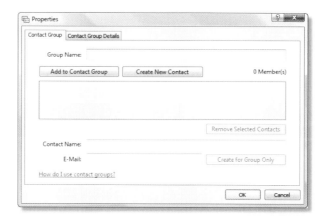

2. In the Contact Group tab, type the name of the group in the Group Name box; then click Add to Contract Group.

    A list of all your contacts displays in the Add Members to Contact Group dialog box.

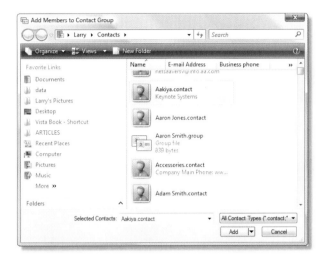

3. Select the name of a contact you want to add to the group, and click Add.

    The person is added to the group, and you return to the Add Members to Contact Group dialog box.

4. Repeat step 3 until you have added all the contacts to your group and click OK when finished.

Using Windows Calendar

New to Windows, the Calendar function not only helps you keep up with your schedule, but also allows you to create task lists and subscribe to other public calendars (such as the game schedule for a sports team).

The Calendar program, along with Windows Mail and Windows Contacts, completes the trilogy that gives Vista users the personal management tools that previously required buying additional software (such as Microsoft Office). It also helps Microsoft catch up with Apple, which has long offered these functions in its Mac OS X operating system.

Launch Windows Calendar

To launch Windows Calendar:

■ Type windows calendar in the Start menu's Search box, and press Enter.

or

Choose Start > All Programs > Windows Calendar.

Windows Calendar launches.

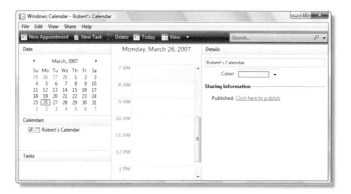

Schedule an appointment

To schedule an appointment:

1. Navigate to the date and time when you want to make the appointment by clicking the date in the mini-calendar near the top-left corner of the Calendar window.

NOTE —— If the month isn't showing, click the left or right arrow at the top of the mini-calendar to navigate to the appropriate month.

The calendar for the selected day is displayed.

2. Double-click the time slot when you want to make the appointment.

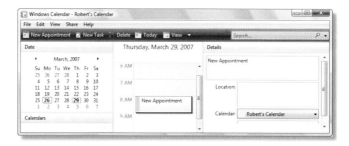

New Appointment appears where you want to enter your new appointment.

3. Replace New Appointment with the name of the appointment by typing over it.

4. In the Details pane (right column), set the location, URL (if you need to include a reference to a Web site), and duration of the appointment.

    Appointments default to one hour, but you can use the up and down arrows to adjust the amount of time.

Create tasks

Calendar also lets you create and track tasks to remind you that you have something to do. These tasks appear in your calendar until you check them off as having been completed.

To create a task:

1. Click New Task in the taskbar.

    The Details pane appears on the right side of the window.

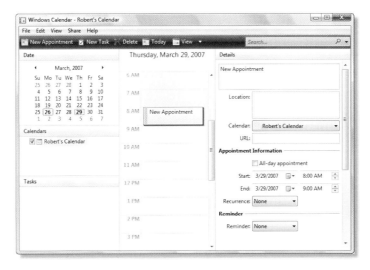

2. Replace New Task in the bottom-left corner of the window by typing the name of the new task over it.

3. Select a priority by making a choice from the Priority drop-down menu in the Details pane.

continues on next page

Your choices are Low, Medium, High, and None.

4. Set a start date, a due date, or both.

5. If you want to set a reminder that will pop up to remind you about the appointment, choose On Date from the Reminder drop-down menu.

Change the calendar view

You can view your calendar in several ways. The default is by day, but you can use the View menu to change it to work week, week, or month.

Other Tools

As with previous versions of Windows, you'll find plenty of other useful productivity tools including some accessories such as Wordpad, Calc, and Paint. Windows also has a very cool speech recognition program that you can learn about by typing Speech Recognition into the Windows Help section. Also check out Windows Meeting Space to share documents or your entire PC with others.

What You've Learned

- How to set up an email account in Windows Mail

- How to write, read, reply to, and send email

- How to deal with junk mail and dangerous phishing mail

- How to create message rules in Windows Mail

- How to add and find contacts

- How to create a contact group

- How to set up appointments and tasks in your calendar

13

GOALS

Discover the simplest way to access Vista's mobile computing features

Optimize Vista's power settings for mobile computing

Keep files and documents synchronized between devices and other computers

Transmit information to external screens and devices

Find and use features specific to Tablet PCs

Go Mobile

If you're using Vista, odds are good that you're using it on a notebook computer. Portable PCs now routinely outsell desktops, thanks to falling prices, more muscular mobile hardware, and the rising ubiquity of Wi-Fi Internet. With a notebook PC, you can take your system with you and do so without sacrificing power and connectivity.

This trend is reflected in features Microsoft has added to Vista that make using a mobile PC a more pleasant experience. In past versions of Windows, mobile users often felt as though they were using the operating system in spite of having a portable. Vista is the first Windows version that actively facilitates mobile use through features such as Mobility Center, better power management, Windows SideShow, Sync Center, and new Tablet PC capabilities.

Be aware of one gotcha: The best features come in the most expensive editions of Vista. If you want to be mobile to the max, it's going to cost you.

Using Vista on a Notebook

Vista has two types of mobile-related features: those that install only when the operating system is installed on a portable computer, and those that benefit mobile computing but are available to all Vista users. The features are:

- **Windows Mobility Center.** This mini control panel is one convenient spot from which you can control key aspects of portable computing. It provides quick access to a variety of features, including presentation settings, Wi-Fi, external displays, and presentations. You'll see Mobility Center only on a portable system.

- **Power management.** Vista lets you fine-tune how your computer handles power. Compared to past versions of Windows, you can control many more aspects of your notebook's energy consumption and customize power plans for different computing scenarios. This feature can also be used on a desktop PC.

- **Windows SideShow.** Working with screens and devices that are enabled for it, Windows SideShow can display specific bits of information on external screens even when the computer is not open or fully powered up. A small LCD screen on the outside of a notebook lid might show you how many email messages are waiting for you, for example. This feature also is available to nonmobile PCs.

- **Sync Center.** Here's a central location for making sure that your key files, folders, contacts, and devices are synchronized. It helps establish relationships among devices and folders so that, as far as your data is concerned, they're all on the same page. This feature also is available to nonmobile users.

- **Tablet PC.** Previously, the pen-based features of Tablet PC computers required a special tablet edition of Windows XP. Now those features are included in the higher-end versions of Vista: Home Premium, Business, and Ultimate.

Diving into Windows Mobility Center

Windows Mobility Center is at the heart of the mobile computing experience in Vista. From here, you can control most aspects of using a computer on the go.

To get to Mobility Center:

1. Click the Start button.

2. Type Mobility Center in the Search box.

3. Click Windows Mobility Center in the results list that appears at the top of the Start menu.

   Mobility Center includes separate control panels for a variety of mobile features; exactly which ones you'll see depends on the features in your notebook and on the manufacturer.

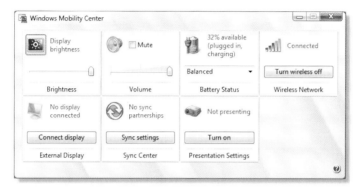

Mobility Center is designed so that PC makers can extend its capabilities with additional panels. Hewlett-Packard, for example, includes a module for its own Wi-Fi utility, and Toshiba has a component that lets you lock access to the notebook—handy if you need to step away from a notebook briefly in a public place.

Each module in Mobility Center has at least two features—one or more basic functions you can control from the module and a button that that takes you to more advanced controls. The following sections look at the individual components of Mobility Center to show you what each module does.

Display Brightness

- Move the slider to control the screen's brightness. Dimming the screen can conserve battery life.

- Click the screen icon to bring up a window that lets you edit power settings related to the display. We talk about power management later in this lesson.

Volume

- Move the slider to control the audio level coming from the speakers.
- Check the Mute check box to silence the speakers.
- Click the speaker icon to open the Sound control panel.

Battery Status

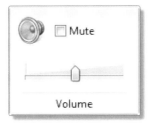

- The module shows you the current charge level of the PC's battery.
- Click the drop-down menu to display preconfigured power plans. The default options are Balanced, Power Save, and High Performance. If you've created and are using a custom plan, it will replace one of the three defaults.
- Click the Battery icon to go to the Power Options control panel. Again, we look at the details of power management later in the lesson.

Wireless Network

- This module (present only on notebooks that have a Wi-Fi adapter) shows the quality of a wireless connection, if one is present, by turning the bars in the icon green. More green bars means a better signal.

- Click the wide horizontal button to turn the Wi-Fi adapter on or off.

- Click the signal-indicator button to launch the Connect to a Network control panel. We talk about networking in Lesson 14.

Screen Orientation

- Click the Rotate Screen button in this module (available only to Tablet PC users) to change the display from landscape to portrait orientation.

- Click the dual-screen icon to display the Tablet PC Settings control panel. This lets you change the order in which the screen rotates between its primary and secondary portrait and landscape modes.

External Display

- If you connect an external monitor to the notebook, click Connect Display so that your desktop appears on that display.

- Click the monitor icon to bring up the Display Settings control panel, which allows you to change the screen resolution and specify the primary display.

> ## Want More Mobile Choices?
>
> Although Mobility Center is a powerful tool, it's actually just a subset of your choices. As we discuss in Online Resource A, which you can access by visiting www.peachpit.com/vistalearningseries, Vista's main Control Panel has a series of subpages that group its modules by type, and one of them is called Mobile PC.
>
> To find the Mobile PC group:
>
> **1.** Choose Start > Control Panel.
>
> **2.** Make sure you are using the Home view of the Control Panel. If you're in Classic view, click the Home View link in the left pane.
>
> **3.** Click the Mobile PC option in the right pane of Home view.
>
> The Mobile PC window displays.

Sync Center

- The Sync Center module shows which synchronization partnerships— between folders, files, or devices to be synced—are active.

- Click either the Sync Settings button or the Sync icon to display Sync Center, which we explore later in this lesson.

Presentation Settings

This module controls how your computer behaves during a presentation and is the only module with settings that aren't accessible elsewhere. For that reason, we go into some detail on it in this section.

1. Click the projector icon to display the Presentation Settings dialog box.

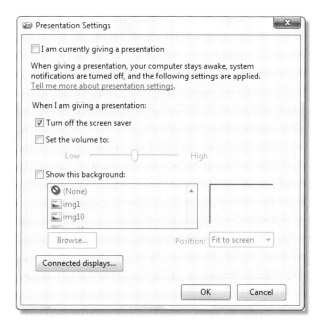

2. In the When I Am Giving a Presentation section, check the Turn Off the Screen Saver check box to make sure that your screen saver doesn't kick in while you're presenting.

continues on next page

3. To set the volume to a specific level for the presentation, check the Set the Volume To check box, and move the slider to the position you prefer.

4. If you want your display to have a certain background during the presentation, check the Show This Background box and then select an image in the list box.

5. If you use different monitors or projectors when you display, click the Connected Displays button to display the Current Displays dialog box; select the display you want to use; and click OK.

   or

   If you always use one display for presentations, select that display, check the check box, and then click OK.

6. Click OK to close the Presentation Settings dialog box.

Keyboard Shortcut

Windows logo key+X	Open Mobility Center

Managing Power

Mobile computing is often about trade-offs, and nothing illustrates this fact as starkly as the yin and yang of balancing performance and battery life. Want a fast machine with a screen so bright, you gotta wear shades? Fine; expect to spend a lot of time tethered to a power adapter. Need your battery to last the length of a New York-to-Los Angeles red-eye flight? Keep the display on maximum dim, and don't even *think* about watching those episodes of a TV show you burned to DVD.

Vista can't stabilize this balancing act completely, but it does provide tools for better control of your notebook's power consumption. All the new power-management features are available to desktop PC users, too.

Turn on to a new way to turn off

In Windows XP, users had three ways to shut down their PCs:

- **Shut Down.** All programs closed, the operating system's files and services were terminated, and the power turned off.

- **Hibernate.** What was currently active in the computer's memory—running programs, the operating system's state, and any files or data being worked on—was written to the hard drive, and the power was shut down. When the computer was restarted, everything was pulled off the hard drive and put back in memory. The computer resumed exactly where it left off.

- **Standby.** The computer was put into low-power mode. The screen was blanked, the processor's activity ratcheted down, and the hard drive stopped spinning. A small amount of power continued to be expended to keep the system active. When a key was pressed or a mouse button was clicked, the system went into full power mode, and all activities resumed.

In Vista, Shut Down and Hibernate are still present, but Standby has been replaced by Sleep, which Microsoft describes as being a hybrid of Standby and Hibernate. Here's how Sleep works in Vista:

- Like Standby, Sleep puts the computer into a low-power state, with current system activity held in memory.

- At the same time, the information in the computer's memory is written to the hard drive, as in Hibernate.

- Upon return, the system wakes up as it did from Standby. But if power is lost or the battery's charge runs out, the system can be restored from what's been saved to disk.

Choose how Vista turns off

When you are ready to walk away from your computer, you have quite a few choices as to what to do. Here's how to access those choices:

1. Click the Start button, then click the button with the right-pointing arrow on it at the bottom-right corner of the Start Menu.

2. Choose an option from the menu.

   The menu includes the three previously mentioned power-down choices: Shut Down, Hibernate, and Sleep. In addition, you have the following options:

   - **Switch User.** As in Windows XP, this option allows you to switch to another user account quickly without powering down or logging off.

   - **Log Off.** This option closes programs and logs you out of the session, taking you to a login screen showing the available accounts on the computer.

   - **Lock.** This option takes you to a lockout screen. If your account requires a password, you'll need to enter it to return to the desktop; if not, a simple

continues on next page

Sleep and Hibernate: Decidedly Flaky

Using anything other than a simple shutdown procedure on Windows-based PCs has been a hit-or-miss proposition. Windows' Standby option has often caused trouble for users, with problems ranging from machines mysteriously waking up on their own to not waking up at all. Hibernate has similar issues.

We hoped that Vista would be different, but both of us have experienced problems with Sleep and Hibernate on a variety of machines, both new and older. This may be the result of buggy drivers that are still in development for the nascent operating system, or it may just mean that Vista has inherited the same problems from its predecessors.

In either event, simply powering down the system will likely be your best shot at a trouble-free way to turn the computer off.

mouse click will get you back in. This feature is handy if you need to walk away from your computer in a public place. Alternatively, simply click the Lock button 🔒 in the Start menu.

- **Restart.** This option shuts down all programs, closes the operating system, and reboots the computer.

NOTE —— Unlike Windows XP, Vista doesn't display a confirmation dialog box when you turn the computer off. When you choose Sleep, Hibernate, Shut Down, or Restart, the PC simply performs that action, so you'd better mean it when you choose any of those options. After one of these processes starts, it can't be stopped.

Program the On/Off button

If you have a preferred way of turning off the computer, you can program the On/Off button ⏻ in the Start menu to use that method.

This exercise also provides a first look at the menus used to manage power, which we explore in the next activity.

1. Click the Start button, type Power Options in the Search box, and press Enter.

The Power Options control panel appears. In the center pane, you see several choices for power plans.

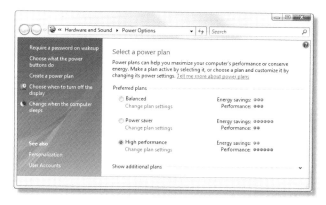

2. Click the Change Plan Settings link below the selected option.

   Unless you or your PC's manufacturer changed the default, Balanced is likely to be the default plan.

   NOTE ——— You may be tempted to click Choose What the Power Buttons Do in the left pane. That option, however, controls what happens when you push the physical buttons on your computer's case–not the software buttons in the Start menu. We deal with physical power buttons later in this section.

   The Edit Plan Settings dialog box appears.

3. Click Change Advanced Power Settings.

   The Advanced Settings dialog box appears.

4. Expand the Power Buttons and Lid item by clicking the plus sign next to it.

continues on next page

5. Expand the Start Menu Power Button item.

Vista's default setting is Sleep.

6. Click the blue word to the right of Setting to open a drop-down menu, and choose the shutdown method you prefer.

For this lesson, choose Hibernate.

7. Click Apply; then click OK to close the Advanced Settings dialog box.

8. Click Cancel to close the Edit Plan Settings dialog box.

Your setting is saved.

9. Click the red X in the right corner to close the Power Options window.

Now when you click the Start menu's Power button, your computer will always hibernate.

Configure the power buttons

As mentioned in preceding section, you can also configure the physical power buttons on the computer's case:

1. Click the Start button, type `Power Options` in the Search box, and press Enter.

The Power Options control panel appears.

2. In the left pane, click Choose What the Power Buttons Do.

The Define Power Buttons dialog box appears.

3. Make a choice from the When I Press the Power Button drop-down menu to determine what happens when you press the Power button on your PC's case.

4. If your computer also has a Sleep button, make a choice from the When I Press the Sleep Button drop-down menu to change that setting.

5. Click Change Settings That Are Currently Unavailable. If a User Account Control prompt appears, click Continue.

6. Select the Require a Password radio button to force the entry of a password to get back to the desktop upon wakeup.

    or

    Select the Don't Require a Password radio button to go straight to the desktop upon wakeup.

7. Click Save Changes.

Tweak and create power plans

Vista starts with three preconfigured power plans. You can not only make changes to them, but also create additional custom plans for specific purposes. The three starting points are:

- **Balanced.** Balances performance with energy savings.

- **Power Saver.** Emphasizes low power use over performance—the best way to conserve a portable's battery life.

- **High Performance.** Emphasizes performance at the cost of increased power use.

Change a power plan

1. Click the Start button, and type Power Options in the Search box.

    or

    With a notebook computer, click the battery icon in the notification area to open a small window that shows battery status, your current power plan, and menu options. Click More Power Options.

continues on next page

281

The Power Options dialog box appears.

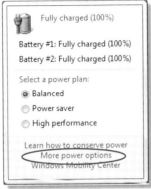

2. Choose the power plan that's closest to your goal.

For this exercise, create a custom plan that ratchets back the High Performance plan a bit. Below High Performance, click Change Plan Settings.

The Edit Plan Settings dialog box appears.

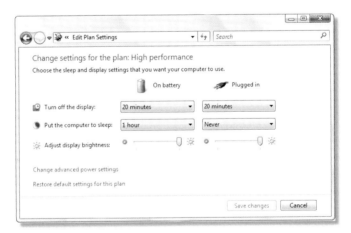

3. If you want to make the simplest of changes, you can do so from here, using the drop-downs next to "Turn off the display" and "Put the computer to sleep" to change when these events happen. On a portable computer, you can make changes based on whether the PC is plugged in or running on battery power. The time choices range from 1 minute to never.

4. Click Change Advanced Power Settings.

The Advanced Settings dialog box appears.

You can change many settings in this dialog box, some of them fairly advanced, falling into the category of "If you don't know what they are, leave them alone." But for this exercise, you'll change when Vista runs its indexing feature for improving search.

5. Expand the Searching and Indexing item.

6. Expand the Power Savings Mode item.

7. Click the blue High Performance text next to On Battery or Plugged In.

8. Change the setting to your preference.

9. Click Apply; then click OK to close the Advanced Settings dialog box.

10. Click Cancel to close the Edit Plan Settings dialog box and return to the Power Options control panel.

    Your change is saved.

11. Click Show Additional Plans to see your tweaked version of High Performance, which will be labeled My Custom Plan 1.

Create a power plan

1. In the left pane of the Power Options control panel, click Create a Power Plan.

    The Create a Power Plan dialog box appears.

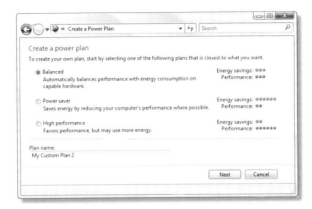

2. Select one of the three preconfigured plans as a starting point.

3. Type a name for your plan in the Plan Name box.

4. Click Next.

    The Edit Plan Settings dialog box appears, but without a link for changing advanced settings.

5. Specify when to turn off the display and/or when to put the computer to sleep, and click Create.

    You return to the Power Options control panel, with your new plan at the top of the list and active.

6. Click Change Plan Settings to go back to the Edit Plan Settings dialog box.

    The Advanced Settings link becomes available.

7. Complete steps 4 through 8 of the preceding exercise to change advanced settings in your custom plan.

Keyboard Shortcut

Alt+F4	Begins the shutdown process

Seeing the SideShow

One of the most intriguing new features of Vista is Windows SideShow, which can beam information to additional screens on a notebook computer or external devices, such as cell phones and MP3 players. At this writing, few of these devices are available; expect to see more later in 2007.

SideShow uses a form of the gadgets discussed in Lesson 8. These gadgets grab specific information—calendar items or email from Microsoft Outlook, email from Windows Live Mail, songs from Windows Media Player, news items from an RSS feed—and pass it on to the displays.

This feature requires that the computer be turned on or be operating in Sleep mode with settings that allow the PC to wake briefly to update the information. If you use SideShow, keep in mind that it will drain battery power faster than if the computer remained asleep.

Manage SideShow gadgets

Vista installs two SideShow gadgets, one each for Windows Live Mail and Windows Media Player. Other programs, such as Microsoft Office 2007, install their own gadgets. Gadgets that come with SideShow-compatible external devices need to be installed before the gadgets can talk to the PC. Also, computer makers may install gadgets that are required for communication with their products' secondary displays.

Gadgets are managed through a Control Panel module:

1. Click the Start button, type sideshow in the Search box, and press Enter.

   The Windows SideShow Manager dialog box appears.

   The following screen shot shows the SideShow gadgets installed on a Toshiba Portégé R400 notebook computer. The R400, which is also a Tablet PC, has a small screen on the front edge of the keyboard called the Toshiba Edge Display.

continues on next page

285

This screen shows the time, battery level, Wi-Fi signal strength, number of email messages, and volume level.

Note that only one of the gadgets is compatible with Toshiba's SideShow device. You'll need to experiment with gadget-and-device combinations to find out which are compatible on your machine.

2. If a gadget is compatible with a SideShow device or display, click it to change its settings.

   What settings you can change depend on the gadget and on the display's capabilities.

Get more SideShow gadgets

As you can with Windows Sidebar, you can download more gadgets from the Web for use with SideShow:

1. Click the Start button, type sideshow in the Search box, and press Enter.

   The Windows SideShow Manager dialog box appears.

2. Click the Get More Gadgets Online link.

Microsoft's SideShow Web site (http://vista.gallery.microsoft.com/SideShow.aspx) launches.

3. When you find a gadget you like, select it and then click the Download button.

The gadget downloads to your PC.

4. Install the software as outlined in Lesson 4.

5. Check the Windows SideShow Manager dialog box to see whether the gadget is compatible with your device.

If so, you can configure the gadget's settings by clicking it. What settings you can change depend on the gadget and on the display's capabilities.

If the gadget is not compatible, you can remove it by using the Programs and Features module in the Control Panel. See the next activity for instructions on how to do this.

Remove a SideShow gadget

1. Click the Start button, type `programs and features` in the Search box, and then press Enter.

The Programs and Features window appears.

2. Find the reference to the gadget you just installed, and double-click it. If a User Account Control prompt appears, click Continue.

3. Click Yes at the confirmation prompt that appears.

4. Click the red X in the upper right corner to close the Programs and Features window.

Syncing Up with Sync Center

As computer users become more mobile—using notebooks and handheld PCs when they're away from their desktops—keeping documents, contacts, email, and other files can be a serious challenge. Sync Center in Vista is a stab at sorting out this information chaos.

Sync Center allows you to monitor the status of synchronization between folders, start the synchronization process, choose how conflicts are handled, and launch other synchronization programs.

Access the Sync Center

Accessing the Sync Center is easy. Just click the Start button, type `sync center` in the Search box, and press Enter.

Synchronize folders, files, or devices

If you haven't set up any relationships that require synchronization, you need to do so by using Sync Center. To see how the process works, synchronize a folder from a computer on a home network.

1. Right-click a folder on another machine on your network that you want to sync—in this case, a folder called graphics—and choose Always Available Online from the shortcut menu.

    Vista begins copying files to your computer, and the Always Available Online dialog box appears, showing the synchronization process.

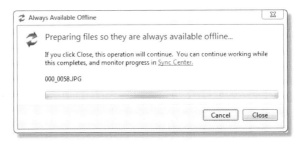

> **TIP** —— You can also watch the progress in Sync Center.

Now when you change anything in the synchronized folder on either computer, both folders will be updated so that the contents match. Note the Sync Center icon that appears on the remote folder.

2. Click the Conflicts button in Sync Center to see conflicts among files in different locations, if any, and resolve them.

3. Click the Sync Results button to get a log of synchronization activity.

4. If you've added new devices to your PC, such as a PDA, click the Sync Setup button to begin the process of synchronizing them with data on your computer.

Getting in Touch with Tablet PCs

Vista's Home Premium, Business, and Ultimate editions all come with tablet features that used to be limited to Windows XP Tablet PC Edition, which was available only on new Tablet PCs.

Tablet PCs are notebook computers with a touch screen. Typically, they work with input from a traditional mouse-and-keyboard combination or from a stylus or pen. The stylus or pen lets you click, point, move items, draw, and write directly on the screen. Tablets require specialized, under-the-hood software components that enable the pen features.

Although most of Vista's features indeed work best on a Tablet PC, you can use some of them on a standard notebook or even a desktop. The handwriting-recognition feature, for example, can be used with a USB-based drawing tablet.

Vista includes three applications designed to work with tablets:

- **Sticky Notes.** This desktop version of the familiar yellow notes lets you create both handwritten and voice-based notes.

- **Tablet PC Input Panel.** Use this application to convert handwritten notes to text that can be inserted into almost any Windows program.

- **Windows Journal.** This simple note-taking program mimics paper but can also be edited in word-processor fashion.

Opening any of the Tablet PC applications involves three steps:

1. Choose Start > All Programs.

2. Click Accessories.

3. Click Tablet PC to see the programs in this program group.

4. Double-click the icon for the tablet application you want to open.

   The following sections look at what each application can do.

Write or speak a Sticky Note

To use Sticky Notes:

1. Follow the steps in the preceding exercise to launch Sticky Notes.

2. To create a note, write on the area in the center with the stylus, just as you would a pen on paper.

Vista automatically saves the note for you.

3. To create a voice note, click the red Record button near the bottom of the window; say what you want to say; then click the middle left button, which is Stop.

   Voice notes can be stand-alone items or can accompany handwritten notes.

4. To step through notes you've left, click the Back and Forward buttons in the top-right corner of the window.

5. To delete an individual written or voice note, select it and then click the red X in the toolbar.

A handwritten note is actually an image that can be pasted into other applications, such as a picture editor or a word processor. Click the Copy button in the toolbar and then paste the note into an application that will accept it.

Insert text by using the Tablet PC Input Panel

The Tablet PC Input Panel lets you use a variety of methods for inserting text into a program with a stylus. This panel features a free-form writing area and an onscreen keyboard.

> **NOTE** —— On most Tablet PCs, the Tablet PC Input Panel application runs when Vista boots up. You'll usually see it peeking out from the left side of the desktop. If you click it, it slides to the middle of the screen.

Drop converted handwriting into an application

To add handwriting converted to text to a program:

1. Follow the steps earlier in this section to launch the Tablet PC Input Panel, or if the panel is partially visible on the left side of your screen, click it to move it to the center.

   The Tablet PC Input Panel opens with the free-form entry method displayed by default.

2. Write anything above the line.

   The panel changes shape and displays an Insert button in the bottom-right corner. Other buttons appear below your handwriting, showing what the handwriting-recognition engine thinks you mean.

3. To see more details about the recognition and to get suggested alternatives, click the button that corresponds to one of the words you wrote.

4. If handwriting recognition doesn't seem to be doing a good job of interpreting your chicken scratches, you have two other options for entering text:

- Click the Character Pad button ⊔⊔ to enter individual letters, each letters in its own space. This feature helps the recognition engine if your handwriting is not very good.

- Click the Keyboard button ⌨ to change the panel to an onscreen keyboard. Use this feature if your handwriting is really, really bad.

5. To insert the text into an application (such as a word processor), launch that application and then click the Insert button in the Tablet PC Input Panel.

   The text appears in your application.

Teach handwriting recognition a thing or two

Want to improve the handwriting-recognition engine's ability to interpret your handwriting? Here's how:

1. In the Tablet PC Input Panel, choose Tools > Personalize Handwriting Recognition.

   The panel slides away, and the Handwriting Personalization wizard appears.

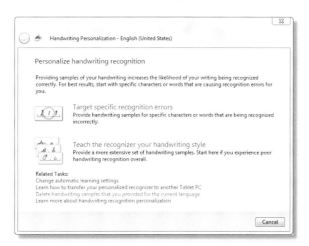

continues on next page

This wizard provides two methods for training Vista's recognizer to improve its capabilities: targeting specific errors and teaching the recognizer to interpret your handwriting better.

2. Click Target Specific Recognition Errors if the recognizer misses the same words repeatedly.

3. Click Teach the Recognizer Your Handwriting Style to launch a series of screens in which you show the system, letter by letter, how you write.

4. If you have a Tablet PC, click the Change Automatic Learning Settings link to tweak how Vista's recognizer learns automatically.

NOTE —— This step won't work on a notebook or a desktop computer with an attached tablet.

Over time, the handwriting recognition will improve as the software learns how you write. The more you use it, the better it becomes.

Take smarter notes using Windows Journal

Windows Journal combines the convenience of handwritten notes with the power of basic word processing. You can do almost anything with handwriting that you can with a word processor, from cutting, copying, and pasting notes to searching for specific words.

Convert handwriting to text

1. Follow the steps earlier in this section to launch Windows Journal.

   Journal launches with a blank page.

2. Use a stylus to write something on the "paper."

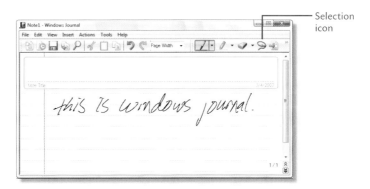

Selection icon

3. To start the conversion to text, click the Selection button in the toolbar, and draw a box or oval around the text you want to change.

   The text changes, and a box appears around it.

4. To convert the selected handwriting to text, choose Actions > Convert Handwriting to Text.

   An editing window appears.

5. Make any corrections that need to be made, and click OK.

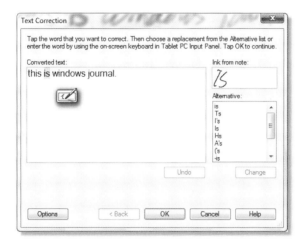

6. In the next window, indicate whether you want the converted text to be placed in the clipboard or pasted into the note (for this exercise, select the latter option), and click Finish.

   The handwriting converts to text.

Find a word in handwritten notes

Journal makes it easy to find what you're looking for, even if you need to scan several pages of scrawl. Even if you don't convert your writing to text, Journal does this in the background. When you search for a word, it uses this information to help find the word.

1. In the Journal toolbar, click the Find button.

   The Find toolbar appears.

continues on next page

295

2. Enter the word you want to find, and click Find.

Journal highlights the word that it thinks you want.

3. If that's not the right word, click Next until you find it.

What You've Learned

- How to configure Vista to shut down the way you prefer

- How to change power plans and set up custom plans of your own

- How to use Sync Center to keep documents and files synchronized between devices and computers

- How to install and manage gadgets used with Windows SideShow

- How to access and use the applications designed for use with Tablet PCs

14

GOALS

Connect to the Internet using Windows Vista

Build a home/small-business network

Share files, folders, printers, and drives

Vista on the Network

The days of the stand-alone computer are long gone. Machines once used mostly to crunch numbers and rearrange text are now primarily devices for communication and creativity. But computers can't communicate if they aren't connected.

Past versions of Windows made more allowances for machines that weren't part of a network. But Vista presumes from the start that the user is at least connected to the Internet, if not to a local area network (LAN). In fact, unless Vista can talk to the Net, some features won't work properly, such as Windows Update, the advanced help system, and even parts of the installation routine.

Users who are familiar with Windows XP's networking will want to follow this lesson closely, because a lot has changed in Vista—and not all for the better. Microsoft made improvements in some areas, but in others, it seems to have opted for change for the sake of change, with some confusing results.

Our emphasis in this lesson is on Internet connectivity, with a secondary focus on home networks. In a further nod to the changed computing landscape, we'll touch on dial-up networking only briefly; those days are almost over.

Understanding Networking

At first glance, network computing seems daunting. People spend a lot of time and money learning its intricacies, but it has advanced to the point where hooking PCs together is not that difficult. Understanding some basic concepts helps, however.

At its core, a computer network is simply a group of machines talking to one another. In doing so, they can share files and information, as well as some of the devices connected to them. Because some of the shared information may be sensitive, permission to access that information (and the devices that contain it) can be restricted in different ways.

A typical network is simply a cluster of machines linked together. The Internet is a network of networks—millions of machines, each in their own networks, which in turn are talking to other networks.

A typical small network-to-Internet configuration is set up this way:

- An individual computer connects to a router, hub, or switch, which acts as a central switching station for data moving among all the computers. A *router* is an active device that intelligently moves data where it needs to go, kind of like a traffic cop. A *hub* or *switch* is more passive—more like a central lobby where many hallways intersect. Often, switches and hubs are built into routers.

- The router, hub, or switch in turn connects to a gateway device that acts as a liaison between the small network and a larger one—such as the Internet. The gateway may be a cable or DSL modem.

- That gateway in turn connects to a similar device on the larger network of an Internet service provider (ISP).

- The ISP's network, using gateway devices of its own, talks to still larger networks and (depending on the scale of the ISP) possibly to one of the *backbones*, or major pathways of the Internet.

NOTE —— Even dial-up networking follows this model. When you use a dial-up modem, it uses the telephone network as its gateway, connecting to another gateway at your ISP.

One of Vista's cooler features lets you see this basic structure in a map of the network to which you're connected. We show you how to access this map later in the lesson, but here, the image serves to illustrate the basics of networking.

The following illustration shows five computers connected to a Wi-Fi router named 9302. Three of the computers are talking to the router via Wi-Fi. (The dotted lines indicate a wireless link.) The other two computers are connected to a switch using Ethernet cable (the solid lines), which in turn is connected via Ethernet to the router. The router connects to the Internet via a cable modem (not shown).

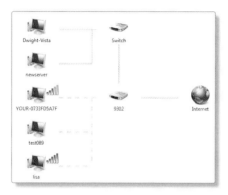

Connecting to the Internet

All personal computers use one or more methods to connect to a network or the Internet:

- **Ethernet**, which uses wiring to connect to a router or directly to a broadband Internet service. Internet access may be provided over DSL, which is a fast connection over phone lines; cable-modem service, which uses the same coaxial wiring as cable TV; business-level access over dedicated network lines; or satellite-based services.

- **A wireless network**, or Wi-Fi, which uses radio frequencies to establish a connection and transmit information. Wi-Fi may be used in homes or businesses as part of a LAN, which in turn talks to an Internet gateway.

- **High-speed cellular phone networks** in what's known as a Wireless Wide Area Network (WWAN). This is primarily used with mobile computers.

- **Standard telephone lines** in a process known as dial-up networking.

Connect via Ethernet

Ethernet is a venerable networking technology that's been around for more than three decades. It's stable, fast, and inexpensive. Almost all modern computers come with an Ethernet port, which looks like an oversize phone jack.

If you have a choice between connecting to the Internet via Ethernet or a wireless connection, Ethernet is almost always the better choice. It's less prone to disconnects and doesn't suffer from the same interference issues as Wi-Fi, and it's certainly faster than dial-up.

Windows has long made connecting to the Internet via Ethernet a snap. As far back as Windows 98, the process has been about as Plug and Play as things get—largely a matter of plugging a working Internet connection into your computer. Windows sees the connection and automatically makes the necessary changes to settings. That's it; you're online.

But Vista treats the process a little differently. The growing use of portable computers means that people may connect to different types of networks with the same PC. Security issues differ when you're connected to your home network versus, say, to Wi-Fi at your neighborhood coffee shop or to an Ethernet connection in a hotel room.

When you connect, Vista basically asks, "Where are you?" Here's how to connect to the Internet using Ethernet:

1. Connect an Ethernet cable to your computer.

   Vista establishes a connection to the network, and the Set Network Location window appears.

2. Choose one of the following:

- **Home or Work.** Functionally, there's not much difference between Home and Work locations. Both allow you to see other computers on the network, and if you allow it, those computers can see yours. The Work option, in editions of Vista that support it (Business, Ultimate, and Enterprise), allows you to join a *domain,* which is a set of network resources that have been given a specific name. The Work location is typically used only in large enterprise networks.

- **Public Location.** This option hides the presence of your computer from others on a network. Use it when you're connected away from home—in hotels, coffee shops, libraries, and airports. It's also a good choice if your PC is connected directly to the Internet via a cable or DSL modem, because it tightens the security settings of Vista's firewall (see Lesson 6).

For this exercise, we chose the Home option.

If a User Account Control prompt appears, click Continue. The Successfully Set Network Settings window appears.

3. Click Close.

Connect via Wi-Fi

Wi-Fi is a wonderfully versatile way to connect to the Internet. You can use it at home, on the road, and (if your employer allows it) at work. Both desktop and portable PCs can use Wi-Fi, and even some handheld computers, such as PDAs and gaming devices, are Wi-Fi enabled. Because it allows users to connect without wires, Wi-Fi also has become the method of choice for an increasing number of home networks.

We deal with using Wi-Fi for a home network later in this lesson, but here's how you connect directly to the Internet (usually in a public place) using Wi-Fi:

1. With your PC powered up, make sure that you're in a location where a wireless connection to the Internet is available and that your Wi-Fi adapter is turned on.

NOTE ———— You may find a physical switch or button on the case, or you may need to turn on the adapter via specialized software. Check your computer's documentation for details

continues on next page

When the Wi-Fi adapter is active, the Network Connection icon  is displayed in the notification area of the taskbar.

2. Click the connection icon to display the Not Connected window.

3. Click Wireless Networks Are Available.

A dialog box displaying a list of available networks appears.

The networks will be labeled either Security-Enabled or Unsecured. Access to the former type of network requires some kind of passphrase or a letter–number combination string that the network operator will give you. (The passphrase is used to encrypt or scramble the signal, making it more secure.) Access to the latter type of network—which is the most common type found in public places—is via a direct connection without a passphrase. This type of network is convenient but not secure.

The strength of the signal is indicated by the number of green bars shown in its listing—an indicator similar to that found on cell phones.

4. For the purposes of this exercise, select the unsecured network with the best signal; then click Connect.

A warning box appears, saying that the network is unsecured.

5. Click Connect Anyway to connect.

A window showing the progress of the connection appears, followed by a Successfully Connected window.

6. If you think you may visit this Wi-Fi hotspot regularly, check the Save This Network check box.

The next time you are within range of this hotspot, Vista will connect to it automatically as a preferred network.

7. Click Close.

The Set Network Location window, mentioned in step 1 of the preceding exercise, appears.

8. Choose Public Location.

The Successfully Set Network Settings dialog box appears.

9. Click Close.

10. Launch your Web browser.

You may be redirected to a sign-in screen that requests basic information.

NOTE —— Some free networks, such as those in hotels and restaurants, may require you to get a password and login name from an employee there. Pay networks show you a screen that may require a credit-card number to bill you for usage.

Stay Secure in Public

If you're not connected to a secured Wi-Fi network, exactly how exposed are you?

It's true that a Wi-Fi connection that's not encrypted can be hacked. Someone with the technical skills and the right software can capture the information you're sending and receiving between your PC and the Wi-Fi router at the hotspot. Vista's firewall settings make it harder for hackers to access your PC itself, but it is possible for someone to see what you're transmitting.

That's why it pays to be careful. If you're doing any kind of e-commerce transaction   say, buying something over the Web—make sure that the site you're using requires an encrypted link from your browser. Even though the Wi-Fi connection isn't encrypted, sessions between a browser and a specific Web site can be encrypted, allowing for secure transactions.

Also, be sure that you're connecting to the real access point offered by the location. Some hackers set up look-alike connections in which they ask for credit-card or other personal information. Ask an employee for the name of the Wi-Fi connection before you log in.

Finally, keep in mind you're in a public place; other people may be able to see what's on your screen. Be careful what you leave up on your screen when you walk away to talk to someone or take a bio break. You can lock your computer's screen by pressing Ctrl+Alt+Delete and then choosing Lock Computer before you wander away.

Connect via cellular broadband

In a new use for a relatively old technology, cellular phone companies have started offering Internet connections over their networks at speeds that approach the lower end of home-based broadband.

This type of connection works through a card or USB-based adapter attached to the PC, or through a built-in WWAN adapter available in some higher-end business-oriented notebooks. In almost all cases, the hardware you buy ties you to a specific cellular provider. If you buy an add-on WWAN PC card that works with Verizon, for example, that card won't work on Sprint's network.

The benefit is that in areas where cellular broadband is available, you don't have to worry about finding a Wi-Fi hotspot or available Ethernet connection to get a speedy link to the Internet.

Cellular broadband is available in most major metropolitan areas, making it a good choice for business travelers. But it's also fairly expensive, usually running $40 to $80 per month, depending on whether you get an unlimited plan or pay by the kilobyte.

After you install the hardware and software in accordance with the manufacturer's instructions, you may see an icon on your desktop or in the Start menu that allows you to connect to the network. If you see this icon, use it to connect; then follow the steps provided by the software.

If you don't get an icon for connecting, here's how you access cellular broadband:

1. Right-click the Network Connection icon ▤ in the notification area of the Vista taskbar, and choose Connect to a Network from the shortcut menu.

   The Connect to a Network dialog box displays.

   At the top of the list of available networks is Dial-Up and VPN, and your WWAN connection should be visible.

2. Select the WWAN connection; then click Connect.

   The Successfully Connected window displays.

3. Click Close.

Connect via dial-up

Even though broadband Internet is now the dominant connection in the United States, a fair number of people are still stuck on dial-up. Usually, they have several reasons for sticking with dial-up connections: Broadband isn't available in the area; they're on a budget, and low-cost broadband isn't available; their older hardware can't handle a dial-up connection; they don't feel a need for speed; or they're change averse.

But even broadband users may hold onto a dial-up connection as a backup ISP or for use on the road on those rare occasions when a high-speed connection can't be found.

As a result, Vista still supports dial-up connections.

The process for setting up a connection and accessing it is similar to that used in previous versions of Windows:

1. Make sure that your computer's dial-up modem is connected to a working phone line.

2. Choose Start > Connect To.

   The Connect to a Network dialog box appears.

3. Click Set up a Connection or Network.

4. In the Set Up Connection Option dialog box, click Set up a Dial-Up Connection; then click Next.

   The Set up a Dial-Up Connection dialog box appears.

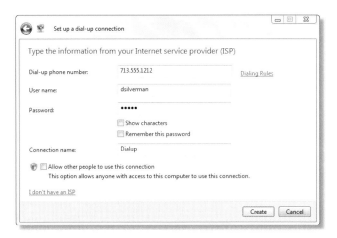

5. Enter the information given to you by your ISP: your phone number, your user name, and your password.

6. Click Create.

    A connection-progress window appears, followed by the Successfully Connected window.

7. Click Close.

The next time you need to use that connection, repeat step 2. The dial-up connection you created appears in the Connect to a Network dialog box.

Now that you've gotten one computer on the Internet, you're ready to connect more than one computer in a network and get all of them online.

Networking with Vista

Although setting up a home or small business network is a lot simpler than it used to be, it can still be daunting for the novice, particularly if something doesn't go according to plan. At a surface level, Vista has made this process simpler. But those who are familiar with the process in Windows XP may find the changes confusing, particularly when it comes to troubleshooting. Vista relies more on automated processes, and in some cases, advanced users may have to drop to a command prompt to get a real fix done.

In this section, we show you how to set up a typical home network with a mix of Wi-Fi and Ethernet-connected machines. Just to keep things interesting, we include computers that use Vista, Windows XP, and even Mac OS X.

Gather your gear

You need certain hardware components before you build your network. Some of them are likely to already be in your PCs.

- **A router.** As mentioned earlier in this lesson, a router acts like a traffic cop, directing information where it needs to go on a network. In a home or small-business network, the router makes the initial connection to your ISP through a cable or DSL modem. It receives the *IP (Internet Protocol) address,* a numerical assignment that identifies a PC or a network on the Net. Then the router hands out its own IP addresses to the computers on the network. Most routers also serve as firewalls, blocking intrusion attempts from the Internet.

A router can be wired or wireless. Most Wi-Fi routers include at least one wired connection; many routers have four. Wireless routers are usually advertised as supporting a specific variant of the Wi-Fi standard, usually designated as 802.11 followed by a letter—a, b, g, or n. At this writing, the most common is 802.11g, though a new standard under development, 802.11n, is considered to be its successor.

You may also want to look for a router that is certified to work with Vista, which has a feature that allows you to configure a router without installing software on your PC or accessing the router's built-in configuration Web pages.

NOTE —— At this writing, 802.11n is still being developed by an international standards committee. This standard allows for dramatically higher transfer speeds–up to 300 megabits a second–and a signal with much better range. Because the standard is still being finalized, however, the details of how it works may still change. Hardware sold as 802.11n may not be able to be upgraded with the final specification when it's available. Check with the maker of what's known as *draft-N* hardware to see whether it will guarantee that the hardware has a future.

- **Ethernet adapters.** Chances are very good that any computer you have already has an Ethernet adapter installed in it. If not, most electronics stores carry inexpensive adapters that come with simple installation instructions. Both Vista and Windows XP have built-in drivers for most common Ethernet cards, so it's usually a matter of just plugging them in and waiting for the operating system to recognize them.

- **Wi-Fi adapters.** Many kinds of Wi-Fi adapters are available, in terms of design and the types of Wi-Fi they employ. A Wi-Fi adapter may plug into the PCI slot on a computer's motherboard, into a USB port on the case, or into a PC Card slot in the side of a notebook (though most modern portable PCs come with a built-in Wi-Fi adapter). Add to that the different flavors of 802.11, and the selections become confusing. For a desktop PC, we mostly recommend USB-based adapters, as they are easy to install and, depending on the design, may allow you to move the antenna for a better signal.

- **Cables, switches, and hubs.** If you plan to connect any of your PCs via Ethernet, you need cables. You can buy networking cables—look for a type called Category 5 or simply Cat 5—at any computer store. If you plan to hard-wire more computers than you have ports in your router, you need a hub or a switch. The latter option is better if you think you'll have a lot of activity on your network.

NOTE —— This lesson doesn't pretend to be a comprehensive guide to building a home network. We're here mainly to show you how to get a network up and running with Vista, describing the basics of connecting all the hardware involved in establishing a connection to the Internet. This explanation is not exhaustive, so if you need more guidance, turn to the various hardware manuals or check PracticallyNetworked.com, an excellent source for general information about setting up computer networks.

Add computers to a network

Vista makes adding computers to a network simple. Just keep a few things in mind:

- Just as your computer has a name, so does the network. Windows calls small networks (such as those found in a home) *workgroups.* For your computers to see one another on the network and to share files and a printer, they must have the same workgroup name. The default name in most versions of Windows XP and Vista is WORKGROUP; in Windows XP Home, it's MSHOME.

- If you are connecting to a network using Wi-Fi, the router to which your PCs connect will broadcast a name as well so that you can find it. The name is not the same as your workgroup name (though it could be, if you like), and it is not seen by computers that use a wired connection to the router.

- When your computers are connected, you need to give permission on each machine to share drives, folders, files, and peripherals (such as printers) with other computers on your network. If you don't, other users in your network will see the computers but won't be able to access anything on them.

Check and change the workgroup name

Begin the process by ensuring that all the PCs have the same workgroup name:

1. Choose Start > Computer > Properties.

continues on next page

The System window appears, with the workgroup name displayed at the bottom of the screen.

2. If the workgroup name is correct, close the window; you need do nothing else.

   or

   If the workgroup name is not correct, proceed to step 3.

3. Click Advanced System Settings in the left pane. If a User Account Control window appears, click Continue.

   The System Properties dialog box appears.

4. Click the Computer Name tab.

5. Click the Change button.

   The Computer Name/Domain Changes dialog box appears.

6. Change the text in the Workgroup box to the workgroup name you prefer, and click OK.

   A confirmation screen appears.

7. Click OK.

   A prompt displays, stating that the change will take place when you restart the computer.

8. Click OK.

9. Restart your computer.

Add computers via Ethernet

Connecting a PC to a network using Ethernet is just as easy as the exercises in this lesson about connecting a PC to the Internet. In fact, the steps are the same! Reread the "Connect via Ethernet" section, and return to this section when you're ready to learn about connecting computers via Wi-Fi.

Add computers via Wi-Fi

The process for adding computers to a network using Wi-Fi is very similar to the process for connecting to the Internet via Wi-Fi. The main difference is that if you are setting up a network yourself, you'll want to set up some kind of security to control who has access.

Wireless network security can be accomplished in several ways, or the approaches can be combined.

- **Encryption.** This process essentially scrambles the information moving between a Wi-Fi-enabled device and the wireless router. The two most common types of encryption are Wired Equivalent Privacy (WEP) and Wi-Fi Protected Access (WPA). Variations of each type exist, but both forms of encryption work by matching a passphrase or string of letters and numbers on both the router and the adapter. WPA is considered to be harder to crack than WEP, though WEP is more universal.

- **MAC filtering.** Every networking adapter—wired and unwired—has a unique number called a Media Access Control (MAC) address. You can set up a router to accept only certain MAC addresses. How you do this depends on the router; check its manual. If someone figures out one of your MAC addresses, it's easy for him or her to set another computer to use that same address.

- **Not broadcasting the SSID.** A wireless network needs a name, known as the Service Set Identifier (SSID). Most Wi-Fi routers have a feature that lets you turn off or not broadcast the SSID; again, check the manual. Someone who has the right hardware and/or software can still find your network, so this security method should not be your only choice. You should use it in conjunction with encryption and/or MAC filtering.

In this exercise, you connect a wireless-enabled notebook computer to a Wi-Fi network using WEP (as almost all Wi-Fi adapters support it), with the SSID broadcast publicly.

1. Follow the steps in your router's manual for setting up a network using WEP encryption, and replace the default SSID (often, the brand name of the router) with a unique identifier.

2. Follow steps 1 through 3 of "Connect via Wi-Fi" earlier in this lesson.

   When you see the list of available networks, look for your router's SSID, which should be labeled Security-Enabled Network.

3. Select your network; then click the Connect button.

A progress window briefly displays as an initial connection is made, followed by a dialog box that lets you enter your security key or passphrase.

4. Type the same security key (a string of letters and numbers) or passphrase that you entered during your router's security setup process.

> **TIP** —— If you want the characters to display as you type, rather than appear as bullets, check the Display Characters check box.

5. Click Connect.

   A window shows your progress; then a window displays to let you know that a connection has been made.

6. Check the Save This Network check box if you'll connect to the network regularly.

7. Check Start This Connection Automatically if you want your computer to connect to this network without your intervention in the future.

   Both this option and the option in step 6 are recommended if you're adding computers to your home network.

8. Click Close.

Now that you've got computers connected to your network via both Ethernet and Wi-Fi, you're ready to manage the network you've built.

Manage your network using Network and Sharing Center

Configuring, understanding, and managing your network begin in Network and Sharing Center, a hub for everything related to networking in Vista.

From Network and Sharing Center, you can manage your network connections as well as how you share the files and devices on your computer with others on a network.

To access Network and Sharing Center:

- Right-click the Network Connection icon ![icon] in the notification area of the Vista taskbar, and choose Network and Sharing Center from the shortcut menu.

  or

  Click the Start button, type network and sharing in the Search box, and press Enter.

The Network and Sharing Center window appears.

The top half of the window is the network part; the bottom half deals with sharing. We'll start with the top half.

Explore your network

The three large icons at the top of Network and Sharing Center are a much-simplified version of the network map shown earlier in this lesson. Combined, they show your particular computer's relation to the overall network and the Internet. Clicking each icon will give you more information, as well as access to tools related to that part of the map.

- Clicking the This Computer icon launches the Computer folder, which shows all your physical and network drives; shared folders; and attached storage devices, such as USB flash drives and memory cards.

- Clicking the Network icon brings up a folder showing the devices on your network, including all computers and your router.

- Double-click any of the computer icons to access drives, folders and files on those systems. If Universal Plug and Play (UPnP) is enabled on the router (check the router manual to see how to do this), you'll be able to double-click the router and access its built-in configuration Web page.

- Clicking the Internet globe icon launches a Web browser window with your start page.

Navigate the network map

You can also display an expanded view of your network with the complete network map:

- Click the View Full Map link above the Internet icon in Network and Sharing Center.

continues on next page

The Network Map window appears. You may have a slight delay while Vista searches for devices on your network and gathers information from them.

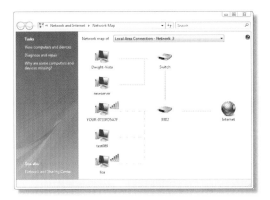

Depending on what the icons represent and the permissions on the computers shown, you may be able to click the icons and get access to settings, information, or files. Clicking the router, for example, if it supports UPnP, will launch its configuration page; clicking the switch won't do anything, because that device isn't configurable. Also, any of the computers that don't have file or printer sharing turned on will not be accessible.

If you have computers connected via Wi-Fi to your network, you may be able to see the quality of the wireless connection, as noted by the set of signal bars next to the Wi-Fi-connected PCs in the map. This feature is handy for troubleshooting from afar.

Manage your network

The settings in the middle section of Network and Sharing Center let you customize your network and change some of the settings for your current PC's connection to it.

Click Network to reconfigure your PC's connection settings.

To change features of your network:

1. In Network and Sharing Center, click Network; then click Customize.

The Customize Network Settings dialog box appears.

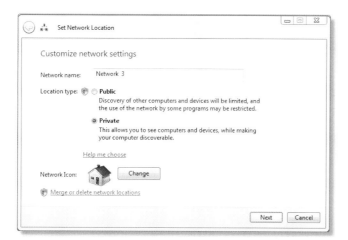

2. To change the name of your network, replace the text in the Network Name box.

3. To change the network type from Private to Public (which will automatically change Vista's firewall settings to prevent file sharing and discovery by other computers), click Public.

4. To change the icon used to represent your network, click the Change button to open the Change Network Icon dialog box; choose a new icon; and click OK.

5. To combine multiple networks (if you are connected to a Wi-Fi network at the same time an Ethernet cable is plugged in, for example), click Merge or Delete Network Locations to open the Merge or Delete Network Locations dialog box; then follow the remaining steps in this exercise.

   or

   If you don't have multiple networks or don't want to combine them, and you are finished reconfiguring your settings, click Close.

6. In the Merge or Delete Network Locations dialog box, select one of the networks you want to merge and then click Merge.

   A window displaying a list of available networks appears.

7. Do one of the following:

   • To add another network you want to merge, select that network and click OK.

   • To delete a network, select that network and click Delete; then click Yes in the confirmation dialog box that appears.

   continues on next page

8. When you finish, click Close.

Now that you have set up some network connections, let's work with them. To manage your network connections:

1. In the Tasks pane on the left side of Network and Sharing Center, click Manage Network Connections.

The Network Connections folder appears.

2. Double-click the connection you want to manage.

For this exercise, choose Wireless Network Connection.

The Wireless Network Connection Status dialog box appears.

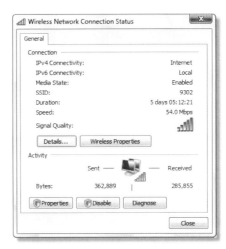

3. Click Details to get detailed information about the current connection.

4. Click Wireless Properties to change the settings you established when you set up the current connection, including the passphrase and whether the network connects automatically.

5. Click Properties to access settings related to the protocols and technologies used to establish the network connection.

   Unless you're a fairly advanced network user, we advise you not to mess with these settings.

6. Click Diagnose if you are having problems with your connection.

   A box appears to show progress, and if there are any issues, you'll be prompted to take actions.

7. Click the Disabled button if you want to turn off the wireless connection.

8. Click Close when you are finished.

Share folders, files, and printers

The main reason for creating a network is to share files and connected peripherals among computers. Network and Sharing Center contains most of what you need to accomplish this task. The bottom half of the Network and Sharing Center window lets you control how different aspects of sharing work. In Vista, you can turn on some types of sharing and leave others off from this one location.

The Sharing and Discovery section of Network and Sharing Center.

Hey! Where'd "Repair" Go?

Regular users of Windows XP's Wi-Fi networking are used to solving many wireless connection problems by right-clicking the wireless network icon in the notification area of the taskbar and choosing Repair from the shortcut menu.

In Vista, that method has been replaced by an automated process that, in our opinion, leaves a lot to be desired. Here's how it works:

1. Right-click the network icon in the notification area, and choose Diagnose and Repair from the shortcut menu.

   A Windows Network Diagnostics window appears; then a result window appears. What this window says depends on what the issue is.

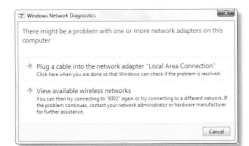

2. Select the option that best fits your issue.

   If the fix worked, you see a success window, which you can close. If the fix didn't work, you see the following message.

Although convenient, this automated process seems to be hit or miss. Don't you wish you had good ol' Repair back to fix this problem? Well, it's still there—just hidden. Here's how to bring it back:

1. Follow steps 1 and 2 of "Manage your network" on page 318.

2. In the Wireless Network Connection Status dialog box, click Diagnose.

   The Wireless Network Diagnostics dialog box appears.

3. Click Reset the Network Adapter to begin a repair. If a User Account Control prompt appears, click Continue.

   A status window shows the progress, followed by a second window.

   If the repair worked, the Problem Has Been resolved window displays; if the repair didn't work, a prompt advises you to contact your ISP.

Clicking any of the down arrows gives you access to more information and lets you change some file-sharing settings. In the image above, the Media Sharing category is opened to show more information.

The following sections explore these categories.

Turn on to Network Discovery

The Network Discovery setting allows you to see other computers on your network and lets other computers see you. When you use the Private Network setting in Vista, this setting is on by default; it's off when you are connected to a public network.

To toggle Network Discovery on or off:

1. In Network and Sharing Center, click the down arrow next to Network Discovery.

2. Click Turn on Network Discovery to see other computers on the network and allow them to see you.

    or

    Click Turn off Network Discovery to be invisible to other computers on the network. (You will not be able to see them, either.)

3. Click Apply. If a User Access Control (UAC) prompt appears, click Continue.

4. Click Change if you want to change the workgroup name.

    The Computer Name/Domain Changes dialog box appears.

5. Change the text in the Workgroup box, and click OK.

Enable File Sharing

You must turn this option on to allow file sharing generally. Only one folder—called the Public folder in Vista—is shared by default; thus, it is the only folder initially accessible to others on your network. You still need to enable sharing for other folders. We show you how to do that later in this lesson.

To toggle File Sharing on or off:

1. In Network and Sharing Center, click the down arrow next to File Sharing.

2. Click Turn on File Sharing to allow any folders, files, and printers you've designated as shared to be seen by others.

    or

    Click Turn off File Sharing to hide shared folders, files, and printers from others on the network.

3. Click Apply. If a UAC prompt appears, click Continue.

Limit access to the Public folder

The Public Folder Sharing option lets you control when and how others can access your Public folder. You can think of this folder as being a dropoff spot that anyone can get to without gaining access to other folders on your PC. If you want to share a file, place a copy in this folder, and anyone on your network can access it.

At times, though, you may want to block access to the Public folder while leaving file sharing on in general, or you may want to change what others on your network can do with the file.

To do that:

1. In Network and Sharing Center, click the down arrow next to Public Folder Sharing.

2. Do one of the following:

    *   Click Turn on Sharing So Anyone with Network Access Can Open Files.

        This option allows other users to look at files but not change, delete, or add them in the Public folder.

    *   Click Turn on Sharing So Anyone with Network Access Can Open, Change, and Create Files.

This option provides the most access. Other users can make changes, add new files, and delete existing files.

- Click Turn off Sharing.

  This option hides the Public folder from other users on the network. Other users with accounts on the computer can still access your Public folder when they physically sit down at the machine, however.

3. Click Apply after making any of these choices. If a UAC prompt appears, click Continue.

Share your printer

Use the Printer Sharing option to determine whether others on your network have access to your shared printer. You still must designate a printer to be shared. We show you how to do that later in this lesson.

To toggle printer sharing on or off:

1. In Network and Sharing Center, click the down arrow next to Printer Sharing.

2. Click Turn on Printer Sharing to give others access to printers connected to your PC.

   or

   Click Turn off Printer Sharing to hide your printer from others on the network.

3. Click Apply. If a UAC prompt appears, click Continue.

Password-protect your content

The Password Protected Sharing option requires anyone who wants to access files, folders, and printers on your PC to have a password-controlled user account on the machine. If you turn this option off, anyone can access your PC from any other machine on the network without entering a password.

To toggle password-protected sharing on and off:

1. In Network and Sharing Center, click the down arrow next to Password Protected Sharing.

continues on next page

2. Click Turn on Password Protected Sharing to require anyone accessing your shared files, folders, and printer to input a password.

   or

   Click Turn off Password Protected Sharing to allow anyone to access shared files, folders, and printers without entering a password.

3. Click Apply. If a UAC prompt appears, click Continue.

Share media

If you have music, photos, or video files on your PC, you can allow others to access them by using Windows Media Player. This feature does not apply to files that have Digital Rights Management restrictions that tie the use of media files to a specific machine. These files cannot be played on other PCs even if the Media Sharing option is enabled.

To enable media sharing:

1. In Network and Sharing Center, click the down arrow next to Media Sharing.

2. Click the Change button.

   The Media Sharing dialog box appears.

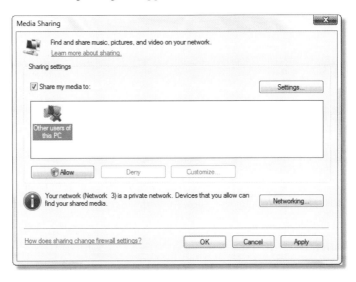

3. Select the category or device with which you want to share media files.

This device may be a music player (such as an MP3 player), a Media Extender (a product that lets you stream music, stills or video from your PC to a TV), or another computer.

4. Click Allow. If a User Access Control Prompt appears, click Continue.

5. To specify which types of media can be shared, select the device or category and click Customize.

   The Media Sharing - Customize dialog box appears.

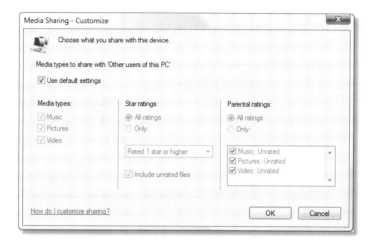

6. Select the type of media you want to share and whether to restrict available media by star ratings or parental ratings.

7. Click OK.

   You return to the Media Sharing dialog box.

8. Click Apply; then click OK.

After file sharing is turned on, you still need to enable specific folders and printers on your computers so other users can access them.

Share folders and drives

In Vista, as in past versions of Windows, you can open folders and entire drives to access by other users. You can specify who on your network will have access, including individuals and groups.

To share a folder:

1. Open the folder you want to share.

2. Click the Share button in the folder's headers at the top of the folder window.

The File Sharing dialog box opens.

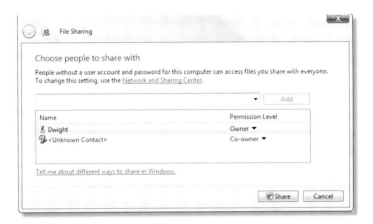

3. If you want a specific person on your network to access the folder, type that person's name at the top of the dialog box; then click Add.

   The person must have an account on your computer. (Use the User Accounts module in the Control Panel to create an account.)

4. To enable access for anyone, choose Everyone from the drop-down menu at the top of the dialog box; then click Add.

5. In the Permission Level column, make a choice from the Everyone drop-down menu.

   You have three choices for permissions, which control what users can do with this folder:

   • **Reader** lets users view files but not change them.

   • **Contributor** lets users add files and then change or delete them. They cannot change or delete files that they did not create, but they can view all files.

   • **Co-Owner** lets users do anything with any files—change, delete, or add.

6. Click the Share button.

7. If a UAC prompt appears, click Continue.

   A window appears that lets you email a link to the folder to the network users who can access that folder.

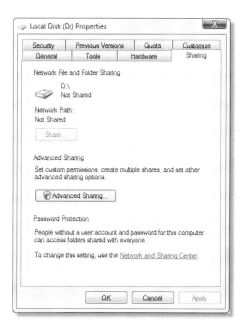

8. If you don't want to email anyone, click the Done button.

   or

   To email the link, click the E-Mail link and follow the remaining steps.

   Your default email client launches, with a message alerting the recipient that he or she now has access to a folder.

9. Fill in the email address; then click Send.

10. When you finish emailing the link to users, click the Done button in the File Sharing dialog box.

Although it's generally not advised, you can also share a complete drive. You might do this if you have more than one hard drive, and one contains files you want to share with others.

To share a whole drive:

1. Choose Start > Computer.

2. Right-click the drive you want to share, and choose Share from the shortcut menu.

   The Local Disk Properties dialog box appears.

3. Click the Advanced Sharing button. If a UAC prompt appears, click Continue.

   The Advanced Sharing dialog box appears.

4. Click Share This Folder.

5. Click Apply; then click OK.

6. Click Apply; then click OK.

   NOTE —— Think twice before sharing your C drive, which is likely to contain all your data. Unless you have a compelling reason to share the entire drive, you may be better off sharing specific folders that don't contain sensitive information. If you need remote access to files that are not in those folders, you can copy them to a shared folder on an as-needed basis.

Share printers

You can enable sharing for any printer attached to your computer. In most cases, a printer shared on a Vista-based PC will be accessible to a Windows XP system, but the reverse may not be true. You may need to install additional drivers.

To share a printer from a Vista PC:

1. Click the Start button, type `Printers` in the Search box, and press Enter.

The Printers folder appears.

2. Right-click the printer you want to share, and choose Sharing from the shortcut menu.

The Properties dialog box for the printer you selected displays.

3. Click the Change Sharing Options tab. If a User Account Countrol prompt appears, click Continue.

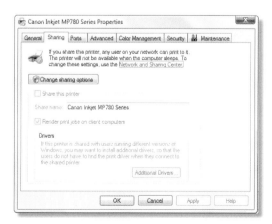

continues on next page

4. Select Share This Printer.

5. If you have a PC on your network that uses an Intel Itanium processor or a 64-bit version of Windows, click the Additional Drivers button; in the Additional Drivers dialog box that appears, check the Itanium or x64 box; then click OK.

6. Click Apply; then click OK.

NOTE —— Before you can use a shared printer from a specific machine, you may have to install drivers on that machine.

What You've Learned

- How to connect to the Internet

- How to build and manage a computer network

- How to share files, folders, drives, and printers on your PC with others on your network

15

GOALS

Understand how Vista's Games folder works

Explore the games that come with Vista

Prepare your system to play graphic-intensive games

Get into Games

OK, we've been serious enough for long enough. It's time to let our hair down, cut loose, have a little fun—maybe even a *lot* of fun.

Despite the increasing power and capabilities of console games—such as Microsoft's Xbox 360, Nintendo's Wii, and Sony's PlayStation 3—the PC remains the gaming platform of choice for millions. With Windows Vista, Microsoft hopes to hold onto those gamers with improvements both in how games look and perform, and how they're managed.

Here's how serious Microsoft is about Vista as an operating system to attract gamers. The company went so far as to redesign what's arguably the most-played computer game in the world: Solitaire.

In this lesson, we look at the changes in the games that come with Vista and show you some new ones. We also look at how Vista's new Games folder makes it easy to manage your games. And we tell you what you need to do to make high-powered, graphics-intensive games run well under Vista.

Using the Games Folder

At the heart of Vista's gaming experience is the Games folder. This folder stores shortcuts for games and gives you detailed information about them. Newer games will even tell you how well they'll run on your particular system.

The nine games that come with Vista already have shortcuts in the folder, and many games—particularly newer ones—add their shortcuts to it upon installation. Even if they don't, you can add a shortcut manually; we show you how to do that later in this lesson.

The Games folder can download information from the Internet about the games in the folder. It also serves as a gateway to a Microsoft Web site devoted to Windows games, which also includes a gaming blog and support information.

Take a tour of the Games folder

The Games folder has many unique features not found in other specialized folders in Vista. It's powerful, but using it is simple.

To access the Games folder:

1. Click the Start button.

    The Start menu opens.

2. Click the Games item in the right pane of the Start menu.

    The Games folder opens. The left side of the folder contains shortcuts for games; the right side displays your PC's performance rating, which we mention in Lesson 2.

3. Click a game shortcut.

The right pane changes to show information about the game—in the following image, Mahjong Titans, a new game that comes with Vista.

The right pane shows you several things:

■ **Game recommended rating.** This display is the recommended rating for decent performance. The game will run as it's supposed to if your PC has this performance rating or better.

■ **Game required rating.** This display is the minimum required for the game to run at all. Some features and visual elements may not work on machines with this rating, however.

■ **Current system rating.** This display is your PC's performance current rating. So long as its rating is at or better than the recommended and/or required rating, you can play the game.

■ **Content rating.** As we outline in Lesson 6's section on parental controls, Vista can display and even restrict games based on different ratings systems. In the example above, the folder shows the Entertainment Software Ratings Board's rating for Mahjong Titans. The game gets an E, which means it's suitable for all ages.

The bottom pane of the folder also contains information about the game, including:

- The game's title

- Its publisher and developer, with links to their respective Web sites

- When the game was last played

- The version of the game

- The game's genre

The folder also lets you sort games based on a variety of criteria. Click the headers across the top of the folder to sort by name, when the game was last played, its product version, publisher, developer, rating, and more.

Finally, the row of buttons across the top of the folder gives you more capabilities.

In addition to the common folder functions mentioned in Lesson 3, the Games folder has some specialized features:

- **Play.** After selecting a game in the Games folder, click this button to play it.

- **Community and Support.** Click this button to go to Microsoft's Games for Windows Web site at www.gamesforwindows.com. From here, you can get technical support for some games; read and comment in the Gamerscore blog (http://gamerscoreblog.com); and access the Microsoft Game Advisor, a tool that will tell you the system requirements for specific games (http://gameadvisor.futuremark.com). This tool can also test your system and tell you whether it can handle a specific game.

- **Options.** Clicking this button brings up a window that lets you control some of the Games folder's features.

To access the folder's specialized features:

1. Click the Options button in the Games folder.

    The Set up Games Folder Options dialog box appears.

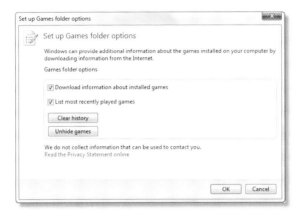

2. Check the Download Information about Installed Games check box to download and display details about a game, including its performance and content ratings.

3. Check the List Most Recently Played Games check box to see recently played games.

4. Click the Clear History button to clear the played-games list.

5. If you have hidden a game so that it does not display in the Games folder, click the Unhide Games button.

    NOTE —— To hide a game, right-click its icon in the Games folder and choose Hide Game from the shortcut menu.

6. Click OK to close the dialog box.

Add games to the Games folder

Newer games place a shortcut in the Games folder when you install them, using the basic procedures for program installation discussed in Lesson 4. Older games that aren't aware of the folder will not place an icon there automatically.

To add an icon manually:

1. Open the Games folder as outlined earlier in this lesson.

2. If the game has placed a shortcut on your desktop, drag it into the Games folder.

    or

    If no shortcut is immediately available, click Start > All Programs, navigate to the game's program group, click the game's icon, and drag it into the Games Folder.

If Microsoft's games database has information on the title, and if you have the folder options set to download information automatically, you should see ratings information appear in the right pane of the Games folder.

Playing Vista's Games

From the start, Windows has come with games. Version 1.0 came with Reversi, a strategic board game that also goes by the name Othello. But Windows is best known for games like Solitaire and Minesweeper, which were originally included to teach users how to work with a mouse.

In Vista, all the familiar Windows games have been redesigned with improved graphics and new features, and several new games are included. (For fans of Pinball, which came with Windows XP, we have bad news: It's been dropped from Vista.)

In this section, we look at the new games and examine what's changed in some of the old ones. We don't go into detail about how to play each one; half the fun of a game is figuring it out on your own!

Play Chess Titans

Frankly, there's not much that's titanic about Chess Titans. It's a very basic chess game, albeit one with pleasant 3D graphics and features common to most commercial chess titles. You can tweak difficulty levels and appearance, and set the game to play against either the computer or another human. Unfortunately, it doesn't allow for Internet play.

To start Chess Titans and set some options:

1. Choose Start > Games.

2. Double-click the Chess Titans icon to launch the game.

    The game launches.

    You can specify whether you want to play a game against the computer or another human, change the board's appearance, see your play statistics, and tweak the options. For this exercise, you'll set options.

3. Choose Game > Options.

    The Options dialog box appears.

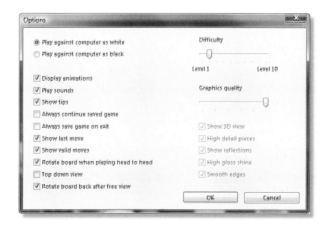

continues on next page

4. Drag the Difficulty slider to the right to make the game harder or to the left to make it easier.

5. Drag the Graphics slider to the right to increase the visual quality or to the left to decrease it.

   On less-powerful machines, the game may perform sluggishly if you push the slider too far to the right. As you drag the Graphics slider to the left, the boxes checked below it are unchecked.

6. Set the check-box options the way you want them.

   Most of the check boxes are self-explanatory, but here are some notes on some of the options:

   • If Always Continue Saved Game is checked, Chess Titans launches with the last saved game displayed on the board.

   • If Always Save Game on Exit is checked, the current game is saved automatically when you close the program.

   • If Rotate Board When Playing Head to Head is checked, the board rotates between the black and white sides when you're playing against another human.

   • If you check the Top Down View box, the board no longer tilts toward you; it appears as though you are looking straight down at it.

7. Click OK when you're done changing settings.

Keyboard Shortcuts

New game against the computer	F2
New game against a human	F3
Undo a move	Ctrl-Z
Show statistics	F4
Options	F5
Change the game's appearance	F7
Help	F1

Play InkBall

The goal of InkBall is to maneuver a colored ball into its corresponding hole on a board. Using a mouse or, if you have a Tablet PC, a pen, you draw lines of electronic ink to try to force the ball toward the right hole. When a ball hits a line you've drawn, it bounces away, and the line disappears. This game is simple, fun and frighteningly addictive, and it is best played on a Tablet PC.

To play InkBall:

1. Choose Start > Games.

2. Double-click the InkBall icon.

   The game launches, and balls are released onto the board.

3. Draw a line to block the ball's progress and direct it toward its color-coordinated hole.

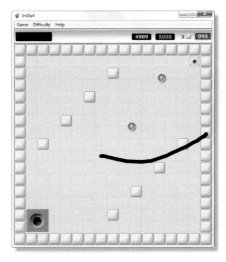

4. Make choices from the Game menu to pause or restart a game, or to clear the ink you've drawn off the board.

5. Make choices from the Difficulty menu to change how hard the game is.

   Your choices run from Beginner to Expert. Harder games feature more balls that move faster and provide more holes to navigate.

Keyboard Shortcut

New game	F2

Play Mahjong Titans

Like Chess Titans, this game is a modest rendering of its classic counterpart (in this case, the tile game mah-jongg), although the graphics are superb. Players match two tiles that have either their left or right side freed, removing both tiles from the board. In this version, the tiles vanish in a glimmer of light or, in some cases, a flash of fire.

To play Mahjong Titans:

1. Choose Start > Games.

2. Double-click the Mahjong Titans icon.

    The game launches.

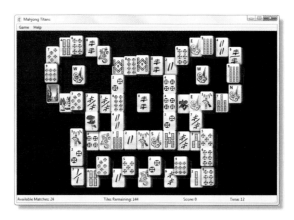

    The Game menu lets you start a new game, undo a move, get a hint, check statistics. and change options and appearance. For this exercise, you'll set options.

3. Choose Game > Options.

    The Options dialog box appears.

4. Choose the settings you want, and click OK.

    The settings in the Options dialog box let you display animations and play sounds, show tips, and always start with the last saved game.

And hey—when you win, you get fireworks!

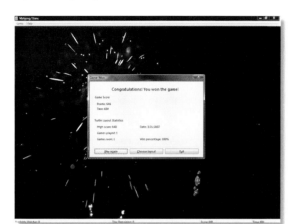

Keyboard Shortcuts

New game	F2
Undo a move	Ctrl-Z
Show statistics	F4
Options	F5
Change the game's appearance	F7
Help	F1

Play Purble Place

Purble Place is a puzzle game for small children, but adults who give it a try may find that they can't tear themselves away. Players are shown a cartoon village with three buildings, and clicking any one of them takes you to one of three different games.

To play Purble Place:

1. Choose Start > Games.

2. Double-click the Purble Place icon.

   The game launches.

continues on next page

3. Click the building corresponding to the game you want to play.

The games are:

- **Purble Shop.** Reminiscent of Mr. Potato Head, players place facial features on a blank Purble, trying to guess what a Purble behind a curtain looks like. As difficulty levels increase, you must choose among a greater number of options to build your perfect Purble.

- **Comfy Cakes.** Remember the classic "I Love Lucy" episode in which she's assembling cakes that pass by on a conveyor belt? Well, in this game, you're essentially playing the role of Lucy, and you must build a cake according to specs before it passes you by. If you get it wrong, you're chastised severely by the head cook.

- **Purble Pairs.** This game is a version of Concentration, in which you must match pairs of items by flipping tiles one at a time. Increasing the difficulty increases the number of tiles on the grid. You get a break from time to time, as a "sneak peek" tile appears without costing a turn, allowing you to find its match before time runs out.

Keyboard Shortcuts

New game	F2
Main menu	F3
Hint	H
Show statistics	F4
Options	F5
Help	F1

Rediscover old favorites

Classic Windows games are still here in Vista, but they have been given facelifts. Four card games—FreeCell, Hearts, Solitaire, and Spider Solitaire—now benefit from 3D graphics, realistic sound effects, added features, and (in some cases) hints.

Minesweeper, in which you try to uncover tiles without also uncovering exploding mines, now sports a brushed-aluminum look, 3D graphics, and stereo explosion sounds. (Hint: Turn your speakers *way up* when playing this one.)

We won't talk you through each of these games, but as an example of what's new, we offer a quick tour of the greatest office-productivity killer of all time: Solitaire.

To play the redesigned Solitaire:

1. Choose Start > Games.

2. Double-click the Solitaire icon.

   Solitaire launches.

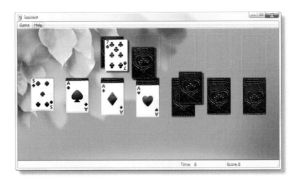

3. Double-click a single card to move it up; right-click the playing felt to move multiple cards at the same time.

   You no longer have to drag cards to the top row, but you must still drag cards around in the bottom row.

   TIP —— Need a hint? Press the H key, or choose Game > Hint. Solitaire highlights cards that can be matched.

4. To adjust settings, choose Game > Options.

The Options dialog box appears.

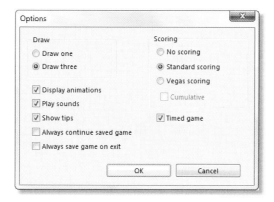

You can adjust many of the same scoring and play settings that were in the previous version of Solitaire, as well as continue saved games and turn sounds and animation on or off.

5. Click OK when you're done changing settings.

The most gratifying part of playing Solitaire, of course, is winning and getting to watch the cards jump off the deck. That still happens, but if you have Aero enabled, the cards shatter when they hit the bottom of the window.

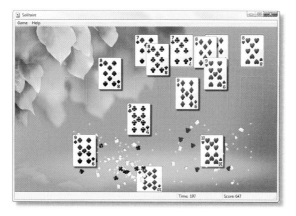

Just so you know, it took us more than a half-hour of solid playing to get that screen shot. The life of a computer-book author is so hard!

Keyboard Shortcuts	
New game	F2
Undo	Ctrl+Z
Hint	H
Show statistics	F4
Options	F5
Change the game's appearance	F7
Help	F1

Getting Your Game On

As we discuss in Lesson 1, Vista's Aero look uses the same 3D techniques used in modern computer games. Displaying the Aero interface requires a fairly powerful graphics card, so if your PC can display Aero, chances are that it can play many graphic-intensive games.

For the serious gamer, Vista goes a step further: It supports a new version of Microsoft's DirectX 3D graphics system. At this writing, only one graphics-card line supports DirectX 10, and that's the GeForce 8800 series from NVIDIA. Advanced Micro Devices, which recently acquired ATI Technologies, is working on a DirectX 10–capable line as well. Not many games use DirectX 10 yet; most of them rely instead on the older—but still technically impressive—DirectX 9.

The technical details on DirectX 10 will make most users' heads swim, so we won't delve into them here. Suffice it to say that games that support it look spectacular, and Microsoft says DirectX 10 also improves overall game performance.

Load up on hardware

In Lesson 1, we list Microsoft's minimum recommended system specifications for Vista's Home Premium edition—the hardware needed to enable Aero. That's also the minimum you need to play games decently. But we'd also like to offer our recommended specifications for a decent gaming experience with Vista:

- **2 GB of system memory.** When it comes to playing graphics-intensive games, you can't have too much memory. If you're a gamer, consider 2 GB the minimum, and consider jumping to 3 GB or 4 GB if you can afford it and your system will support it. Ideally, this memory should not be shared with the memory used by your graphics cards—a configuration often used in lower-priced systems but avoided by gamers.

- **256 MB DirectX 9 or DirectX 10 graphics card.** This card doubles the recommended memory for a video adapter, allowing the card to handle more visual information and allowing for more graphical capabilities at higher screen resolutions. If you can afford a DirectX 10 card (fairly expensive at this writing, starting at several hundred dollars), getting one is a good idea. In the interim, a DirectX 9 card with Vista drivers will do fine, because that's what the majority of current games support.

- **300 GB, 7,200 rpm Serial ATA hard drive**. Today's high-end games don't come on CDs; they come on DVDs, and sometimes on more than one. If you're playing lots of games, you'll want the hard-disk real estate to store them. You'll also want one that spins rapidly and transfers data quickly, which is why we recommend a 7,200 rpm serial drive.

- **5.1 stereo sound card.** You want to be able to hear bad guys creeping up behind you, which means that you want an audio card that's capable of producing surround sound. The specification *5.1* means four corner speakers, a subwoofer, and a center speaker. Need more speakers than that? There are 6.1 and 7.1 configurations as well.

Tweak your system

You want to keep your PC in top shape, and you can do several things to make sure that it's running at its most efficient. Vista also has features that can enhance performance.

Update your drivers

Make sure that you have the latest hardware drivers for the key components of your system, especially the sound and video cards. Hardware manufacturers update drivers often, and because Vista's new, its drivers are getting even more frequent updates. Check the manufacturers' Web sites at least once a month for new drivers. In theory, Microsoft will be pushing new drivers for hardware through Windows Update, but it's been our experience so far that drivers get posted to support sites well before Microsoft makes them available. Download and install them in accordance with the instructions on installing new software that we give in Lesson 4.

Defragment your hard drive

Under normal use, Windows' files become scattered across your hard drive. The read/write head of the hard drive, which looks like the tone arm of an old-fashioned record player, must jump all over the drive to read data. When you defragment a drive, the files are placed sequentially on the drive, so the head doesn't have to go as far to find them, which means that it pulls data off the drive faster.

In Vista, you can schedule defragmentation to run automatically, in the background, while you work on other things. Here's how to set that up:

1. Choose Start > Computer.

    The Computer window opens.

2. Right-click the icon representing your hard drive, and choose Properties from the shortcut menu.

    The Local Disk Properties dialog box appears.

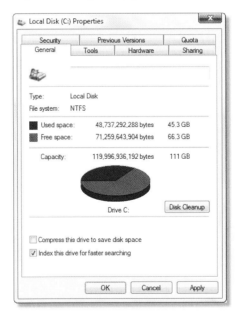

3. Click the Tools tab.

4. Click the Defragment Now button. If a User Access Control prompt appears, click Continue.

The Disk Defragmenter dialog box appears.

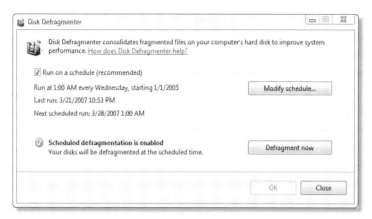

5. Check the Run on a Schedule check box.

    The default is every Wednesday at 1 a.m.

6. To change the default, click the Modify Schedule button.

    The Modify Schedule dialog box appears.

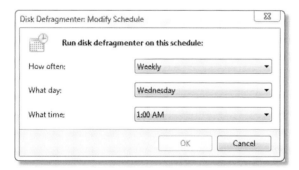

7. Make choices from the three drop-down menus on the window to specify how often and when defragmentation should occur, and click OK when you are done.

    You return to the Disk Defragmenter dialog box.

8. Click OK.

9. Click OK to close the Disk Properties box.

Use ReadyBoost

As mentioned in Lesson 1, the ReadyBoost feature moves parts of Vista's system from the hard drive to a removable storage device, such as a flash memory card or a USB 2.0 flash drive. Because this type of memory is very inexpensive, it can be a low-cost way to make dramatic performance gains. Some caveats apply, however:

- The removable storage must be fast enough to support ReadyBoost, and some devices that you think would support it do not. If you're using a USB flash drive, for example, ReadyBoost requires that it meet the USB 2.0 specification, but not all USB 2.0 drives are fast enough for ReadyBoost.

- It's a good idea to match the amount of system memory with the amount of ReadyBoost memory. If you have 2 GB of RAM, for example, try using a 2 GB flash drive. You can always use more memory, though larger flash drives cost more.

Here's how to set up ReadyBoost (for this exercise, we presume that you're using a USB flash drive):

1. Insert a USB 2.0 flash drive into one of your PC's USB slots.

   When you plug the drive in, Vista conducts a quick test behind the scenes to determine whether the drive will work with ReadyBoost.

   If AutoPlay is turned on for flash drives, an AutoPlay window appears. If the drive passed the test and is ReadyBoost–capable, the option Speed up My System Using ReadyBoost is listed.

If AutoPlay is not enabled, stop here and instead follow the steps in the next exercise.

2. Click Speed up My System Using Windows ReadyBoost.

   The Properties dialog box for your flash drive appears.

3. Click the ReadyBoost tab.

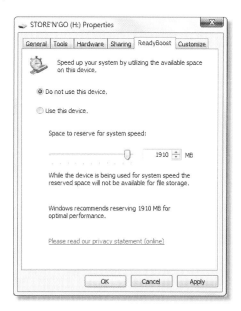

This tab allows you to activate ReadyBoost and set the amount of space to reserve for data.

4. Select the Use This Device radio button and then set the slider to the amount of space to use.

   Leaving the slider at its default setting is a good idea.

5. Click Apply; then click OK.

   ReadyBoost places a large cache file on your flash drive.

You can remove the drive whenever you like without losing data, but the big cache file remains (it's encrypted, so no one can snoop through it, looking for personal information). Delete the file if you want to use the drive to store other items.

> **TIP** —— On a 2 GB drive, the cache file can be as much as 1.9 GB, which won't leave room for much else. You can adjust the slider in the Properties dialog box to provide more room for other files, but it's a good idea to devote a flash drive just to ReadyBoost.

If you don't have AutoPlay turned on, you need to access the drive manually before you can use ReadyBoost. Here's how:

1. Choose Start > Computer.

   The Computer window appears.

2. Right-click the flash drive's icon, and choose Properties from the shortcut menu.

   The Properties dialog box for your flash drive appears.

3. Follow steps 3 through 5 of the preceding exercise.

Find games

Now that your machine's ready to play games, where can you find games that work with Vista?

Games for Vista are everywhere. The same advice we gave in Lesson 4 about software compatibility pertains here: If a title works with Windows XP, chances are good that it will run in Vista, particularly if your drivers and operating-system patches are up to date. Since Vista's release, Microsoft has released compatibility-related patches, and many of those fixes relate to games.

In "Take a tour of the Games folder" earlier in this lesson, we mention the Microsoft Game Advisor Web site, which lets you search for Windows games based on genre, age-appropriateness, or title. The site can also help you keep track of patches and updates for games you own.

Other Web sites we recommend for learning about games include:

- GameSpot (www.gamespot.com)

- GameSpy (www.gamespy.com)

- 3D Gamers (www.3dgamers.com)

- PC Gameworld (http://pcgames.gwn.com)

- GameZone (http://pc.gamezone.com)

Concerned about a game your child wants to play? You can learn more about it on the Entertainment Software Rating Board's site (www.esrb.org), which lets you look up the rating and a brief description of the game's content. For in-depth reviews of kids' games, check out Common Sense Media (www.commonsensemedia.org), which rates games as well as movies and other media.

What You've Learned

- How to use the Games folder to manage your games
- Which games are new to Vista and which favorite games have been redesigned
- What kind of hardware you need for the best gaming experience
- How to make sure your computer is running in top shape for gaming

16

GOALS

Understand the components of the PC and what can go wrong with each

Get basic strategies for troubleshooting a PC

Discover the troubleshooting tools available in Vista

Troubleshoot Vista

When something goes wrong with your computer, trying to find the problem and fix it can be maddening. That's because PCs are complex machines. When something breaks down, the symptom may not necessarily point directly to a cause.

That's particularly true of operating systems. In and of itself, Windows Vista is very complicated. Fortunately, it also comes with a set of tools for tracking down and eliminating issues.

It also helps to understand something about how a computer works in general. Knowing the genesis of common problems can give you a leg up on figuring out where to start looking.

In this lesson, we first look at the most frequent types of computer problems and their causes. Then we show how you can use the tools that come with Vista to track down and solve these issues.

Understanding Common Problems

We often refer to PCs as *systems,* and that's an apt word. A system is a collection of components that interact in a unified way, and each of the main parts of a computer is itself a system. This is why a PC is complex—and why it can be so hard to troubleshoot.

But if you understand that certain types of issues are symptoms of problems in specific parts of the computer, you'll know where to start looking. Because of a PC's complexity, where you start may not ultimately be the source of the problem, but it will get you closer to the source.

We start this section by breaking a PC into its two main subsystems—software and hardware—and then look at the problems common to the various components within them.

Examining hardware problems

Hardware problems can be especially difficult to troubleshoot. They may mimic software issues, and finding them may require special equipment or software tools. But the nice thing about most PCs—particularly desktops—is that their parts are easy to remove and replace. Simple trial and error works well when you suspect failed hardware.

Different hardware components show different symptoms when they go bad:

- **Memory modules.** The computer's memory modules are a set of small circuit boards with memory chips mounted on them. They're inserted into slots on the main system board, also known as the *motherboard.*

  A friend of ours jokingly refers to defective memory modules as "the silent killer." They frequently are the cause of some of the most frustrating and mysterious computer problems. Symptoms of bad memory include sudden screen lockups or crashes; garbled data; file corruption; distorted screen displays (which also can be caused by a failing video card); crashes during startup; and stop errors, also known as the Blue Screen of Death.

But when you suspect bad memory, testing for it is actually fairly simple. In fact, Vista has a hidden, built-in memory tester. We tell you how to activate it later in this lesson.

■ **Power supply.** The power supply converts AC current to the DC current that powers the parts in your computer. Power-supply issues are often intermittent and unpredictable. The most common symptom of a faulty power supply is a spontaneous reboot, but you may also see system lockups, restarts during power fluctuations (such as brownouts), and some of the same errors that occur when memory is going bad.

If you bought a computer from a major manufacturer and added new hardware—including power-demanding parts such as a high-end video card—your power supply may be underpowered. Many PC makers cut corners on the power supply, which can cause problems for those who upgrade their systems.

■ **Hard drive.** Hard drive problems range from the subtle—files become corrupted or go missing, programs won't launch, or you see error messages about problems with system files—to the more obvious, as in your PC won't boot at all. The one message you don't want to see is "Operating system not found" or something like it. That message means that your PC has failed completely or that the operating system is so corrupt, the computer can't even begin to start up.

■ **Motherboard.** Problems with the motherboard are often the hardest to troubleshoot, because they can mimic issues with other hardware components. All the computer's other subsystems plug into the motherboard, and it has components that interact and control all of them. So bad slots into which you'd plug memory modules can cause the same problems as bad memory. Motherboards contain chips that control the hard drives, so when those chips go bad, the result can look like a hard drive failure.

Motherboards have their own diagnostic software, which you can find via the setup routine at startup. Check the manual that came with your computer or motherboard to see how to access the setup.

Exploring software problems

In almost all cases, a software problem can be traced back to a change of some kind. You've installed something new (intentionally or, in the case of malware, unintentionally), updated a driver, or patched a program or the operating system. Fixing the problem is a matter of going back to find the change and then tweaking or reversing it.

■ **Malware.** The introduction of viruses, Trojan horses, worms, and spyware into a PC may be the most common software issue today. The symptoms range from slow performance to offensive and frequent pop-ups to system instability and crashes. You can avoid most malware by following the safe-software practices we mention in Lesson 6. Malware can and does slip through, however, which is why Vista comes with Windows Defender—software that helps prevent spyware. You still need to install an antivirus program.

■ **Drivers.** *Drivers* are software programs that act as go-betweens for the operating system and hardware; they're partly responsible for getting images on your screen from your video card, for example. Drivers with bugs are a major cause of stop errors, or Blue Screens of Death; in fact, that's where you should look first when you see one of these screens. Video drivers in particular are frequent culprits.

As we mention in Lesson 14, Vista is new, so hardware manufacturers are still fine-tuning their drivers. Check the manufacturer's Web site early and often for new drivers for all your hardware components, but particularly for video and audio cards.

- **Startup programs.** When Vista boots up, a series of programs launches with it. As you install other programs, they may add modules that launch at startup as well. Over time, startup programs can slow the boot process and, if you have enough programs launching, become a drag on overall system performance. In some cases, issues with startup programs can prevent Vista from launching completely. Vista has excellent tools for managing these issues, and we explore them later in this lesson.

- **Software conflicts.** Simply put, a software conflict is a case of one software program not knowing what the other is doing. In theory, well-written programs don't conflict, but conflicts happen from time to time. In addition, some programs are simply buggy. The most common symptoms of software bugs and conflicts are individual program crashes and lockups.

  Software conflicts may be hard to troubleshoot, because one of the programs in conflict could be one of the startup items mentioned in the previous item and could be running in the background. It's a good idea to check for updates for your most commonly used software to get the latest bug fixes and compatibility tweaks.

- **Operating-system bugs.** Believe it or not, these bugs are relatively rare causes of major software issues, even in a new operating system such as Vista. Sure, the OS has its share of bugs, but they usually appear in very specific circumstances that most users won't experience. More than 2 million people tested Vista before its release, and so-called "show-stopper" bugs were hammered out. Still, bugs do remain, which is why it's a good idea to turn on Windows Update (refer to Lesson 6) to make sure you get fixes as they become available.

Now that you've learned about what can go wrong, you're ready to look at the tools Vista offers for fixing problems.

Fixing Problems

Regardless of the operating system, you should do some general things when troubleshooting. Take these steps first before you begin making changes in an attempt to fix a problem:

- **Document the details.** Too often, when users see an error message, their eyes glaze over, and they click OK just to get rid of it. But the details in the message—presuming that there are any, of course—matter a lot. When you spot an error message, take a minute to write down what it says, along with some general notes about what you were doing at the time. If you don't want to take the time right then to troubleshoot, the notes will help reinforce your memory of the event when you return later. If the error state hasn't locked up your system completely, consider using the Snipping Tool (see Lesson 10) to copy the part of the screen where the error message appears.

- **Use a search engine.** Here's a little secret: The best tool for troubleshooting computer problems is the Internet, particularly search engines. Seasoned technicians know that a site like Google is your best friend when your computer is acting up. Remember that error message you wrote down in the preceding item? Enter it word for word into your favorite search engine. Chances are that someone has had the problem you're experiencing, and you can find information about it somewhere online.

- **Use Usenet.** Microsoft has a collection of Usenet discussion groups that it calls Windows Communities. Everyday users mix with Windows experts and even Microsoft staff members to come up with solutions for problems. It's a great place to get help. Find the Windows Vista Community at http://windowshelp.microsoft.com/communities/newsgroups/en-us/default.mspx.

- **Try the obvious.** There's a reason why tech-support types often tell you to reboot before trying any other fixes: It often works! Turning components off and back on again often clears minor problems. Rebooting a PC can solve a temporary software conflict; restarting a DSL or cable modem can fix a sluggish Internet connection. Try the simple things before getting fancy.

The troubleshooting tools that come with Vista are rich and varied. Some require advanced knowledge of Windows and can be dangerous even in the hands of experienced users. The last thing you want while troubleshooting a problem is to do something that makes it worse or causes a new problem. With that in mind, in the following sections we discuss the tools that are most useful for the majority of users.

System Restore: Let your computer fix itself

System Restore has been available in Windows since the unfortunate Windows Me. (In fact, it's one of the few good things to come out of that debacle of an operating system.) This feature rolls your system settings and files back to a predetermined state.

Suppose that you install a program and begin to experience problems a few hours later. You uninstall that program, but the problems continue. There's a good chance that the program made changes to your system and didn't undo them during its uninstallation. System Restore can go back to a point in time before you installed the problematic program and restore your system settings.

In the past, System Restore has not always worked well. It was hit or miss in Windows Me and marginally better in Windows XP. So far, our experience with System Restore shows it to be much improved, thanks to its use of a technology called Shadow Copy backup.

To restore your PC to a previous point in time:

1. Click Start, type `system restore` in the Start menu's Search box, and press Enter. At the User Account Control (UAC) prompt, click Continue.

    The System Restore window appears. By default, Vista recommends the most recent restore point it created before a system change.

2. To accept the default selection, click Next and skip to step 5.

    or

    To choose a different restore point, select Choose a Different Restore Point, and click Next.

    continues on next page

The Choose a Restore Point dialog box appears.

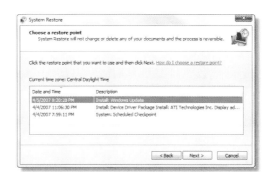

3. Click the restore point you want to use.

   To see even more restore points, check the check box titled Show Restore Points Older Than 5 Days.

4. Click Next.

   A confirmation window appears.

5. Click Finish to start the restore process.

   A warning message indicates that the process cannot be stopped after it starts and cannot be undone when it's complete.

6. Click Yes to continue.

   The restoration process begins, with a progress bar showing the status. Then your computer will begin to reboot; before it does, a screen appears indicating that a system restore is in process.

After your computer restarts, a message appears on the desktop indicating that the system restore was successful.

Use Shadow Copies to Restore Individual Files

The same Shadow Copy feature that makes System Restore so much better in Vista also lets you restore versions of files you have changed. We mention in Lesson 10 that Vista's Photo Gallery lets you undo changes to photos all the way back to the original, untouched picture. You do that via Shadow Copy, and it works with almost any file.

Suppose that you've made some changes in a word processing document, and you want to restore some text you deleted. You can use Shadow Copy to go back to an earlier version and retrieve the text.

1. Right-click the file you want to restore, and choose Restore Previous Versions from the shortcut menu.

   The document's Properties dialog box appears, set to the Previous Versions tab.

2. Select the version you want, and click Restore.

   A progress dialog box appears, followed by a warning that you're about to replace a newer version with an older one.

3. Select Copy, but Keep Both Files to create a new copy.

4. Click Finish when the success window appears.

Let Microsoft fix it

Windows XP users are familiar with the error message that occurs when a program or Windows itself crashes or locks up. This message invites users to send information to Microsoft to help fix the problem. Sometimes, a Web page pops up afterward, suggesting possible fixes or (in rare cases) pointing you to something to download that may ease your pain.

In Vista, that process has been expanded and refined. Every time a problem occurs, Vista notes it and, if you allow, automatically sends information about the issue in the background. Vista keeps tabs on whether there's a solution and can alert you. It keeps track of issues and potential fixes via a feature called Problem Reports and Solutions.

To use Problem Reports and Solutions:

1. Click Start, type `solutions` in the Start menu's Search box, and press Enter.

2. Click Problem Reports and Solutions, which should top the results list.

    The Problem Reports and Solutions window appears.

3. Click Check for New Solutions in the left pane.

    A dialog box appears and shows the progress of the check.

4. If the dialog box asks whether you'd like to send more information, click Send Information.

This option gathers program data and error-log information about the problem; no personal information is sent to Microsoft.

When all the information is dispatched, you return to the Problem Reports and Solutions window.

5. Click any of the items in the Information about Other Problems section to learn more about possible solutions.

Some of the reports are purely informational; they often say, "This problem is being researched." In other cases, you're encouraged to download a new hardware driver or a fix for a software program.

Unfortunately, the process isn't always refined enough. Some of the error reports may not even say which issue the reported problem is related to.

continues on next page

369

6. If you don't have error reporting set to automatic—or if you do and prefer to approve each report sent—click Change Settings in the left pane.

   Check for Solutions Automatically should be selected.

7. If you want to handle the process manually, select Ask Me to Check If a Problem Occurs.

8. Click OK when you are done.

Manage running programs with Task Manager

Task Manager, another veteran application in Windows, lets you halt running programs and *processes*, which are instances or components of a program, if they're causing problems. You can use Task Manager when you have a program that won't close or that seems to be conflicting with other software. Sometimes when a program won't start, it's because a portion of that program is already running. Closing that program component in Task Manager could solve the problem.

To launch Task Manager:

1. Right-click an unoccupied area of the taskbar, and choose Task Manager from the shortcut menu.

   Task Manager appears, usually open to the Applications tab, which shows running programs.

2. Do one of the following:

   - To close a program, select it and then click End Task.

   - To bring a program to the fore, select that program and click Switch To.

   - To launch an executable file manually, click New Task. In the Create New Task window, enter the name of an executable file and press Enter to launch the program.

3. Click the Processes tab to show running processes.

4. To halt a process, select it and click the End Process button.

TIP —— Right-click a process to launch a shortcut menu that gives you many more choices as to what you can do with that process. Most options are for advanced users, but choosing Properties gives you detailed information about the process, including the program to which it's related.

5. Click the Services tab to display the list of running services, which are low-level programs that are crucial to the operations of Windows and its applications.

6. Right-click a service to display a shortcut menu that lets you start or stop the service.

7. Click the Performance tab to see CPU and memory activity.

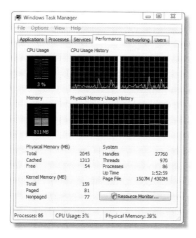

continues on next page

8. Click the Network tab to show your computer's activity on your network.

9. Click the Users tab to see which users are logged onto your computer.

10. Select a user; then click Disconnect to kick a networked user off your PC, or click Logoff to log off a user who has logged on to your PC but may be inactive due to User Switching.

11. When you are done, click the red X in the top-right corner to close Task Manager.

Start in Safe Mode

Like past versions of Windows, Vista has the ability to launch in Safe Mode, which starts the operating system with a bare minimum of drivers and running programs. This mode is best used when you have trouble booting into Vista at all, such as when the operating system halts in the middle of the startup process and won't continue.

When you're in Safe Mode, you can use some of the other tools mentioned in this lesson to attempt a fix, such as MSCONFIG or System Restore. Sometimes, just the process of successfully starting up via Safe Mode and then restarting allows you to get back into the operating system normally.

Here's how to launch in Safe Mode:

1. Start your PC.

   When the computer first boots, it may show either a logo (for the PC vendor or motherboard manufacturer) or diagnostic startup information.

2. Begin pressing the F8 key rhythmically, about once a second.

   If you see the Vista startup progress bar, you were unsuccessful in getting to Safe mode. Restart your computer and try again.

   If you were successful, you see the Advanced Boot Options screen.

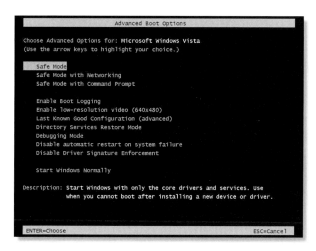

3. Choose an option:

   - **Safe Mode.** This option starts Windows with a very simple graphical interface and the minimum drivers and services needed to start up. In most cases, this is the choice to make.

   - **Safe Mode with Networking.** This option allows you to boot into Safe Mode but also includes network drivers, providing access to a network and potentially the Internet.

   - **Safe Mode with Command Prompt.** This option (for advanced users only) takes you to a DOS-style command prompt, from which you can run some low-level system applications.

   continues on next page

For this exercise, choose Safe Mode, and then press Enter.

Vista shows you which drivers and files it's loading.

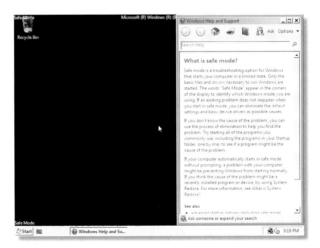

```
                    Loading Windows Files
  Loaded: \Windows\system32\drivers\volmgr.sys
  Loaded: \Windows\System32\drivers\mountmgr.sys
  Loaded: \Windows\system32\drivers\intelide.sys
  Loaded: \Windows\system32\drivers\PCIIDEX.SYS
  Loaded: \Windows\system32\drivers\volmgrx.sys
  Loaded: \Windows\system32\drivers\atapi.sys
  Loaded: \Windows\system32\drivers\ataport.SYS
  Loaded: \Windows\system32\drivers\fltmgr.sys
  Loaded: \Windows\system32\drivers\fileinfo.sys
  Loaded: \Windows\system32\drivers\ndis.sys
  Loaded: \Windows\system32\drivers\NETIO.SYS
  Loaded: \Windows\system32\drivers\msrpc.sys
  Loaded: \Windows\System32\Drivers\ntfs.sys
  Loaded: \Windows\System32\Drivers\ksecdd.sys
  Loaded: \Windows\system32\drivers\volsnap.sys
  Loaded: \Windows\System32\Drivers\spldr.sys
  Loaded: \Windows\System32\Drivers\partmgr.sys
  Loaded: \Windows\System32\Drivers\mup.sys
  Loaded: \Windows\System32\drivers\ecache.sys
  Loaded: \Windows\System32\DRIVERS\fvevol.sys
  Loaded: \Windows\system32\drivers\disk.sys
  Loaded: \Windows\system32\drivers\CLASSPNP.SYS
  Loaded: \Windows\system32\drivers\crcdisk.sys
Please wait...
```

Next, Vista launches into Safe Mode, showing a Windows Help file explaining Safe Mode and how it can be used to solve problems. Safe Mode uses the older, Windows 2000-style interface.

4. When you complete your troubleshooting—uninstalling a problem program or driver, turning off startup programs or services using MSCONFIG, or launching System Restore—you can exit in the usual way, via the Start menu.

Test for bad memory

If you suspect the memory in your PC may be bad, you can use a new diagnostic feature in Vista that's incredibly handy—and also incredibly hard to find.

Windows Boot Manager, which normally comes up only when you have more than one operating system on your computer, gives you access to the Windows Memory Diagnostic, which can conduct a set of tests on your system's memory modules.

Here's how to access the Windows Memory Diagnostic:

1. Start your computer.

2. After the initial startup screen, and before Windows begins its startup screen, begin pressing the spacebar, about once a second.

    Getting the timing right may take several tries.

    If you see the startup progress bar, you need to go back and try again. If you're successful, Windows Boot Manager appears.

3. Press the Tab key to select the Windows Memory Diagnostic item; then press Enter.

continues on next page

The Windows Memory Diagnostic Tool window appears.

The test begins running, placing different kinds of data in all the addresses in your computer's memory. Next, it removes the data and checks to see whether that data has been corrupted. If so, the program alerts you to the problem.

Troubleshoot startup with MSCONFIG

We show you in Lesson 4 how to use MSCONFIG (aka the System Configuration utility) to turn off programs that run when Vista starts up. This utility is useful when you want to troubleshoot issues with startup programs or want to determine which programs may be conflicting.

The discussion in Lesson 4, however, dealt with only one part of MSCONFIG, specifically the Startup tab. In this section, we look at some of its other capabilities.

To use MSCONFIG:

1. Click the Start button, type `msconfig` in the Start menu's Search box, and press Enter.

   The System Configuration dialog box appears.

2. Click the General tab.

What If the Diagnostic Tool Reports Errors?

If the Windows Memory Diagnostics Tool reports an error, you need to determine which of your memory modules is the culprit. If you have just one memory module, of course, you're in luck; simply open the case, remove the faulty memory, and install a new module.

Things get tricky if you have more than one module. Many PCs that come with 1 GB of RAM may have it in two modules of 512 MB each, or a 2 GB system may have two 1 GB modules. Here's the strategy to use if you have more than one module:

1. Shut down your computer.

2. Unplug the power cable, and ground your-self before touching inside your computer to prevent static electricity from damaging components.

3. Remove all but one of the memory modules.

4. Rerun the Windows Memory Diagnostics Tool.

   If you don't get errors, that module is fine.

5. Turn off your computer, remove the good module, put the next one in, and repeat the test.

6. Repeat steps 4 and 5 until you find a module that produces an error.

   You'll know that one is faulty. If you have others you haven't tested yet, continue the process with those modules; more than one may be faulty.

When replacing memory, you need to match the specifications of your remaining modules.

The General tab features a quick-and-dirty way to test Vista's startup processes. Each option changes the way Vista starts.

continues on next page

3. Choose one of the following options:

- **Normal Startup** launches Vista with all drivers, services, and startup programs and is Vista's default startup setting.

- **Diagnostic Setup** loads the bare minimum necessary to launch Vista.

- **Selective Startup** lets you choose which programs and services to run at bootup and which to turn off. You can also select the services and startup items to narrow further what gets launched. When you use the technique outlined in Lesson 4, Selective Startup is automatically selected.

4. Click the Boot tab, which lets you further configure how Vista starts up.

5. Select your configuration options.

Here are the most important ones for troubleshooting:

- **Safe Boot/Minimal** starts Windows in Safe Mode with a very basic graphical desktop and minimal services. You won't have access to your network.

- **Safe Boot/Alternate Shell** starts Windows with a simple, DOS-style command prompt.

- **Safe Boot/Active Directory Repair** is for use on a corporate network, when you need to boot into Safe Mode but still need access to Microsoft's Active Directory server.

- **Safe Boot/Network** boots into Safe Mode but gives you access to the network.

- **Boot Log** creates a log of actions that Windows takes during the startup process. The log is stored in the root directory—usually, C:\—and named Ntbtlog.txt. It can be read with any text editor, such as Notepad.

- **OS Boot Information** shows you which drivers are loading as Vista launches.

6. Click Apply.

7. Click the Services tab.

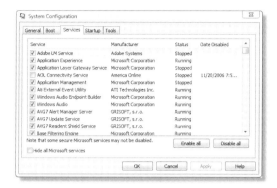

8. Uncheck items that you don't want to launch.

NOTE —— Be warned: Services, which are mini-programs that enable specific functions in Vista, can be critical. Uncheck the wrong ones, and your PC may not work properly.

9. Check the Hide All Microsoft Services check box to see only services installed by other programs.

10. Click Enable All to turn on all services or Disable All to turn all of them off.

11. Click Apply to save your changes.

12. Click the Tools tab.

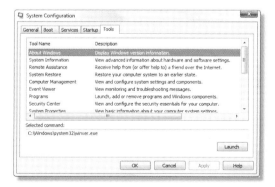

continues on next page

The Tools tab provides access to a slew of useful troubleshooting modules, including:

- **About Windows.** Tells you which version of Windows Vista you're using.

- **System Information.** Provides detailed information about your PC's hardware and software.

- **Remote Assistance**. Lets someone working from another Vista or Windows XP computer connect to your machine and access the desktop remotely. It's excellent for letting a savvy friend (whom you must trust!) troubleshoot your PC for you.

- **Computer Management.** Gives you access to system and security settings at an advanced level. Dive into this program only if you are an advanced, knowledgeable Windows user.

- **Event Viewer.** Gives you access to error and system logs.

- **Programs.** Lets you uninstall or change programs on your computer. This feature is the Add/Remove Programs module from Windows XP.

- **Security Center.** Gives you access to settings for Windows Defender, the Windows firewall, antivirus programs, and other security features (refer to Lesson 6).

- **System Properties**. Takes you to the System module from the Control Panel for basic system information.

- **Internet Options.** Lets you tweak settings for Internet Explorer. These controls are the same set of controls mentioned in Online Resource A (www.peachpit.com/vistalearningseries).

- **Internet Protocol Configuration.** Launches a command-prompt window with a program commonly known as IPConfig already launched. This program lets you control and tweak aspects of your Internet connection.

- **Performance Monitor.** Allows you to check your current system state—memory, CPU usage, hard drive activity, and more—and see a graph of your system's reliability over time. We look at this tool later in this lesson.

- **Task Manager.** Shows lists of running programs and processes, and provides a subset of the system-state information shown in Performance Monitor. This feature is discussed earlier in this lesson.

- **Disable UAC/Enable UAC.** Allows you to turn the User Account Control prompt feature on or off.

- **Command Prompt.** Lets you launch a DOS-style command prompt.

- **Registry Editor.** Lets you make manual changes in the Windows registry, a database of settings for Windows and the programs that run on it. It's powerful—and dangerous. Delete or add the wrong thing, and your system could become inoperable. This feature is for advanced users only.

13. Click Apply.

14. Click OK when you are finished working in MSCONFIG.

> **NOTE** —— A prompt to launch MSCONFIG may appear the next time you start your computer. Unless you want to undo the changes you've made, check the check box titled Don't Show This Message or Launch the System Configuration Utility When Windows Starts, and click OK. If you just click OK, the utility launches again. Click Cancel.

Roll back drivers

Generally, it's a good idea to update your PC with the latest drivers, but a new driver can cause a problem sometimes. Most Windows drivers come with uninstall routines, and you can remove them by using the Programs and Features module from the Control Panel mentioned in Online Resource A (www.peachpit.com /vistalearningseries). But occasionally, you won't find an entry there for a driver.

When that happens, you can roll back to the previous driver by using Device Manager. Here's how:

1. Click Start, type device manager in the Start menu's Search box, and press Enter. If a UAC prompt appears, click Continue.

   Device Manager appears, grouping your hardware devices by category.

continues on next page

2. Click the small plus sign to the left of a category to open it and see the devices.

3. Right-click the device you want to change, and choose Properties from the shortcut menu.

   The Properties dialog box for the device appears.

4. Click the Driver tab.

   The dialog box gives you several options that let you see more information about the driver, update the driver, disable the device, or uninstall the driver. For this exercise, click Roll Back Driver.

5. Click Yes in the confirmation window that appears.

   When the process is complete, the Roll Back Driver button is grayed out.

6. Click OK.

7. If you are prompted to restart your computer, click Yes.

Use Reliability and Performance Monitor

Reliability and Performance Monitor is the Swiss Army knife of troubleshooting and monitoring tools. This feature, new to Vista, is a very powerful application for learning about what's happening with your computer. Most of its features are aimed at advanced users, but it's helpful for everyday users to understand its potential.

The first thing you want to do is familiarize yourself with Reliability and Performance Monitor.

1. Click Start, type `reliability` in the Start menu's Search box, and press Enter.

   Reliability and Performance Monitor appears.

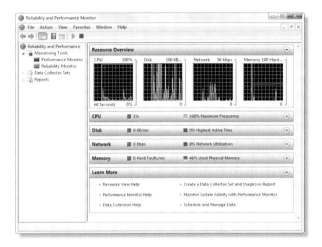

   The window is split into two panes. The left pane lets you choose which tools to use; the right pane lets you see and work with information.

   The monitor has three primary components:

   - **Monitoring Tools.** Lets you keep an eye on what your system is doing now (Performance Monitor) and how it's performed over time (Reliability Monitor). In this section, we focus on the monitoring tools, as they are what most users would encounter when troubleshooting.

   - **Data Collector Sets.** Lets you collect certain types of information about the computer's behavior over time.

   - **Reports.** Displays detailed reports on your PC's activity, generated from the collector sets.

   The monitor's main screen shows four activity panels: CPU, Disk, Network, and Memory. These panels are essentially the same as the monitoring screens in the various tabs of Task Manager. The preceding screen shot shows Resource View.

   Below the panels are a series of bars related to each panel.

2. Click the down arrow on the right side of any of the bars to see more detailed information on that topic.

continues on next page

Clicking the arrow on the CPU bar, for example, shows what programs are running and how they are using the computer's CPU.

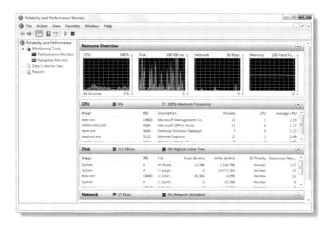

3. Click any of the categories in the headers below a bar to sort by that category.

If you click the CPU category, for example, the list will be sorted with the programs that are hitting the CPU hardest listed at the top.

Meet Performance Monitor

Now you're ready to look at Performance Monitor.

1. Click the Performance Monitor item in the left pane.

The Performance Monitor appears in the right pane, showing a line chart of processor activity.

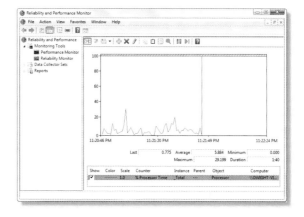

2. To change the kind of graph being displayed, click the Change Graph Type button 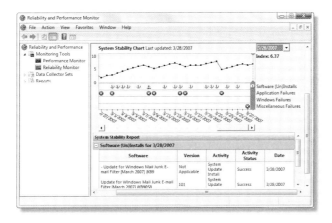 ▼.

3. Select Line, Histogram Bar, or Report.

   The display changes.

4. To add other types of information to the display, click the green plus button 🟢.

   The Add Counters window that appears.

5. In the Add Counters window that appears, double-click any of the categories in the top-left pane to see what's available to add.

6. Select a counter, and click the Add button.

7. Click OK.

   The counter is added to the display.

Take a tour of Reliability Monitor

Reliability Monitor looks at the way your system has performed over a longer period. It allows you to look for trouble areas and can show you system events that may have caused problems in the past.

To access Reliability Monitor:

1. Click the Reliability Monitor item in the left pane.

   The System Stability Chart appears in the right pane.

continues on next page

The chart shows five categories of system issues:

- **Software installs and uninstalls.** Programs that were added and/or removed.

- **Application failures.** Programs that crashed.

- **Hardware failures.** Hardware components that quit working as they should.

- **Windows failures.** Operating-system crashes.

- **Miscellaneous failures.** Other components that quit working properly.

2. Click any of the icons in the top-right chart to see details about that event in the list below it.

    By default, the chart shows the past month's activity, but you can change months or zoom in on a specific day.

3. Make a choice from the Select a Date drop-down menu near the top-right corner of the chart to get a calendar that lets you select a different 30-day period or an individual day.

What You've Learned

- How to recognize where problems may originate in a PC

- How to carry out basic troubleshooting strategies

- What Vista tools are available for troubleshooting

Index

dex